CW00601241

Business Relationships for Competitive Advantage

Business Relationships for Competitive Advantage

Managing Alignment and Misalignment in Buyer and Supplier Transactions

Andrew Cox

Chris Lonsdale

Joe Sanderson

and

Glyn Watson

First published 2004 by
PALGRAVE MACMILLAN
Houndmills, Basingstoke, Hampshire RG21 6XS and
175 Fifth Avenue, New York, N.Y. 10010
Companies and representatives throughout the world

PALGRAVE MACMILLAN is the global academic imprint of the Palgrave Macmillan division of St. Martin's Press, LLC and of Palgrave Macmillan Ltd. Macmillan® is a registered trademark in the United States, United Kingdom and other countries. Palgrave is a registered trademark in the European Union and other countries.

ISBN 1–4039–1904–6

This book is printed on paper suitable for recycling and made from fully managed and sustained forest sources.

A catalogue record for this book is available from the British Library.

Library of Congress Cataloging-in-Publication Data
Business relationships for competitive advantage: managing alignment and misalignment in buyer and supplier transactions/by Andrew Cox ... [et al.].
p. cm.
Includes bibliographical references and index.
ISBN 1–4039–1904–6 (cloth)
1. Business logistics. 2. Industrial procurement. 3. Supply and demand. 4. Business logistics – Case studies. 5. Industrial procurement – Case studies. 6. Supply and demand – Case studies. I. Cox, Andrew W.
HD38.5.B87 2004
658.7′2—dc22 2003061155

10 9 8 7 6 5 4 3 2 1
13 12 11 10 09 08 07 06 05 04

Printed and bound in Great Britain by
Antony Rowe Ltd, Chippenham and Eastbourne

Contents

List of Figures

Preface

All organisations have to manage relationships with customers and suppliers. Sometimes they must also manage relationships with direct competitors. Relationship management is, therefore, a key aspect of effective business management and the search for competitive advantage.

While there have been many books on the subject of business-to-business relationship management it is clear that few volumes exist that link theoretical insights about the possible forms of relationship management with the empirical experience of success and failure by companies in managing their relationships, so that a comprehensive framework can be created to guide managers in the ways in which they can align their business relationships more effectively, either as buyers or as suppliers.

This book seeks to achieve this practitioner-focused goal. The volume is the result of a fusion of insights gleaned as a result of both academic and consulting activities. Part of the work that has made this volume possible was undertaken by the authors at the University of Birmingham as part of a two-year study funded by the Engineering and Physical Sciences Research Council (Project No. GR/L86395) into how competitive advantage can be achieved through the alignment of buyer and supplier relationships in supply chains. The work was undertaken with the support of a number of major public and private sector organisations. The case material and theoretical insights on which this work draws are indicated clearly in the text by reference to the copyright of the Centre for Business Strategy and Procurement (CBSP) at Birmingham University.

The book also benefits from a wealth of consulting experience by Andrew Cox, working directly with companies managing their relationships either as buyers or as suppliers, and the material and theoretical insights of this work are clearly indicated in the text by reference to the copyright of Robertson Cox Ltd. When the work has been jointly undertaken the copyright is so indicated with the major contributor appearing first in the assignment.

For commercial reasons the names of the organisations involved in this study are not disclosed in what follows. We do not however believe that this will detract significantly from the understanding of success and failure in business relationship management that can be gleaned from reading about these case studies. We hope that the book will be of interest to managers in all types of organisations (both private and public). The book has been specifically written for a practitioner audience but we hope that it will also be of wide interest in the academic community as well.

As always in writing a book one has an enormous debt of gratitude to express to all of those who have assisted with what has been produced. Obviously this book could not have been written without the active participation of the individuals from the organisations that have given so freely of their time. The authors of this volume thank everyone, while recognising that any sins of omission or commission in this volume are the authors' alone.

In preparing this volume a special vote of thanks is due to the researchers who have participated in the empirical research work for the EPSRC study. Without the diligent efforts of Dan Chicksand and Rachel Farmery, as well as the sterling administrative support of Michelle Donovan, Jackie Potter and Carol Levy, this work could not have been completed.

ANDREW COX
CHRIS LONSDALE
JOE SANDERSON
GLYN WATSON

The publishers and authors wish to thank Earlsgate Press for permission to reproduce Figures 2.2, 3.2 and 3.9, and the IMP Group for Figure 1.5.

Notes on the Contributors

Andrew Cox is Chairman of Robertson Cox Ltd and CIPS sponsored Professor and Director of the Centre for Business Strategy and Procurement in the Birmingham Business School, University of Birmingham. Amongst other publications he is the author of *Business Success* (1997), and co-author of *Innovations in Procurement Management* (1996), *Advanced Supply Management* (1997), *Outsourcing* (1998), *Strategic Procurement in Construction* (1998), *Contracting for Business Success* (1998), *Strategic Procurement Management* (1999), *Privatisation and Supply Chain Management* (1999), *Power Regimes* (2000), *The E-Business Report* (2001), *Supply Chains, Markets and Power* (2002), and *Supply Chain Management: A Guide to Best Practice* (2003).

Chris Lonsdale is Lecturer in Supply Chain Management in the CBSP in the Birmingham Business School, and author of *The Equity Gap* (1997) and co-author of *Outsourcing* (1998), *Supply Chains, Markets and Power* (2002), and *Supply Chain Management: A Guide to Best Practice* (2003).

Joe Sanderson is Lecturer in Supply Chain Management and Deputy Director of the CBSP in the Birmingham Business School. He is co-author of *The Political Economy of Britain* (1997), *Power Regimes* (2000), *Supply Chains, Markets and Power* (2002), and *Supply Chain Management: A Guide to Best Practice* (2003).

Glyn Watson is Lecturer in Supply Chain Management in the CBSP in the Birmingham Business School, and co-author of *Power Regimes* (2000), *Supply Chains, Markets and Power* (2002), and *Supply Chain Management: A Guide to Best Practice* (2003).

Part I

Business Relationship Management in Theory and Practice

1
Current Approaches to the Analysis of Business Relationships

This book discusses the appropriate management of business-to-business relationships. It is not, therefore, a book about how humans beings can or should manage all of their personal or their economic relationships. The book focuses instead on buying and selling relationships between organisations, whose purpose (at least theoretically if not always in practice) is to maximise the returns for their shareholders or owners. While this activity may sometimes involve individuals acting as buyers from, and suppliers to, business organisations the primary focus is on buying and selling relationships between organisations.

This chapter is divided into two main sections. The first section presents a critical appraisal of the current literature on business relationship management. The second section focuses on what is meant in theory and practice by a business relationship in the context of an exchange transaction between a buyer and supplier. This is provided as a starting point for a theoretical and practical understanding of appropriateness in ways of managing business relationships from both the commercial and operational perspectives of the buyer and the supplier. This latter issue – aligning business relationships appropriately – is the subject-matter of the remainder of the book.

1.1 Current approaches to business relationship management

The general criticisms that can be made about current approaches to business relationship management are fourfold:

- They tend to be descriptive rather than analytical.
- They tend to focus on one side of the relationship, emphasising the buyer or supplier perspective, without considering the transaction between the two parties holistically.

- They tend to be prescriptive rather than predictive.
- They tend to focus on operational management issues, without fully explaining the complex interconnections between the commercial and operational preferences of both the buyer and the supplier in any exchange relationship.

Not all current approaches to business relationship management have all of these four weaknesses, and all of them in different ways provide major contributions to our understanding of the structure and purpose of business relationships. In order to outline the strengths and weaknesses of current approaches to business relationship management the discussion that follows is divided into a review of two major ways of thinking in the current literature.

- *One-dimensional dyadic approaches*
  These are approaches that focus primarily on one side of the business relationship and emphasise how either the buyer or the supplier can improve what they obtain from any transaction. On the buyer side this approach encompasses most of the current literature on Procurement Improvement, including recent discussions of Lean and Agile Supply Chain Management, as well as the Transaction Cost Economising School. On the supplier side this approach encompasses most of the current literature on Customer Portfolio Management and Relationship Portfolio Mapping, as well as the Resource-based school in business strategy thinking.
- *Holistic dyadic approaches*
  These are approaches that focus equally on the motivations of buyers and suppliers when they interact and that seek to ascertain to what extent buyers and suppliers can or cannot work together to achieve their respective goals. These approaches include the work of the Industrial Marketing and Purchasing (IMP) Group and the Power Perspective on buyer and supplier relationship management.

(i) One-dimensional dyadic approaches

Historically the major problem with business relationship management thinking and practice has been the failure to think holistically about what business involves entrepreneurially. Ultimately business is about the ability to buy something cheap and then sell it dear. In the absence of this it is unlikely that any company or entrepreneur can survive for very long in business. This means that the ability to buy and sell effectively must be at the heart of successful business management.

The problem is, however, that although there has always been recognition that both of these competencies (buying and selling) are important there has been a tendency to address competence in these two areas from a one-dimensional functional perspective. This is not surprising given that most companies create functional departments to manage specific competencies, and most Business Schools reinforce this short-sightedness by insisting on teaching competencies from the same functional perspective.

A one-dimensional approach to competence development has therefore developed in procurement and supply, as well as marketing and sales, thinking. Rather than focusing holistically on the dyadic relationship within exchange transactions between buyers and suppliers, the majority of current thinking focuses on how one side can achieve their goals without necessarily understanding how this impacts on the other party in the exchange. As a result, most of this thinking – whether on the buyer or supplier side – tends to be descriptive rather than analytical, and prescriptive rather than predictive, with a tendency to emphasise operational as opposed to commercial goals. This currently dominant way of thinking about improvement in business relationship management is critically appraised in what follows.

Dominant approaches in procurement and supply thinking

In the procurement and supply literature there are basically three broad schools. These are the *purchasing portfolio management*; the *supply chain management*; and the *transaction cost economising* approaches. Each of these schools of thinking has specific nuances – and these are briefly outlined below – but all of them also have a great deal in common. In particular all of these approaches tend to focus one-dimensionally on the commercial and operational goals of the buyer rather than of the supplier. Furthermore, there is a tendency in this way of thinking to prescriptively encourage relationship management styles that favour transparent and trusting (alliancing or partnering) ways of working.

The *purchasing portfolio management* approach to procurement and supply improvement is perhaps the most well recognised way of thinking by buyers about business relationship improvement, and it informs much of the strategic thinking of the main consultancy companies working with buyers to improve their sourcing competence. The portfolio approach was developed as a way of helping buyers to think proactively about how they could make improvements in their sourcing strategies (Kraljic, 1983).

This approach recognises that the buyer must understand what is happening in the supply market from which they source and manage their suppliers appropriately, given these circumstances. This is achieved by buyers segmenting their spend by reference to the internal value to them of particular supply requirements relative to the market difficulty they experience from the supply market as buyers. The standard portfolio approach is outlined in Figure 1.1.

As Figure 1.1 demonstrates, the segmentation approach advises buyers to mange their suppliers based on the specific circumstances they are in. The approach is not, however, necessarily focused on moving suppliers from one position to another, but rather on focusing the buyer's efforts on the appropriate management of suppliers given the portfolio position they currently inhabit. The hope here is clearly that buyers will recognise what is the most effective way to manage under certain circumstances and not waste their time and effort in inappropriate sourcing strategies. Thus, in the *strategic* quadrant the buyer is expected to develop close and collaborative relationship management approaches with the supplier. In the *leverage* quadrant the buyer is expected to undertake regular market testing techniques. In the *acquisition* quadrant the buyer is expected to focus on operational process improvement and cost reduction internally and externally. In the *critical* box the buyer is expected to undertake contingency planning to avoid potential bottlenecks in supply in the future.

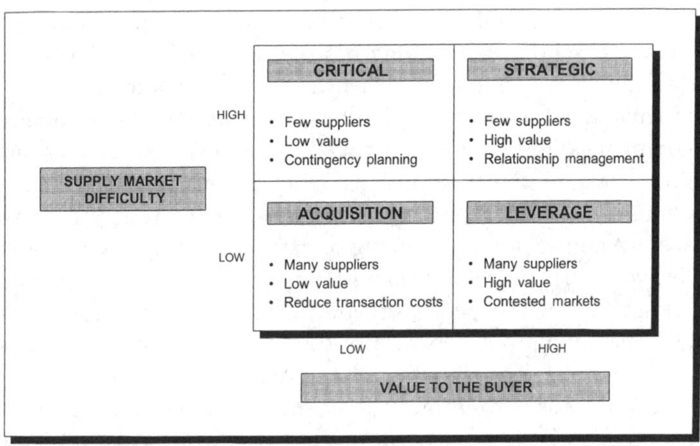

Figure 1.1 Purchasing portfolio management

Source: Adapted from Kraljic (1983).

This approach is, therefore, prescriptive for the buyer based on the current segmentation of supply market difficulty and value for the buyer. It has been widely adopted by buyers in practice, and it is widely taught by academics as a way of improving procurement and supply competence. The problem with this approach, and others that focus on the supplier's attractiveness and relationship strength with the buyer (Olsen and Ellram, 1997), is, however, that they are essentially a one-dimensional way of thinking. While this is a tool that many buyers find useful its major problem is that it is static and does not provide buyers with the necessary thinking to allow them to move to more congenial leverage positions than those they currently experience.

Even when writers attempt to use the approach to suggest ways for buyers to move to more congenial sourcing situations the way of thinking is still one-dimensional (Gelderman and van Weele, 2002). The major reason for this is because the approach focuses only on the current situation of suppliers and assumes that the buyer can devise appropriate strategies without understanding the likely responses of any supplier to the strategies that the buyer may devise in the future, and vice versa.

In recent years an alternative and more prescriptive approach to procurement and supply improvement has developed. This approach is known as *supply chain management*, although it has within it a number of variants. Despite the differences between the thinkers in this school there is, however, substantial agreement about how buyers should effectively manage their business relationships with suppliers. Most writers in this school also tend to focus one-dimensionally on the relationship from the perspective of the buyer, and tend to prescribe the use of a highly transparent and trusting relationship between the buyer and the supplier, using long-term and non-adversarial collaborative relationship management styles.

The supply chain management approach has become something of a dominant way of thinking about best practice amongst buyers. The approach was originally developed in the automotive sector in Japan but has been developed since in other sectors – like supermarket retailing, aluminium and computer manufacturing – where demand and supply and power variables have been conducive (Cox *et al.*, 2003). The basic approach is often referred to as 'lean thinking' because it is based on the copying of Toyota's lean manufacturing process, which historically involved a very high level of outsourcing of sub-assembly and components to suppliers. These supply relationships – focused on improving the value for money that Toyota could pass to its customers – are normally long-term and highly collaborative (Womack, Jones and Roos, 1990; Womack and Jones, 1996).

From this automotive practice a dominant one-dimensional prescriptive view has developed amongst lean writers and many buyers that, because this approach has been successful in the automotive and in other sectors, it must be the best practice approach that all buyers should adopt to improve their sourcing competence (Carlisle and Parker, 1989; Hines, 1994; Macbeth and Ferguson, 1994; Hines and Rich, 1997; Hines *et al.*, 2000). This view, while obviously highly appropriate in some circumstances, is clearly simplistic as a generalisation. This is because buyers have to manage in many different demand and supply and power circumstances from those experienced by automotive, aluminium and computer manufacturers (Ramsay, 1996; Cox, 1997; Cox and Townsend, 1998; Bensaou, 1999; Cox, Sanderson and Watson, 2000; Cox *et al.*, 2002, 2003).

Interestingly enough the lean approach to supply chain management has recently been challenged by an 'agile' school. The agile school contends that the lean approach cannot be the most appropriate way for buyers to source because sometimes the demand and supply variables that have to be managed are not the same (Stalk and Hoult, 1990; Meyer, 1993; Towill, 1996; Mason-Jones and Towill, 1999; Naylor, Naim and Berry, 1999; Christopher, 2000; Harrison and van Hoek, 2002). In highly volatile supply chains (where customer requirements are often unpredictable, and supplier capabilities and innovations are difficult to control) a more responsive agile approach may be required by buyers.

This discussion has led to considerable debate amongst lean and agile proponents of supply chain management, but this debate does not change the basic thrust of the supply chain management school's way of thinking about the best way for buyers to manage suppliers. Essentially both approaches adopt the view that the best way for buyers to mange suppliers is through long-term and highly collaborative relationships, based on non-adversarial, trusting and transparent ways of working. Interestingly, this is exactly the same prescriptive approach adopted by a third variant of supply chain management thinking. This approach is sometimes referred to as 'lean supply'.

The proponents of lean supply move some way from the one-dimensional approach of the lean and agile approaches and attempt to describe the goals and motives of both the buyer and supplier (Lamming *et al.*, 1996, 2001). In doing so this school demonstrates a broad understanding of the range of relationship management approaches that buyers can adopt when they interact with suppliers. While this school clearly understands the holistic nature of business relationships descriptively, the approach does not necessarily fully articulate what the goals and motives of buyers and suppliers are in any business relationship. The reason for this is because it also prescriptively argues that the best way for buyers and suppliers to interact is by developing transparent and trusting business relationships.

While transparency and trust is clearly one way of managing relationships, and one that clearly benefits buyers who do not have full information about supplier strategies and their costs of operations, it is not necessarily clear that there is anything in transparency for all suppliers – sometimes there may be, but sometimes there may not. Whether or not there will be is unfortunately not predicted by any of the current supply chain management thinking. This, plus the failure to properly articulate what the concepts of partnering or alliancing mean to both parties in terms of their operational and commercial goals, plus the tendency to focus one-dimensionally on the needs of the buyer, ensures that this way of thinking is highly limited as a guide to what is best practice for buyers in relationships with suppliers and vice versa.

The final one-dimensional buyer focused approach is that associated with *transaction cost economising*. The transaction cost economising (TCE) school was developed to provide a way of thinking about appropriate governance structures for firms when they deal with the make–buy decision. Williamson developed the idea that there was an alternative governance mode that buyers have to be aware of when they consider insourcing and outsourcing relationships in markets. Essentially Williamson was one of the first economists to realise that while buyers can use market testing governance structures to manage relationships with suppliers, this is only one of the ways in which buyer and supplier relationships need to be managed (Williamson, 1975, 1985).

The basic thrust of the TCE approach to business relationship management is that in many buyer and supplier relationships hybrid forms of governance are required. This is because buyers often wish to reduce the number of suppliers that they do business with pre-contractually; and post-contractually, what started as multi-bidding supply contests may – over time – become limited bidder market places. In these circumstances (of what may be termed 'bilateral governance') Williamson argues that alternative governance structures to those that use pure forms of insourcing or arm's-length market transactions are required to ensure that the transaction costs in the relationship are economised (Williamson, 1996).

There is clearly significant overlap in the TCE approach and the supply chain management school (and, as we shall see later, in the IMP Group approach). This is because all of these approaches focus almost exclusively on extensive, close and collaborative relationships between buyers and suppliers that can exist for lengthy periods of time. The major difference between the TCE approach and the supply chain management school is, however, Williamson's clear understanding that collaboration can pose serious problems for buyers in a world in which suppliers may use opportunism (self-seeking interest with guile) against buyers' suffering from bounded rationality (Simon, 1955).

Williamson was particularly concerned by the fact that in many circumstances of bilateral governance a 'fundamental transformation' could occur in the relationship. This implied that what had been a buyer-controlled relationship could be transformed into one in which the supplier controlled the buyer through the creation by the supplier of unforeseen switching costs that limit the room for manoeuvre of the buyer.

Williamson's concerns are presented graphically in Figure 1.2, which demonstrates that while 'comprehensive contracting' may be possible

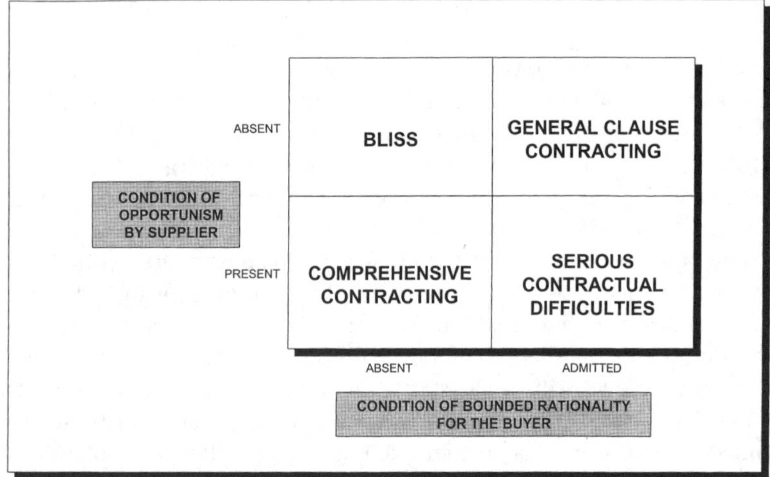

Figure 1.2 Opportunism, bounded rationality and governance mechanisms
Source: Adapted from Williamson (1985, p. 67).

for the buyer in some circumstances, in highly collaborative relationships in which future contingencies are not fully known different governance structures are needed. Williamson calls this 'general clause contracting' – or agreeing how the relationship will operate in the future even though all contingencies cannot be known now. The problem of the 'fundamental transformation' is demonstrated by the fact that buyers can operate with 'serious contractual difficulties' and, if they do not manage their general clause contracting appropriately, they may very well end up operating in this quadrant over time.

The major significance of this insight, when compared with the supply chain management school, is the recognition that long-term collaborative relationships between buyers and suppliers are not necessarily always benign or the ideal to which all buyers and suppliers should aspire. On the contrary, though the supply chain management school tends to prescribe this form of long-term collaboration as the best way to achieve competitive advantage for both parties, and especially for buyers, Williamson's analysis demonstrates that sometimes long-term collaborative relationships can create shifts in control from the buyer to the supplier, that lead to sub-optimal sourcing and transaction cost economising outcomes for the buyer.

Despite these risks of opportunism, the TCE approach contends, with the supply chain management approach, that the best way for buyers and suppliers to interact when they have business relationships is to pursue mutuality (Williamson, 2000). This implies that, despite concerns about opportunism and bounded rationality, the TCE approach is also firmly locked into the view that mutual transparency, focused on finding the most cost economising way to manage transactions, is the best way for buyers and suppliers to work together.

There are of course problems with this viewpoint. The most important of all is the criticism that while buyers may wish to economise on the costs of transactions it is not clear why this should be the case for suppliers. This is a similar criticism to that levelled at the lean supply school above and indicates that the TCE approach is clearly one-dimensionally focused on the interests of the buyer. This fact has been demonstrated by the continuing debate about the relative utility of the TCE approach when compared with the competence perspective in business strategy (Williamson, 1999).

This debate demonstrates quite clearly the problem of writers focusing on different aspects of the business relationship. The TCE approach focuses on what is clearly in the best interest of the buyer; while the competence perspective focuses on the strategies of suppliers to close markets to their competitors and create opportunities to put buyers in situations of serious contractual difficulties, if they can. It is not surprising that neither side can agree on what is the best way to analyse business relationships. This is because both approaches are partial and one-dimensional in their focus.

Despite this, the TCE approach has probably done more than any other to specify the key variables that a buyer must focus on when engaging in transactions with suppliers – particularly in relation to post-contractual sourcing risks when buyers collaborate extensively with suppliers. Nevertheless, the approach suffers from a number of weaknesses. The approach is clearly one-dimensional in that it does not provide a detailed understanding of the motives and goals of the supplier, and tends to argue that economising on the costs of transactions should be the shared goal of both the buyer and the supplier. This demonstrates a somewhat overly buyer-focused way of thinking about the purposes of a business relationship. This school also tends to be overly prescriptive in arguing that mutuality is the preferred way to manage all business relationships, without specifying clearly what mutuality means in practice for the buyer or the supplier.

Overall the fundamental problem with much of this one-dimensional buyer-focused literature is that, apart from the purchasing portfolio management approach, most of the thinking tends to prescribe the benefits of trust, transparency and collaboration, without ever fully specifying what this means in practice for either the buyer or the supplier. There is, as a result, a substantial body of literature that argues that there are significant benefits for buyers if they adopt alliancing or partnering approaches. The problem with this literature is that its proponents do not fully specify what the alternatives for the buyer and supplier are, or articulate what the risks as well as rewards are for both parties from the adoption of this approach.

Dominant approaches in marketing and sales thinking

The first major marketing and sales school discussed here is that focused on supplier leverage improvement through *customer portfolio management*. This approach has a number of variants but is widely adopted operationally by practitioners and also by academics and consultancies seeking to raise the competence of marketing and sales staff. Like its partner on the buying side – purchasing portfolio management – this approach is also one-dimensional. This is because it focuses primarily on the commercial and operational goals of the supplier, without thinking through the likely response of the buyer in any relationship.

Like purchasing portfolio management on the buyer side, however, it does not prescribe just one way of working and provides for a range of alternative choices from which mangers can choose when they act as suppliers in different competitive market circumstances.

One of the most recent developments of the customer portfolio management approach emphasises the importance of managing buyers for profits not just for sales. This approach is similar in many ways to the purchasing portfolio approach developed one-dimensionally for buyers. This approach is outlined in Figure 1.3.

As Figure 1.3 demonstrates, suppliers can think about their relationships with buyers in four major ways:

1 *Carriage trade* – this type of buyer costs a great deal to service but will pay a high net price if high quality is provided.
2 *Aggressive* – this type of buyer is also high cost to service and expects high quality but only wishes to pay the lowest price possible.
3 *Passive* – this type of buyer is relatively low cost to service and allows the supplier to earn a high net price for any given level of quality or service.
4 *Bargain basement* – this type of buyer is also low cost to service but only low net prices can be earned for any given level of quality or service.

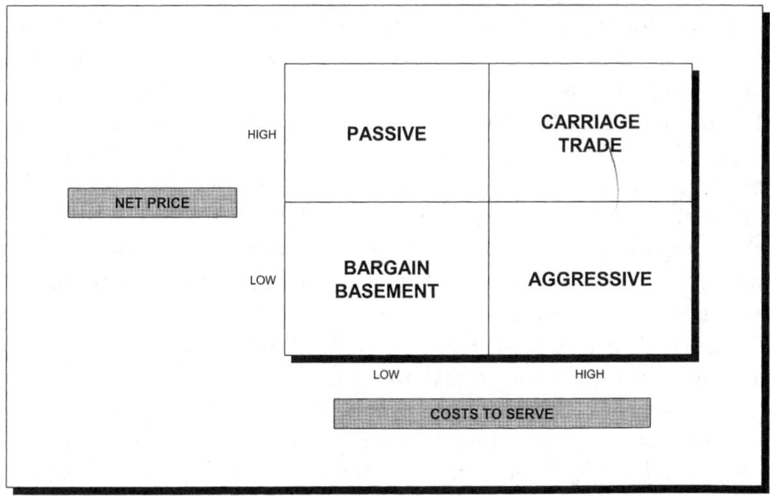

Figure 1.3 The customer classification matrix
Source: Adapted from Shapiro *et al.* (1987, p. 104).

The basic argument developed by Shapiro *et al.* is that over time customers will attempt to migrate from the carriage trade quadrant to other quadrants to the detriment of the supplier's ability to leverage returns for themselves. To counter this they recommend action plans using repeated analysis, the pinpointing of costs, the analysis of profitability dispersions, the production of support systems and the focusing of strategy to maintain the supplier in the most congenial profitability situation from the perspective of the supplier.

Clearly this type of approach to business relationship management, as well as others within this tradition that adopt similar portfolio planning approaches from the perspective of the supplier, is one-dimensional (Turnbull, 1990; Turnbull and Zolkiewski, 1995). This is because, like the purchasing portfolio approach, the analysis focuses only on one side of the relationship and seeks to provide managers with tools and techniques to allow them to leverage their position with the other party (the buyer in this case), but without a proper understanding of the goals and motives of the other party in the exchange relationship. Given this, even though the approach may provide beneficial ways of thinking about leverage for the supplier in isolation, it fails to provide for a full understanding of the interaction between buyer and supplier and therefore does not provide a predictive approach to relationship alignment.

The second major approach considered here is that developed by the *Resource-based* (RB) school. This approach is widely adopted by managers developing their business strategies for competitive advantage, and by academics and consultants attempting to raise corporate competence in business strategy. This approach also tends to be one-dimensional. This is because it focuses primarily on what suppliers should do to achieve sustainable competitive advantage, without necessarily thinking through the likely responses of buyers or customers in any relationship. Furthermore the approach tends to be prescriptive in that it argues that suppliers have only one strategy choice and that is to pursue 'isolating mechanisms' that close markets to their competitors so that they can leverage value from buyers.

There is clearly nothing wrong with this recommendation as an ideal approach for suppliers who seek to achieve above normal returns on a sustainable basis. The major problem, however, is that it provides little guidance about appropriate relationship management choices for suppliers who cannot do this, and who are operating in more or less competitive markets in which supplier leverage over customers and competitors is not sustainable. This, unfortunately for the RB school, tends to be the circumstance under which most companies operate.

This means that the RB school, while able to explain the ideal position for a supplier to dominate business relationships with customers, does not provide any insight into how companies should manage their relationships when they cannot.

There is a wide literature in the RB school, and it currently dominates strategic management thinking academically, but perhaps the most fundamental argument of the RB school is that a supplier can only achieve *rents* (above normal returns) in a business relationship with a customer if it is able to close markets to competitors through the development of isolating mechanisms (Rumelt, 1987; Barney, 1991; Cox, Sanderson and Watson, 2000). The key isolating mechanisms that companies can seek to develop include:

- property rights
- economies of scale
- information impactedness
- causal ambiguity
- reputation effects
- buyer switching costs
- buyer search costs
- communication good effects
- collusive effects

The RB school also focuses heavily on the ability of companies internally to manage their resources more effectively than their competitors, so that a relative superior competence is developed that is difficult to replicate by others (Wernerfelt, 1984; Hamel and Prahalad, 1990; Peteraf, 1993; Penrose, 1995). While this approach clearly provides important insights into how suppliers should operate in pursuit of their own commercial and operational goals, by focusing one-dimensionally on the strategy of the supplier in relation to its competitors and customers it is unlikely to provide a holistic and predictive approach to effective business relationship management. It helps managers understand what they should do to reach the ideal leverage position with their customers, but provides no real guide to action when this cannot be achieved.

In this sense the RB school provides limited practical guidance for managers who will never be able to create isolating mechanisms against their competitors and customers. Furthermore, by focusing on only one approach it tends to be prescriptive (however ideal this may be in theory) and one-dimensional and fails, thereby, to provide guidance for managers about how to deal with buyers when sustainable isolating mechanisms do not exist or cannot be created.

The relationship portfolio mapping approach

This problem has been avoided on the supply-side by writers who have recognised that there is a portfolio of relationship management approaches that suppliers have to use when they interact with buyers. This approach is called *Relationship Portfolio Mapping* (RPM). The RPM approach focuses both analytically and predictively on the relationship management choices that suppliers must make in any transaction. The RPM approach is firmly grounded in political economy, resource dependency, TCE and relational contracting ways of thinking (Krapfel *et al.*, 1991).

Perhaps the most important contribution of the RPM approach has been its development of a comprehensive specification of relationship management choices available for a supplier when interacting with a buyer. The approach is derived from work in political economy and marketing channel management, in which issues such as control, conflict and power are perceived to be of major significance for the choice of relationship management style by suppliers (Zald, 1970; Walmsley and Zald, 1973; Benson, 1975; Stern and Reve, 1980; Achrol *et al.*, 1983; Arndt, 1983; Frazier, 1983; Schul *et al.*, 1983; Anand and Stern, 1985; Dwyer and Summers, 1986; Gaski, 1986; Thorelli, 1986; Heidi and John, 1988; and Dwyer and Sejo, 1987).

As Figure 1.4 demonstrates, four types of relationship are defined in the RPM approach. These are defined as follows:

1 *Partner* – a relationship with high interest communality and high relationship value, with equitable sharing of profits.

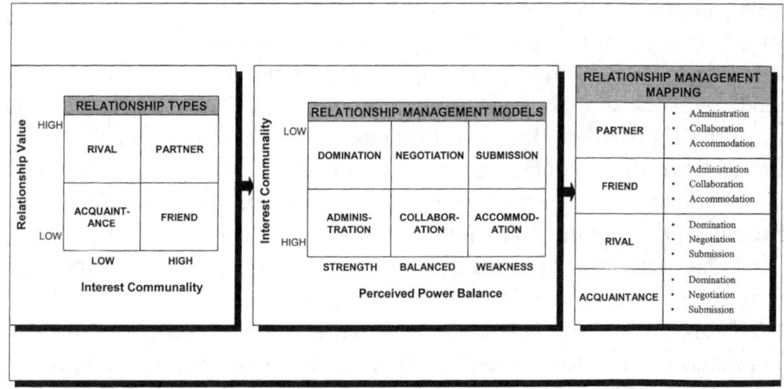

Figure 1.4 Relationship portfolio mapping
Source: Adapted from Krapfel *et al.* (1991).

2 *Friend* – a relationship with high interest communality but low relationship value, with monitoring of future potential opportunities.
3 *Rival* – a relationship with low interest communality and high relationship value, with attempts to find alternative partners.
4 *Acquaintance* – a relationship with low interest communality but low relationship value, with only standard offerings provided.

The RPM approach further develops this segmentation by demonstrating the relationship management modes that may be used in any transaction in relation to the perceived power balance and the level of interest communality between the two parties. The six types are defined as follows:

1 *Collaboration* – a transparent and trusting relationship mode, with extensive information sharing in balanced power situations, with high interest communality.
2 *Negotiation* – an arm's-length relationship mode, with limited information sharing, a balanced power situation, with low interest communality.
3 *Administration* – a uni-directional relationship mode, with the supplier directing information flow but offering promises to the buyer.
4 *Domination* – a uni-directional relationship mode, with the supplier directing information flow and threats rather than promises to the buyer.
5 *Accommodation* – a cooperative relationship mode in which the supplier provides non-sensitive information to the buyer.
6 *Submission* – a non-cooperative, but submissive relationship management mode in which the supplier provides information reluctantly to the buyer.

Relationship mapping occurs when the supplier chooses a relationship management mode that is appropriate for a particular relationship type. The RPM approach concludes that the administration, collaboration and accommodation modes are the most appropriate to link with partner and friend relationship types. In acquaintance and rival relationship types the domination, negotiation and submission types are the most appropriate. Appropriateness is defined by reference to the degree to which the selection reduces conflict and the transaction costs associated with information search, relationship monitoring and contract enforcement.

The strength of the RPM approach is that it deepens our understanding of the need to think about relationships in terms of the appropriateness of particular modes of management under specific circumstances. Furthermore, the RPM approach recognises that power plays a major role in the selection of optimal modes for particular relationship types. This improves our understanding of the complexity of choice for managers in relationships considerably, and begins the process of developing an analytical and predictive way of thinking about managerial choice, when compared with the more descriptive customer account perspective discussed earlier.

Despite this the RPM approach suffers from two major weaknesses. The first is that it is written almost exclusively from the perspective of the supplier and does not consider whether or not the buyer's perspective on relationship management is likely to be different or the same as the supplier's. This is true even though the RPM school recognises that it is desirable for the supplier to match their relationship type and mode to that of the buyer, and signal the mismatch to the buyer. While this demonstrates an understanding of the need to be holistic in thinking about the relationship between the buyer and the supplier, the RPM approach does not provide a clear specification of which specific relationship management types and modes match with particular buyer relationship management types and modes to provide for effective and efficient relationship alignment.

Given this, the RPM approach is not truly holistic and remains one-dimensional on the supplier's side of the relationship, even though it provides a much more sophisticated understanding of the relationship management choices available for both buyers and suppliers. The second major weakness is that while the approach discusses the concept of power it does not fully articulate what the key variables are that shape the power circumstances that buyers and suppliers may find themselves in. Nor does this approach explain how these attributes of power impact directly on the relationship management choices of both parties, or how suppliers (or for that matter buyers) can move to more congenial power circumstances or relationship management types and modes.

This implies that while the RPM approach is a valuable addition to our understanding of business relationship management it fails to properly specify what the impact of power is on both parties to the exchange, and therefore provides only a one-dimensional conceptualisation of relationship alignment. As the discussion that follows demonstrates, it is only by fully understanding the transaction between the buyer and supplier from the perspective of both parties that an holistic understanding can be attained, and a truly analytic and predictive approach to relationship alignment created.

(ii) Holistic dyadic approaches

There are two approaches to business relationship management that do not take a primarily one-dimensional approach. The two holistic dyadic approaches to business relationship management are those associated with the work of the *International Marketing and Purchasing (IMP) Group* and the *Power Perspective School*. Both of these approaches to business relationship management contend that it is necessary to understand the goals and motives of both the buyer and supplier as they interact together. This implies that effective business relationship management can only be achieved if both parties are aware of the goals of the other, and that these are aligned effectively both now and in the future. Despite this agreement on the need for a holistic approach there are significant differences between the two perspectives.

The International Marketing and Purchasing (IMP) Group

The IMP Group is a broad church and has developed its detailed insights into buyer and supplier relationships over twenty years (Hakansson and Wootz, 1979; Ford, 1980; Turnbull and Cunningham, 1981; Hakansson, 1982; Ford, Hakansson and Johanson, 1986; Easton, 1992; Johanson and Mattsson, 1992; Ford, 1998, 2002). The major benefit of the IMP approach has been its unequivocal focus on the need to understand the complex interrelationships between the buyer and the supplier from the perspective of both parties when they interact. Thus the IMP approach has provided an extremely comprehensive descriptive account of the nature of business relationships. This is outlined in Figure 1.5.

As Figure 1.5 demonstrates, the IMP school has provided the most detailed account possible of the factors that impact upon buyer and supplier transactions. The IMP approach contends that the interactions between buyers and suppliers are shaped by 'environmental' factors, which neither party to the exchange can directly control (*limiting factors*). This involves such aspects as market structure; dynamism; internationalisation; channel position; and, social system. The IMP approach contends, however, that there are some elements of the interaction that buyers and suppliers can influence (*handling factors*). These aspects are referred to as 'atmosphere' and include such elements as power/dependence; conflict and cooperation; and, expectations (IMP, 2002).

One of the major benefits of this approach is its inclusiveness. In particular, work by Campbell has demonstrated clearly the need for buyers and suppliers to think about the strategies they should adopt under different types of buyer and supplier interaction (Campbell, 1985). He argues that there are three types of strategy – competitive, cooperative

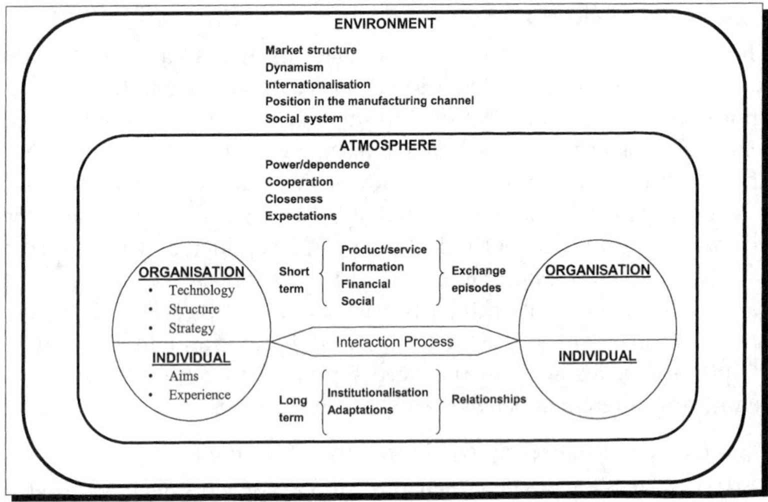

Figure 1.5 The IMP interaction model
Source: D. Ford, *Understanding Business Markets and Purchasing* (2002, p. 29).

and command – that buyers and suppliers can use with one another, and that sometimes these will create a match or mismatch in a relationship depending on the strategies that both sides adopt. This is a valuable contribution because it demonstrates that the relationship between the buyer and the supplier must be understood from the perspective of both the buyer and the supplier. This portfolio approach to buyer and supplier relationships has also been adopted to understand how different types of relationships can be managed in the automotive sector (Bensaou, 1999).

The major weakness of the IMP approach, however, is its lack of predictive focus on the relative importance of any of the variables specified in an interaction between a buyer and supplier. This is another way of saying that the IMP approach is comprehensive but primarily descriptive, providing limited predictive guidance for managers in how to manage relationships in any particular circumstance. The approach also tends to be dominated by marketing and sales writers and demonstrates a lack of comprehensive understanding of the commercial and operational motives of buyers. Empirically buyers often demonstrate an unwillingness or inability to develop the close collaborative relationships that the IMP Group believes are the most conducive for the majority of sourcing requirements.

A further critique that can be made is similar to that levelled against the supply chain management approach. This is that the IMP approach also tends to emphasise the benefits of those interactions between buyers and suppliers that produce the most mutually beneficial outcomes, without explaining in detail what this concept means for buyers and suppliers in practice (Hakansson, 1982). This is undoubtedly due to the research bias of the IMP approach that has focused primarily on long-lasting and highly collaborative buyer and supplier relationships.

That said, the approach has provided considerable insight into the factors that impinge on buyer and supplier choices. The major problem with the IMP approach is that while it is comprehensive in detailing the major factors involved in buyer and supplier exchange and interaction it does not provide any predictive guide for action by managers, nor does it explain fully which variables are likely to be more important than others in determining transactional outcomes in specific circumstances. In fact the IMP Group remains essentially pessimistic about the ability of managers to control many of the environmental factors that impinge on relationships (Ford, 2002).

The Power Perspective

The Power Perspective on buyer and supplier relationship management has a long tradition of its own, and has also been supported by the work of the IMP Group and the RPM portfolio approach. As we saw above, both of these approaches have focused extensively on power and dependence as major concepts and have always accepted that power is central to an understanding of transactions(Zald, 1970; Campbell and Cunningham, 1983; Dwyer and Summers, 1986; Gaski, 1986; Thorelli, 1986; Frazier and Anita, 1995; Hakansson and Gadde, 1997).

The Power Perspective is a holistic approach and focuses explicitly on the exchange relationship between the buyer and supplier. Unlike the IMP approach the Power Perspective has, however, always asserted that the relative power of the buyer and supplier is the determining factor in the operational and commercial outcome in any transaction. This is the approach that is adopted in this volume, which is an attempt to link the thinking in the RPM and IMP approaches with the Power Perspective in order to develop both a predictive and holistic approach to business relationship management.

The Power Perspective is evident in many areas of business management writing. The approach claims many proponents, all of whom have articulated many of the key variables that impact on the relative power of buyers and suppliers (Emerson, 1962; Blau, 1964; Cook, 1977;

Cook and Emerson, 1978; Pfeffer and Salancik, 1978; Porter, 1980; Cook *et al.*, 1983; Provan and Grassenheimer, 1994; Maloni and Benton, 2000). Despite this, the approach has one major weakness, and that is that while many writers use the concept it has never been fully articulated theoretically or in practice. This is the major criticism made of the power school by writers who argue that power may be important but it has never been satisfactorily defined conceptually (Williamson, 1985). There is clearly some truth in this criticism but despite it there is still a wide consensus that power is a significant variable that must be understood in business relationships.

The Power Perspective has, therefore, articulated many of the variables that impinge on buyer and supplier leverage of one another, and these will be discussed in some detail in what follows. Despite this, the approach, while holistically interested in the exchange relationship between the buyer and the supplier, has three major problems. First, writers use the concept without properly defining it (Scott and Westbrook, 1991). Second, they use it but focus on only one party in the exchange (Campbell and Cunningham, 1983; Ramsay, 1994 and 1996). Third, amongst most writers in this school there is no real attempt to link the variables that impinge on buyer and supplier power predictively with relationship management outcomes or strategies.

Thus, while the specification of power variables has become increasingly sophisticated, the analysis of the link between power circumstances and the relationship management strategies that buyers and suppliers can use within them has never been fully developed. This is another way of saying that the existing literature, while providing a way of describing the current power circumstances that exist, does not provide a way of predicting which relationship management approaches are likely to be the most appropriate under specific circumstances for either the buyer or the supplier to adopt to achieve their respective goals.

Despite this, the RPM approach has provided a useful specification of the relationship management styles that can be used under different circumstances (Krapfel *et al.*, 1991), and the Power Perspective has provided an indication of many of the levers that buyers and suppliers can use to move from existing power circumstances to those that are more conducive (Cox, Sanderson and Watson, 2000; Cox, 2001a,b). It seems evident, therefore, that it is through the linkage of the relationship management approach of the RPM school and the specification of power circumstances that a more holistic analytic and predictive approach to the alignment of business relationships between buyers and suppliers will be achieved. Before this can be undertaken it is necessary to specify more closely what buyer and supplier transactions are, and how these can be understand operationally and commercially.

1.2 Business transactions and relationships in theory and practice

Current approaches to the analysis of business relationships provide rich and detailed descriptive information but they also contain major gaps, or tend to emphasise one aspect of the relationship to the exclusion of a more holistic approach. Overall, however, if there is one major criticism of current approaches it is that they fail to provide the analytic basis to allow managers (whether operating as buyers or suppliers) to predict which types of relationship management approaches are the most appropriate to use under different circumstances.

The major reason for this is because current approaches have not fully specified the reasons for business relationships, or the full range of relationship management choices that are available to both parties when they come together in a transaction that exchanges goods and services for money. This is because none of the current approaches properly explains the commercial and operational preferences of buyers and suppliers when they interact with one another. The reason for this malaise is because current approaches fail to properly understand that buyer and supplier preferences are driven by the power circumstances in any relationship.

In other words, what a buyer or supplier chooses to do operationally or commercially in any relationship is contingent on the power circumstances that they find themselves in now, and the power circumstances they believe they can create in the future. Clearly some current approaches recognise the fact of power in relationships but to do so is not necessarily to fully specify what the concept means, or explain how it acts as the driving force in shaping and limiting relationship management choices for both the buyer and supplier.

This book seeks, therefore, to provide an alternative view of business relationship management that is both analytical and predictive rather than merely descriptive and prescriptive. The aim of this volume is to outline in detail the conditions that must be in place for the buyer and supplier to manage business relationships successfully, under the different circumstances of power and leverage that can exist when exchange transactions occur. In doing so we hope to specify clearly what a business relationship entails, both operationally and commercially, and also the full range of relationship management choices that are available to the buyer and supplier when they interact.

We also hope to demonstrate that by understanding the ideal-typical relationship management approaches that work best under different power situations it is possible for managers to understand and predict which types of relationship approaches, and which types of relationship partners, are most conducive for success and which will lead to failure. To achieve success in relationships it is clear, therefore, that one must create an alignment of buyer and supplier commercial and operational goals under specific circumstances of power.

To assist the reader in understanding the argument of the book, Figure 1.6 provides a way of thinking about the theoretical and practical basis for business relationships. As the figure demonstrates, business relationships can be understood *operationally* and they can be understood *commercially*. The key point being made here is that, although both of these aspects are important, the ultimate purpose of a business relationship is always fundamentally about commercial rather than operational outcomes. In other words, success or failure in business relationships must be understood primarily in commercial rather than operational terms.

Clearly these two aspects of relationships are inextricably intertwined, but it is the commercial outcome – the ability of each party in

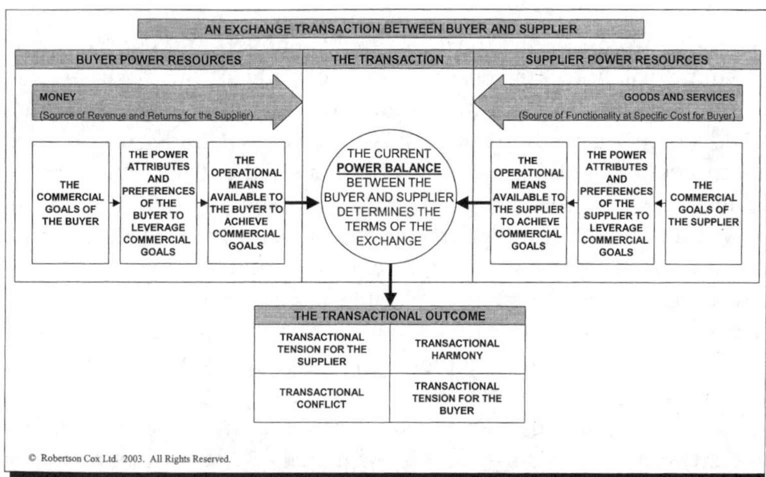

Figure 1.6 Business relationships as transaction and outcome

the exchange relationship to achieve an acceptable commercial outcome – that is the ultimate test of the success or failure of a business relationship for both parties. This does not imply that both sides have to achieve the same commercial outcome to make the relationship successful, only that each party in a transaction must be satisfied with the commercial outcome that they have received.

It follows, however, that in some business relationships (in theory at least) both parties will achieve their commercial goals (*transactional harmony*) and in other transactions one party may be more satisfied than the other with the commercial outcome (*transactional tension*). If both parties are dissatisfied with the commercial outcome then a state of *transactional conflict* will exist. This raises the possibility that conflict and tension is inevitable in business relationships, and that *transactional harmony* may be the exception rather than the rule. What this means is that many relationships occur even though the commercial goals of one or both of the parties involved are not being completely achieved. It is our view that this is likely to be the rule in business relationship management and that *transactional harmony* may be difficult to sustain in many circumstances in the real world.

Indeed it may well be the case that the best commercial outcome for the buyer is to operate with *transactional tension for the supplier* and for the supplier to seek a commercial outcome that has *transactional tension for the buyer*. This is because the aim of both the buyer and the supplier is not to satisfy the commercial goals of the other party to the exchange, but to maximize their own. This does not mean that a buyer or supplier would necessarily reject *transactional harmony* if this maximised or satisfied their own commercial goals, but rather that they would choose whichever outcome provides them commercially with the best outcome from their point of view. This is simply to make the point that nobody enters into a commercial relationship to help the other party – they do it to help themselves (Cox, 2005).

This raises the issue of course of why a buyer or a supplier enters into a relationship in which they do not achieve their commercial goals when the other side is doing so. The answer to this question is what this book is fundamentally about. It is our view that buyers and suppliers often have to enter into asymmetrical commercial arrangements because of the power circumstance they are in.

Both the buyer and supplier have to make complex calculations about what is the best option available to them to achieve their commercial goals. Sometimes they will have extensive power attributes that allow them to leverage continuous improvements in their commercial goals – these will normally be circumstances of *supplier or buyer dominance*. In other circumstances both of the parties will have extensive power resources that force both parties to work together and share the commercial returns created by the relationship.

Whether the buyer achieves more than the supplier and vice versa, or whether they both equally achieve their commercial goals is – as we will demonstrate in what follows – a function of the relative power between the buyer and the supplier, both now and in the future. It is also, as we shall see, a function of the ability of either party to make appropriate operational and commercial choices when they work together in business relationships.

The ability of managers – whether acting as buyers or suppliers – to make appropriate commercial and operational choices about how to align business relationships with other parties is in our view one of the keys to competitive advantage. Many companies – as the case studies that follow in the second part of this volume demonstrate – experience significant problems in aligning their commercial and operational goals effectively. It follows that the misalignment of business relationships must be a significant waste of valuable and scarce corporate time and resources. If companies could find ways of better aligning their commercial and operational goals when they engage in business relationships then they would clearly achieve a competitive advantage over those companies that cannot.

1.3 Conclusion

The chapter has shown that there are many different perspectives on business relationship management, and major differences of opinion about what managers should do to be effective in managing their relationships, either as buyers or suppliers. Overall the analysis has concluded that far too many of the current approaches are one-dimensional, descriptive or overly prescriptive about specific approaches to relationship management for either the buyer or the supplier. Only the IMP, RPM and Power approaches, it has been argued, take a sufficiently holistic approach to analysing the objective circumstances and the full range of relationship management choices available for buyers and suppliers.

Given this, it is clear that it is through a combination of the Power Perspectives specification of the key variables that impact on managerial choice, and the IMP and RPM specifications of relationship management choices, that an inclusive approach to relationship alignment for buyers and suppliers can be achieved. Before this can be achieved it is necessary, first, to fully specify what the commercial goals of buyers and suppliers are. Having achieved this it is then necessary to discuss in detail the full range of operational choices available to the buyer and supplier to achieve these goals.

The next chapter examines the commercial goals (*strategic ends*) of buyers and suppliers, and how these relate to power in exchange transactions. This is then followed by a discussion of the *operational means* available to buyers and suppliers to achieve their commercial goals in business relationships.

References

Achrol, R. S., Reve, T. and Stern, L. W. (1983) 'The environment of marketing channel dyads: a framework for comparative analysis', *Journal of Marketing*, vol. 47, pp. 44–54.

Anand, P. and Stern, L. W. (1985) 'A socio-psychological explanation for why marketing channel members relinquish control', *Journal of Marketing Research*, vol. 22, pp. 365–76.

Arndt, J. (1983) 'The political economy paradigm: a foundation for theory building in marketing', *Journal of Marketing*, vol. 47, pp. 68–78.

Barney, J. B. (1991) 'Firm resources and sustained competitive advantage', *Journal of Management*, vol. 17, no. 1, pp. 99–120.

Bensaou, M. (1999) 'Portfolios of buyer–supplier relationships', *Sloan Management Review* (Summer), pp. 35–44.

Benson, J. K. (1975) 'The inter-organizational network as a political economy', *Administrative Science Quarterly*, vol. 20, pp. 229–49.

Blau, P. M. (1964) *Exchange and Power in Social Life* (New York: John Wiley).

Campbell, N. C. G. (1985) 'An interaction approach to organisational buying behavior', *Journal of Business Research*, vol. 13, pp. 35–48.

Campbell, N. C. G. and Cunningham, M. T. (1983) 'Customer analysis for strategy development in industrial markets', *Strategic Management Journal*, vol. 4, pp. 369–80.

Carlisle, J. A. and Parker, R. C. (1989) *Beyond Negotiation: Redeeming Customer–Supplier Relationships* (Chichester: John Wiley).

Christopher, M. (2000) 'The agile supply chain', *Industrial Marketing Management*, vol. 29, pp. 37–44.

Cook, K. S. (1977) 'Exchange and power in networks of inter-organisational relations', *Sociological Quarterly*, vol. 18, pp. 62–82.

Cook, K. S. and Emerson, J. (1978) 'Power, equity and commitment in exchange networks', *American Sociological Review*, vol. 43, pp. 712–39.

Cook, K. S., Emerson, R. M., Gillmore, M. R. and Yamagishi, T. (1983) 'The distribution of power in exchange networks: theory and experimental results', *American Journal of Sociology*, vol. 89, no. 2, pp. 275–305.

Cox, A. (1997) *Business Success* (Helpston, UK: Earlsgate Press).

Cox, A. (2001a) 'Understanding buyer and supplier power: a framework for procurement and supply competence', *The Journal of Supply Chain Management,* vol. 37, no. 2, pp. 8–15.

Cox, A. (2001b) 'Managing with power: strategies for improving value appropriation from supply relationships', *The Journal of Supply Chain Management* (Spring), vol. 37, no. 2, pp. 42–7.

Cox, A. (2005) *The Rules of the Game: How to Capture Value in Business* (Helpston, UK: Earlsgate Press).

Cox, A. and Townsend, M. (1998) *Strategic Procurement in Construction* (London: Thomas Telford).

Cox, A., Sanderson, J. and Watson, G. (2000) *Power Regimes: Mapping the DNA of Business and Supply Chain Relationships* (Helpston, UK: Earlsgate Press).

Cox, A., Ireland, P., Lonsdale, C., Sanderson, J. and Watson, G. (2002) *Supply Chains, Markets and Power: Mapping Buyer and Supplier Power Regimes* (London: Routledge).

Cox A., Ireland, P., Lonsdale, C., Sanderson, J. and Watson, G. (2003) *Supply Chain Management: A Guide to Best Practice* (London: Financial Times/Prentice Hall).

Dwyer, F. R. and Sejo, O. (1987) 'Output sector munificence effects in the internal political economy of marketing channels', *Journal of Marketing Research,* vol. 24, pp. 347–58.

Dwyer, F. R. and Summers, J. O. (1986) 'Perceptions of inter-firm power and its use within a franchise channel of distribution', *Journal of Marketing Research,* vol. 23, pp. 169–76.

Easton, G. (1992) 'Industrial networks: a review', in B. Axelsson and G. Easton (eds), *Industrial Networks: A New View of Reality* (London: Routledge).

Emerson, R. M. (1962) 'Power–dependence relations', *American Sociological Review,* vol. 27, pp. 31–41.

Ford, D. (1980) 'The development of buyer–seller relationships in industrial markets', *European Journal of Marketing,* vol. 14, nos 5/6, pp. 339–54.

Ford, D. (ed.) (1998) *Managing Business Relationships* (Chichester: Wiley).

Ford, D. (ed.) (2002) *Understanding Business Markets and Purchasing: An Interaction Approach* (London: International Thompson).

Ford, D., Hakansson, H. and Johanson, J. (1986) 'How do companies interact?', *Industrial Marketing and Purchasing,* vol. 1, no. 1, pp. 26–41.

Frazier, G. L. (1983) 'Inter-organizational exchange behaviour in marketing channel: a broadened perspective', *Journal of Marketing,* vol. 47, pp. 68–78.

Frazier G. L. and Anita, K. (1995) 'Exchange relationships and inter-firm power in channels of distribution', *Journal of the Academy of Marketing Sciences,* vol. 23, pp. 321–6.

Gaski, J. (1986) 'Inter-relations amongst a channel entity's power sources: impact of the exercise of reward and coercion on expert, referent and legitimate power sources', *Journal of Marketing Research,* vol. 23, pp. 62–77.

Gelderman, C. J. and van Weele, A. J. (2002) 'Strategic direction through purchasing portfolio management: a case study', *The Journal of Supply Chain Management* (Spring), vol. 38, no. 2, pp. 30–7.

Hakansson, H. (ed.) (1982) *International Marketing and Purchasing of Industrial Goods: An Interaction Approach* (Chichester: John Wiley).

Hakansson, H. and Gadde, L. E. (1997) 'Supplier relations', in D. Ford (ed.), *Understanding Business Markets: Interactions, Relationships and Networks* (London: Dryden Press) pp. 400–29.

Hakansson, H. and Wootz, B. (1979) 'A framework of industrial buying and selling', *Industrial Marketing Management*, vol. 8, pp. 113–23.

Hamel, G. and Prahalad, C. K. (1990) 'The core competence of the corporation', *Harvard Business Review* (May/June), pp. 79–91.

Harrison, A. and van Hoek, R. (2002) *Logistics Management and Strategy* (New York: Prentice Hall).

Heidi, J. and John, G. (1988) 'The role of dependence balancing in safeguarding transaction-specific assets in conventional channels', *Journal of Marketing*, vol. 52, pp. 20–35.

Hines, P. (1994) *Creating World Class Suppliers: Unlocking Mutual Competitive Advantage* (London: Pitman).

Hines, P. and Rich, N. (1997) 'The seven value stream mapping tools', *International Journal of Production and Operations Management*, vol. 17, no. 1, pp. 46–64.

Hines, P., Lamming, R., Jones, D., Cousins, P. and Rich, N. (2000) *Value Stream Management: Strategy and Excellence in the Supply Chain* (London: Financial Times/Prentice Hall).

IMP Group (2002) 'An interaction approach', in D. Ford (ed.), *Understanding Business Markets and Purchasing: An Interaction Approach* (London: International Thompson) pp. 19–34.

Johanson, J. and Mattsson, L. G. (1992) 'Marketing investments and market investments in industrial networks', *International Journal of Research in Marketing*, vol. 2, pp. 185–95.

Kraljic, P. (1983) 'Purchasing must become supply management', *Harvard Business Review*, vol. 61, no. 5 (September–October), pp. 109–17.

Krapfel, R. E., Salmond, D. and Spekman, R. (1991) 'A strategic approach to managing buyer and seller relationships', *European Journal of Marketing*, vol. 25, no. 9, pp. 22–37.

Lamming, R. C., Cousins, P. D. and Notman, D. M. (1996) 'Beyond vendor assessment: the relationship assessment programme', *European Journal of Purchasing and Supply Management*, vol. 2, no. 4, pp. 173–81.

Lamming, R. C., Caldwell, N. D., Harrison, D.A. and Phillips, W. (2001) 'Transparency in supply relationships: concept and practice', *The Journal of Supply Chain Management* (Fall), vol. 37, no. 4, pp. 4–10.

Macbeth, D. and Ferguson, N. (1994) *Partnership Sourcing: An Integrated Supply Chain Approach* (London: Pitman).

Maloni, M. and Benton, B. C. (2000) 'Power influences in the supply chain', *Journal of Business Logistics*, vol. 21, no. 1, pp. 49–73.

Mason-Jones, R. and Towill, D. (1999) 'Total cycle time compression and the agile supply chain', *International Journal of Production Economics*, vol. 62, pp. 61–73.

Meyer, C. (1993) *Fast Cycle Time* (New York: Free Press).

Naylor, M., Naim, D. and Berry, D. (1999) 'Leagility: integrating the lean and agile supply chain', *International Journal of Production Economics*, vol. 62, pp. 46–73.

Olsen, R. F. and Ellram, L. M. (1997) 'A portfolio approach to supplier relationships', *Industrial Marketing Management*, vol. 26, pp. 101–13.

Penrose, E. (1995) *The Theory of the Growth of the Firm* (Oxford: Oxford University Press).

Peteraf, M. A. (1993) 'The cornerstones of competitive advantage: a resource-based view', *Strategic Management Journal*, vol. 14, pp. 179–91.

Pfeffer, J. and Salancik, G. R. (1978) *The External Control of Organisations: A Resource Dependency Perspective* (New York: Harper & Row).

Porter, M. E. (1980) *Competitive Strategy: Techniques for Analysing Industries and Competitors* (New York: Free Press).

Provan, K. and Grassenheimer, J. (1994) 'Supplier commitment in relational contract exchanges with buyers: a study of organisational dependence and exercised power', *Journal of Management Studies*, vol. 31, no. 1, pp. 55–68.

Ramsay, J. (1994) 'Purchasing power', *European Journal of Purchasing and Supply Management*, vol. 1, no. 3, pp. 125–38.

Ramsay, J. (1996) 'The case against purchasing partnerships', *International Journal of Purchasing and Materials Management* (Fall), pp. 13–21.

Rumelt, R. P. (1987) 'Theory, strategy and entrepreneurship', in D. Teece (ed.), *The Competitive Challenge* (New York: Harper & Row).

Schul, P. L., Pride, W. L. and Little, T. L. (1983) 'The impact of channel leadership behavior on intra-channel conflicts', *Journal of Marketing*, vol. 47, pp. 21–34.

Scott, C. and Westbrook, R. (1991) 'New strategic tools for supply chain management', *International Journal of Physical Distribution and Logistics Management*, vol. 21, no. 1, pp. 23–33.

Shapiro, B. P., Kasturi Rangan, V., Moriarty, R. T. and Ross, E. B. (1987) 'Manage customers for profits (not just sales)', *Harvard Business Review*, September–October, pp. 101–8.

Simon, H.A. (1955) 'A behavioural model of rational choice', *Quarterly Journal of Economics*, vol. 69 (February), pp. 99–118.

Stalk, G. and Hoult, T. (1990) *Competing Against Time* (New York: Free Press).

Stern, L. W. and Reve, T. (1980) 'Distribution channels as political economies: a framework for comparative analysis', *Journal of Marketing*, vol. 44, pp. 52–64.

Thorelli, H. (1986) 'Networks: between markets and hierarchies', *Strategic Management Journal*, vol. 7, pp. 37–51.

Towill, D. (1996) 'Time compression and supply chain management – a guided tour', *Logistics Information Management*, vol. 9, no. 6, pp. 41–53.

Turnbull, P. W. (1990) 'A review of portfolio planning models for industrial marketing and purchasing management', *European Journal of Marketing*, vol. 24, no. 3, pp. 7–22.

Turnbull, P. W. and Cunningham, M. T. (1981) 'The quality of relationships', in P. W. Turnbull and M. T. Cunningham (eds), *International Marketing and Purchasing: A Survey among Marketing and Purchasing Executives in Five European Countries* (New York: Macmillan).

Turnbull, P. and Zolkiewski, J. M. (1995) 'Customer portfolios: sales costs and profitability' (Manchester School of Management, UMIST, UK).

Walmsley, G. L. and Zald, M. N. (1973) *The Political Economy of Public Organizations* (Lexington, MA: Lexington Books).

Wernerfelt, B. (1984) 'A resource-based view of the firm', *Strategic Management Journal*, vol. 5, pp. 171–80.

Williamson, O. E. (1975) *Markets and Hierarchies: Analysis and Anti-Trust Implications* (New York: Free Press).

Williamson, O. E. (1985) *The Economic Institutions of Capitalism: Firms, Markets, Relational Contracting* (New York: Free Press).

Williamson, O. E. (1996) *The Mechanisms of Governance* (Oxford: Oxford University Press).

Williamson, O. E. (1999) 'Strategy research: governance and competence perspectives', *Strategic Management Journal*, vol. 20, pp. 1087–108.

Williamson, O. E. (2000) 'Empirical microeconomics: another perspective' (Unpublished paper, University of California, September 2000), 40 pages.

Womack, J. P. and Jones, D. T. (1996) *Lean Thinking: Banish Waste and Create Wealth in Your Organisation* (New York: Simon & Schuster).

Womack, J. P., Jones, D. T. and Roos, D. (1990) *The Machine that Changed the World* (New York: Rawson Associates).

Zald, M. N. (1970) 'Political economy: a framework for comparative analysis', in M. N. Zald (ed.), *Power in Organizations* (Nashville, TN: Vanderbilt University Press).

2
Power, Leverage and the Strategic Purposes of Business Relationships

Having discussed the strengths and weaknesses of the current literature this chapter introduces the conditions that must be in place for successful relationship alignment under changing circumstances of buyer and supplier power. The analysis attempts to provide a holistic account by focusing on the relationship from the perspective of the buyer as well as the supplier. Unlike some previous analyses the approach outlined here starts from the view that there is no one best way for buyers or suppliers to manage business relationships. Although there may be ideal positions for both the buyer and supplier, how any organisation should manage a business relationship in practice depends on the circumstance it is in. This means that buyers and suppliers often have to manage business relationships in circumstances that are far from ideal.

It follows, therefore, that if managers wish to be successful in business relationship management they must understand how to manage appropriately the diversity of relationships that can exist between organisational buyers and their suppliers under different transactional circumstances. Given this, it is necessary to specify clearly *the range of external circumstances* that buyers and suppliers find themselves having to manage and *the range of strategies for leveraging increased value* from any exchange transaction. These are the *strategic ends* that organisations pursue commercially as buyers or as suppliers. This is the subject-matter of this chapter.

For the successful management of business relationships it is also necessary to understand *operational means*. This involves understanding *the type of operational relationship management approaches* that buyers and suppliers can select from; and *the range of management styles* that are available for their effective implementation. This is the subject-matter of the next chapter.

Ultimately, it is necessary for both the buyer and the supplier in any relationship to *internally align their strategic ends with operational means*, as well as to find *an appropriate coincidence of interest* with one another externally. If this is achieved, then, as Figure 2.1 demonstrates, there will be the creation of both internal and external alignment in business-to-business relationships. In the absence of these forms of joint internal and external alignment it is likely that there will be misalignment and conflict in business-to-business relationships between buyers and suppliers. As the figure demonstrates, there are likely to be many more circumstances in which misalignment occurs in business-to-business relationships than does perfect alignment. How external alignment is achieved is the subject-matter of Chapter 4. Internal alignment is discussed in Chapter 8.

In order to understand how to create alignment and avoid misalignment and outright conflict in business relationships this chapter is divided into two major sections. First, *strategic ends* are outlined, through an analysis of the external power circumstances that exist between buyers and suppliers. This is followed by an analysis of the commercial strategies that organisations can use to leverage improvements in their power position with the other parties in an exchange transaction.

2.1 Managing strategic ends in circumstances of buyer and supplier power

There is one major aspect that must be understood when managing any business relationship, and this is true whether one is involved in a transaction as a buyer or as a supplier. This major aspect is the external power structure that exists between the buyer and supplier organisations in any transaction, and whether or not it will support a particular sourcing and relationship management approach.

- For the purposes of this analysis external power refers to the ability of an organisation (whether acting as a buyer or a supplier) to use relationship management strategies and relationship management styles to maximise its commercial interests by participation in a transaction.
- For the buyer this will normally involve the maximisation of use value and the minimisation of exchange cost.
- For the supplier this will normally involve the maximisation of both revenue and returns (profits).

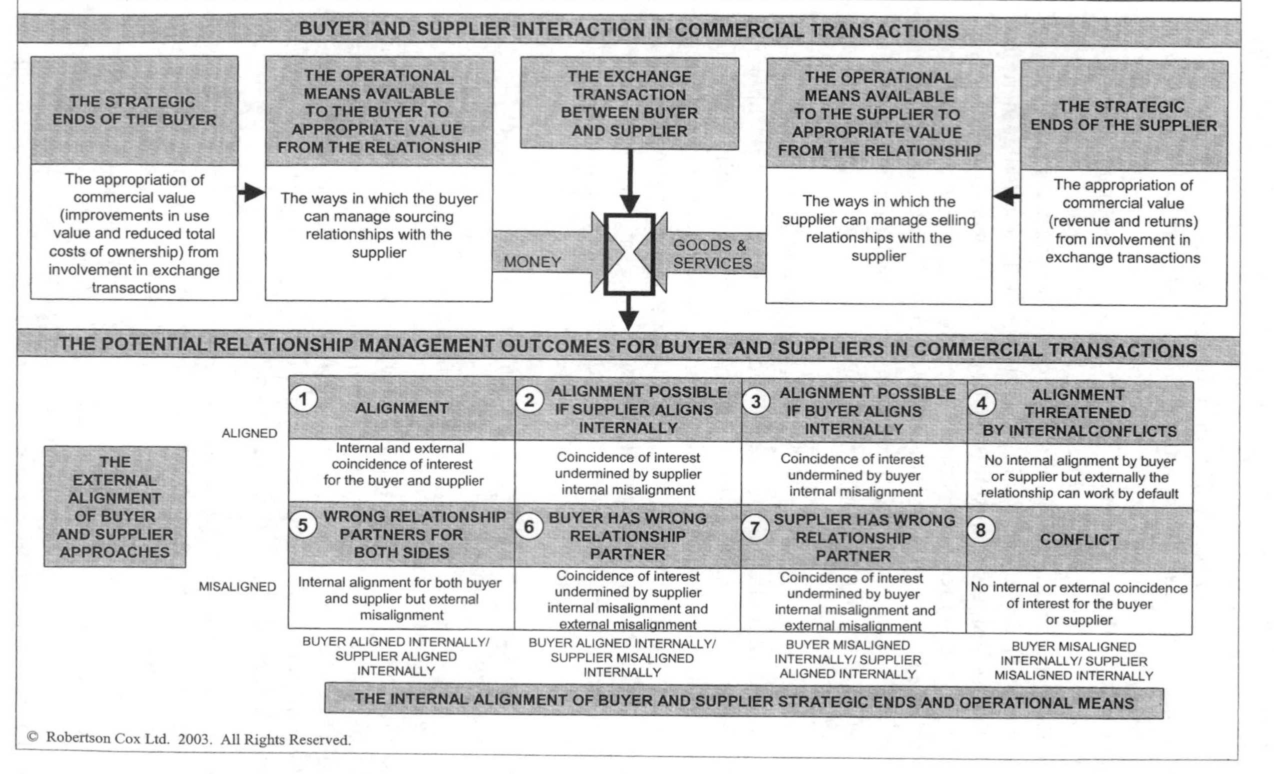

Figure 2.1 Alignment, misalignment and conflict in business relationships

Clearly these definitions do not do full justice to the concept of power in business and economic life. This is because the definitions do not adequately describe the problem of subjective and objective interests for both individuals and organisations (Connolly, 1972; Lukes, 1977; Gallie, 1955/6). These complex theoretical and epistemological issues are not addressed here but are discussed in more detail in a forthcoming volume (Cox, 2005). Despite these theoretical caveats it is clear that the general definition provided can be applied to the motives and goals of buyers and suppliers when they act as organisations in any external exchange transaction. The most important learning points from this general theoretical starting point are as follows:

- Objectively buyers and suppliers have potentially divergent goals when they enter into transactions.
- Ideally buyers seek to maximise the use value (functionality) of a product or service and to reduce their total costs of ownership, while suppliers are normally interested in maximising their revenue and returns.
- This does not mean that there cannot ever be a coincidence of interest between both parties that allows them to work together amicably, but that because of this objective tension in all business relationships it will be difficult for both sides to maximise their respective commercial goals without affecting the other side detrimentally.

To understand this tension one must recognise that when two organisations engage in any exchange relationship there will necessarily be a power circumstance between the two parties involved. The absence of this understanding in much of the current business relationship management literature was discussed briefly in Chapter 1, so it is necessary here to outline in more detail what is meant by power circumstances in buyer and supplier transactions.

When buyers seek to source any supply input from a supplier they are concerned with two aspects of the transaction. First, they are concerned with *increasing use value (functionality)*. This is the ability of the supplied item to meet or surpass the operational purposes or performance characteristics required. Buyers are always concerned about whether the suppliers they might source from have the competence to deliver necessary goods and services that are 'fit for purpose'. This normally means that suppliers are as much concerned with the operational utility of any supply offering as they are with its cost. In some circumstances buyers are clearly prepared to pay more for a particular level of functionality, especially when paying less results in lower quality than it is believed is necessary to deliver the required operational utility.

Thus in the oil industry it is possible to buy valves cheaply or expensively. Few buyers, however, purchase the cheapest valves because they break easily and the threat to the sustainability of operational performance and revenue generation is so high that buyers would rather pay more for better-quality valves. Having said this, however, for whatever level of quality or functionality (use value) that a buyer must source all buyers are interested in the exchange cost of the transaction, and all buyers are normally interested in *reducing the total costs of ownership* of any required quality of supply input.

It follows, therefore, that buyers have power in their relationship with suppliers to the extent that the buyer is able to make the supplier pass value to them in the form of ever increasing use value, as well as ever decreasing total costs of ownership for any given level of functionality. To the extent that buyers are not able to achieve these two aspects it is possible to argue that their relative power vis-à-vis suppliers is diminished. Thus, if, for example, buyers can only achieve reduced costs of ownership without an increase in use value, or increases in use value but with no reduction or only with an increase in costs of ownership, then the supplier is relatively more powerful than if they have to increase use value and reduce exchange costs for the buyer.

The reason for saying this is because suppliers have only two major reasons why they engage in exchange transactions. The first is to achieve a sustainable source of revenue from undertaking the supply of a particular good or service. The second is the ability to earn acceptable and sustainable returns (profit margins) from their participation in an exchange transaction. Ideally, therefore, the supplier wishes to *maximise revenue* and also to *maximise returns*.

How do these two factors link to the relative power of buyers and suppliers to achieve their goals from any exchange relationship? Clearly, if a supplier has to pass value to a buyer in the form of increased use value and lower total costs of ownership it is likely that to do so will have an impact upon the revenue and returns that a supplier receives from a buyer. It is clear that, while increasing the *functionality* (*use value*) of particular goods and services can provide opportunities for suppliers to win large shares of markets, constant innovation of this type may not always lead to this benign outcome, because whether or not any supplier can achieve a large market share is dependent on the nature of competition in any market, which is inextricably related to the ability of suppliers to replicate (copy) the innovations of others.

Thus, in some markets there are *isolating mechanisms* that allow some innovating companies to close the market to competitors so that they can dominate the market as a relative monopolist (Rumelt, 1987). In such markets only one (monopoly) or a few suppliers (duopoly or oligopoly) can achieve the functionality that the customer requires and this results in high barriers to market entry for competitors. In such circumstances it is likely that the buyer will receive the highest use value that is currently available in the market, but not necessarily at the lowest possible costs of ownership. The reason for this is because the supplier or suppliers control the quality being offered to the market and are also in a position to set pricing structures. In such circumstances it is normal for suppliers to have a high level of market share and returns tend to be above normal.

In other words, suppliers are able to earn *rents* (above normal double-digit profit levels). In this circumstance it is clear that the power of the supplier relative to that of the buyer is high and the power of the buyer relative to the supplier is low. This is because the buyer is dependent on the supplier for any given level of functionality as well as the price/cost of ownership, and the supplier is able to control both the level of innovation in use and cost variables and maximise the share of revenue and returns from engaging in any transaction.

But it is not the case that all forms of innovation around use value will lead inevitably to the closure of markets to competitors. Some innovations in the functionality and costs of ownership of goods and services are relatively easy for competitors to replicate. In such circumstances companies find that they are in highly *contested* market places. A highly contested market place is one in which everyone can replicate the innovations of others very quickly and there is little scope for the creation of isolating mechanisms to allow particular suppliers to dominate market share. In such circumstances the scope for suppliers to win market share will normally rest on their ability to constantly innovate on use value and also strive to constantly reduce the cost of ownership for the buyer. This is ideally what a buyer prefers.

When these situations develop supplier profits tend to be *normal*. This means that returns will tend to zero rather than double-digit levels. This is because the supplier can only stay in business by passing all of the value in the exchange relationship to the customer, and, because there are many others who can do the same thing, the supplier (unless they can engage in collusive market behaviour, merge and acquire the competition, or use information asymmetry against unenlightened customers) will receive relatively low commercial returns for doing so.

In this circumstance the power of the supplier relative to the buyer is low and the power of the buyer relative to the supplier will also be low (if they have limited share of the volume in the market) or high (if they have a high percentage share of volume in the market). In either circumstance, however, the supplier is dependent on delighting the buyer in order to receive any given level of volume and must pass all improvements in functionality and costs of ownership to the buyer.

Clearly, if these are the extreme outcomes that may occur for both a buyer and a supplier in any transaction, there must be intermediate power instances. Thus in some instances there will be a limited number of buyers and a limited number of potential suppliers for any goods or services. In such circumstances the buyer and supplier will have restricted choices about transaction partners, and suppliers may only have the ability to provide dedicated supply innovations for particular customers if they develop long-term collaborative relationships with one another. It is clear that when this occurs the power of the buyer and the supplier will have to be shared to some extent.

This is because the buyer is not able to achieve an increase in use value or a reduction in the costs of ownership without developing a close working relationship with a particular supplier, who in turn is able to use this fact to close the market to competitors. In such circumstances it is likely that improvements in use value and reduced costs of ownership will only be achieved if both parties make mutually supportive relationship specific adaptations (Hallen *et al.*, 1991; Cannon and Perreault, 1999). In so far as these post-contractual adaptations create switching costs in the relationship between one another it is likely that a situation of *interdependence* will be created in power terms. What this means is that both the buyer and the supplier develop such a close working relationship over time that they have to agree to share the value in the transaction with one another rather than seek to maximise their individual benefits from the relationship. In such circumstances it is likely that the buyer and supplier will recognise a non-adversarial coincidence of interests and agree to share value with one another over time.

It follows from this discussion that the relationships between buyers and suppliers are complex and can involve conflicts as well as accommodations over the sharing of value. It should never be doubted however that the objective purpose of a business relationship is for either side to maximise all the benefit it can from the exchange (Low, 1996). This fact will always ensure that there is an objective tension in business relationships. This is because buyers will normally seek to maximise their ability to appropriate value, defined as increased functionality, at the lowest possible costs of ownership. Suppliers will normally seek to maximise their ability to appropriate value, defined as increasing revenue shares and above normal returns.

Given this, it seems clear that all business relationships have within them an inherent tension. This is because the buyer and supplier do not necessarily have the same objective goals when they engage in any transaction. This is true even when a power situation of *interdependence* exists. While interdependence may create a need for both sides to work closely together and to share the value created, if either side can find a way of increasing their power in the relationship for themselves (which allows them to increase their share of the value created) then they are likely to do so.

It is clear, therefore, that for buyers or suppliers to undertake the effective management of business exchange transactions they must recognise the objective purpose of any relationship, and not confuse means and ends. A transaction between a buyer and a supplier should be focused on the ability of either party to maximise their commercial objectives. It is not having a particular type of relationship that is important, however, but whether or not any specific type of relationship (which is a *means* to an end) allows the buyer or the supplier to achieve these commercial goals (*the ends* or purpose of the relationship). It seems self-evident that the objective goal of any buyer is to be in a position where a supplier has to pass value to them in the form of increasing *use value* and decreasing *exchange costs*. Similarly it seems obvious that the goal of suppliers is to put themselves in a position where they can maximise their share of *revenue* and their ability to earn above normal returns (*rents*).

The problem for buyers and suppliers is that even though this is the objectively ideal situation for them the reality of business is not so simple. In the real world, business transactions take place with varying degrees of leverage between buyers and suppliers. Sometimes buyers are able to achieve their ideal position and sometimes suppliers can do the same. On many occasions, however, there will be situations when neither the buyer nor the supplier has the capability to create the ideal leverage situation over the other party to the exchange, and both sides have to accept non-ideal situations. On other occasions the buyer and supplier will be able to achieve some of the leverage they desire, but only if they make a conscious effort to work together and share the value created.

This is to state the obvious but even the obvious requires a conceptual framework that allows managers to understand the circumstances that they have to manage. This is necessary because neither buyers nor suppliers can manage their relationships appropriately unless they first understand the power circumstances they are in, as well as the scope for moving that circumstance to one that is more congenial for either party in leverage terms.

2.2 The power matrix: understanding the power circumstance between buyers and suppliers

It is necessary, therefore, for all parties to exchange transactions to understand that there must be power circumstance that exists between buyers and their suppliers and that, assuming that each party to the exchange understands the purpose of business, each side will be attempting to maximise their returns from the relationship in whatever manner is the most appropriate given the power circumstance that currently exist, or that could be created in the future. One way of expressing this reality is to develop a conceptual way of thinking about the power relationships that can theoretically exist between buyers and suppliers. This is achieved in *The Power Matrix* outlined in Figure 2.2.

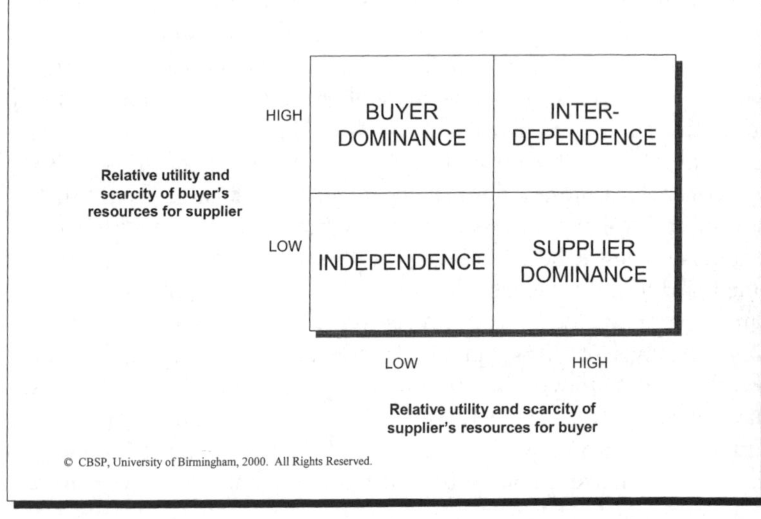

Figure 2.2 The power matrix

Source: Cox, Sanderson and Waston, *Power Regimes* (2000, p. 18).

As the Power Matrix demonstrates, there are two major variables that explain the power of buyers relative to suppliers and of suppliers relative to buyers. These are the concepts of *utility* and *scarcity*, which are explained in more detail elsewhere (Cox, Sanderson and Watson, 2000, and Cox *et al.*, 2002). In very general terms it is clear that these concepts will have different meanings for both the buyer and the supplier, which helps to explain the inherent tension in all business relationships.

From the buyer's perspective the *utility* of a supplier's offering refers to the *use value* (functionality) of the item supplied, plus the perceived risks associated with buying from alternative sources of supply, relative to the operational and commercial goals of the buyer's own organisation. The *scarcity* concept refers to the number of potential or actual suppliers that could be utilised in any exchange relationship. Thus if there are only a few suppliers who can provide the required supply item it is likely that the buyer will have less leverage over the *exchange costs* than if there are many, all of whom are operating in a highly contested market.

On the supplier's side of the exchange relationship it is clear that the concept of *utility* refers to the general attractiveness of doing business with any particular buyer or customer. In general terms suppliers wish to work with buyers who can provide them with large, regular and predictable volumes of work and who can also assist them with their ability to win new orders. In this sense the ability of a buyer to assist a supplier with product or service differentiation (so that they can close markets to their competitors) will be a major benefit for any supplier. Similarly, if work with any buyer provides a supplier with the capability to use brand association to build their reputation so as to win additional orders from other potential customers in the same market, then this will be highly attractive to a supplier. In considering these factors of buyer attractiveness the supplier is concerned with the ultimate goal (*ends*) of maximising *revenue* flow.

The *scarcity* element is also critically important to a supplier. If a supplier is able to make what they do a relatively scarce commodity in ownership (especially when it is required by very many buyers) through the creation of isolating mechanisms, or through the use of information asymmetry to deny valuable information to buyers, then the supplier will be in a position to earn above normal returns (*rents*) from any transactional relationship.

Given these general comments it seems clear that there will be four broad power situations that can exist in any buyer and supplier exchange relationship. These are: buyer dominance; independence; interdependence; and supplier dominance.

(i) Buyer dominance

In this circumstance the power resources favour the buyer relative to supplier. The buyer will be able to fix the trade-off between the use value (functionality) and the costs of the exchange and leverage future improvements in this from relatively dependent and supplicant suppliers. For this to occur it is normal for the buyer to have a relatively high share either of the revenue flow in the market place or of a particular supplier's total business revenue. It is also likely that there will be many suppliers operating within highly contested markets. In such circumstances it is likely that the returns achieved by suppliers will be low, and that suppliers will be forced to innovate on a continuous basis and pass all use and exchange improvements to the customer immediately. Clearly, buyers who have these power resources will be able to achieve improvements in use value and the costs of ownership that other buyers, without these leverage resources, cannot.

(ii) Independence

In this circumstance the power resources of both the buyer and the supplier are relatively low on both sides. In this situation the buyer normally commands a very small share of the potential supply market and cannot provide constant and/or high volumes to any supplier, such that the supplier does not view any particular buyer as more valuable than another. Conversely the supply market is highly contested with few barriers to market entry and the suppliers have to constantly innovate and pass value to the customer in order to keep ahead of the competition. Once again in this circumstance returns tend to be low and there are few isolating mechanisms available for suppliers to make above normal returns. In this context, while buyers have few levers, the natural contestation in the market tends to provide buyers with continual value improvement without their having to do very much to force suppliers to innovate for them. Their problem is that they only obtain the same value from suppliers in the form of current best market pricing that all other buyers in the same circumstance receive.

(iii) Interdependence

In this circumstance there is a coincidence of power resources that tends to force the buyer and supplier into a sharing of the value appropriated from the exchange relationship. Interdependence normally occurs when there are few buyers, each with a relatively high percentage share of the market, and relatively few suppliers who have the ability to use isolating mechanisms to create barriers to market entry. In such circumstances both sides need one another in the relationship and the ability of one side to impose its wishes on the other is limited. In this scenario the buyer and supplier must normally forgo the maximisation of their own economic interests in return for reciprocity.

Thus, the buyer normally offers a high percentage of the revenue it has at its disposal to a supplier in exchange for a long-term commitment by the supplier to work with them to reduce the costs of ownership, while also increasing the use value of the supply offering. In return the buyer normally allows the supplier to earn higher than normal, but not excessive profits. The supplier's interests are served by the fact that it has certainty of demand and a high volume of work, plus by working with the buyer the supplier may improve its capability to differentiate itself from other suppliers. In return for predictability and volume the supplier is normally prepared to be transparent about the trade-off between costs and functionality.

(iv) Supplier dominance

In this circumstance the supplier normally possesses an isolating mechanism that allows for effective market closure against other suppliers. The isolating mechanism also normally provides a sustainable and non-replicable basis for market closure, and the supplier is able to determine the use value (functionality) in the market place. The supplier is also normally in a market place where there is high volume and very many buyers all of whom highly value what it is that the supplier offers. In such situations buyers are dependent on the supplier who can determine what level of exchange costs will be incurred. Obviously in a near monopoly or actual monopoly circumstance the supplier has to be careful (especially in advanced industrial and liberal democratic countries) about pushing the pricing levels too high and earning supernormal profits. This is because in some countries this can create a regulatory control of monopoly pricing.

There is, however, another aspect to supplier dominance and this arises as a result of buyer ignorance through information asymmetry and post-contractual moral hazard. In many circumstances buyers are ignorant of the true state of competition and the true costs and margins being made by suppliers in what appear to be contested markets. In this situation suppliers can achieve above normal returns through standard industry or opportunistic pricing against unenlightened buyers. Post-contractual moral hazard is a situation in which the buyer operates initially in a highly contested market but after signing a contract finds that they are locked-in to a relationship with a particular supplier which they cannot easily exit from, due to high unforeseen sunk and switching costs. When this occurs suppliers can also achieve above normal returns from their relationship and a situation of supplier dominance is created even though it could have been avoided if the buyer had properly understood the power resources available before the event.

Supplier dominance, by whatever means, is clearly the goal of most companies when they develop their corporate strategies because all companies seek uniqueness, competitive advantage and above normal returns as an ideal. This is true even though few can sustain this for very long due to the pernicious impact of competitive imitation by competitors.

This short discussion cannot do justice to all of the factors that allow buyers and suppliers to develop power resources that allow them to leverage their economic objectives against one another in exchange relationships. A more detailed discussion of the key factors that augment the power of suppliers and buyers can be found elsewhere (Cox, Sanderson and Watson, 2000; Cox *et al.*, 2002; and Cox, 2005), but Figure 2.3 provides an indication of some of the key factors that allow practitioners to understand how to position buyer and supplier relationships in *The Power Matrix*.

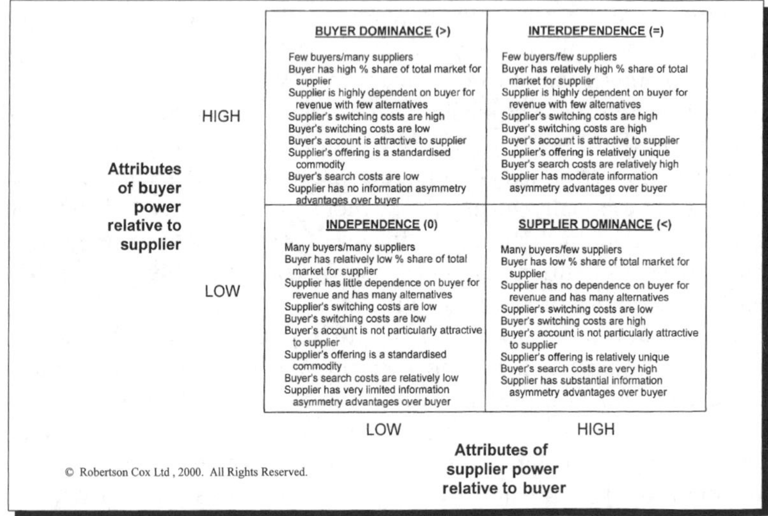

Figure 2.3 Attributes of buyer and supplier power in the power matrix
Source: Adapted from Cox (2001a, p. 14).

2.3 Using leverage to improve power positions and commercial results

It should be clear from the previous discussion that knowing what the power circumstance is for any buyer and supplier in a transaction is one thing, but understanding how to use business relationship management techniques to manage existing power circumstances appropriately and, more importantly, how to use such techniques to create new and more congenial power circumstances, is altogether another.

This is not a minor point. On the contrary – it is one of the major criticisms that can be made of other approaches to the analysis of business relationship management. As was demonstrated in Chapter 1, most current approaches to this topic start from a failure to address the commercial as opposed to the operational aspects of business relationships, as well as arguing that there is often one preferred approach to business relationship management. This approach is either defined as partnering or alliancing, or predicated on the superiority of mutuality as the best way for managers to develop relationships in exchange transactions. There are two major reasons why these interpretations are of only limited value for managers.

Suggesting that there is one best way of managing all types of exchange relationship in all power circumstances is clearly naive. There are many ways of managing relationships and it is obvious that while alliancing/partnering and mutuality are appropriate in some power circumstances (especially *interdependence*) they are unlikely to be desirable in all (Low, 1996; Cox, 1997a,b; Bensaou, 1999). The second criticism is perhaps more profound because suggesting that there is one best way of managing relationships fails to take account of the fact that managers have to manage two realities. The first is the effective management of the power circumstance that currently confronts them as buyers or as suppliers. The second is the ability to develop and use relationships with others that provide for the creation of a more congenial power situation that allows the buyer or the supplier to maximise their ability to achieve their commercial goals.

Thus buyers and suppliers have to recognise that part of their task is not only to manage the current power circumstance, but also to use relationships to create new power circumstances that provide for a more congenial leverage position for them to maximise their often divergent economic objectives. Figure 2.4 demonstrates the way in which practitioners must think when they operate as buyers (Cox, 2001b), while Figure 2.5 demonstrates how they must think when they operate as

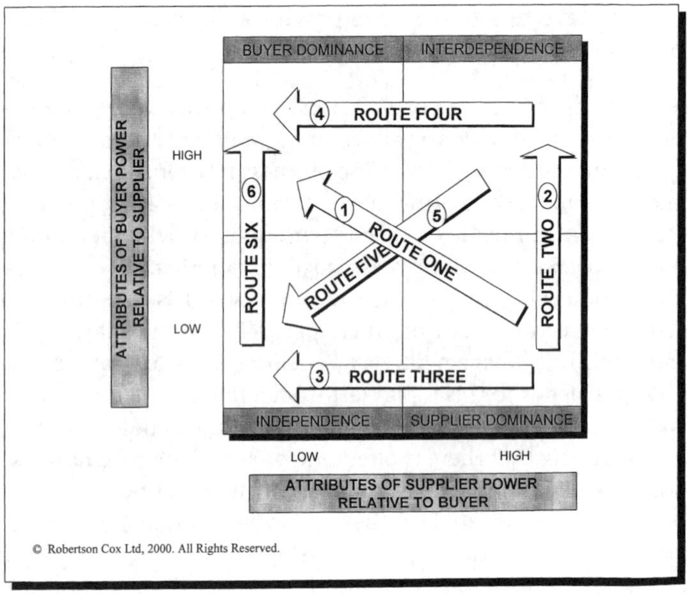

Figure 2.4 Repositioning buyer leverage in the power matrix

suppliers (Cox, 2001b). The goal for each party in the exchange relationship is always the same: it is not to seek any particular *means* (partnering or alliancing) as the goal of relationship management, rather it is to select the best relationship management approach that allows the buyer or the supplier to achieve the maximisation of their own commercial goals (*ends*). Sometimes long-term partnering relationships may be the way forward; in other circumstances short-term opportunism may be the preferred route.

As Figure 2.4 indicates, when organisations act as buyers the worst situation they can find themselves in is to be in supplier dominance. The reason for this is because in this situation, while the buyer may be receiving the currently best available use value in the market, the price and cost of ownership will be largely determined by the supplier, who is likely to be making above normal returns. Furthermore, it is likely that the supplier will determine any future innovation because they will only innovate when they are forced to do so by potential competitors threatening to catch up.

It is clear, therefore, that supplier dominance is the least congenial environment for buyers to operate from when they source from suppliers.

This is true whether one is discussing the use value created in the relationship or the exchange costs involved in the transaction. This is because the supplier will normally set use value and exchange costs to their own advantage. Thus, as Figure 2.4 demonstrates, the ideal situation for the buyer is to move as quickly as possible to locate all of their sourcing relationships into buyer dominance. The reason for this is self-evident. In this situation the buyer has many ways in which to leverage value from the supplier, whether this is in the form of increased use value (functionality), or reductions in the total costs of ownership (by forcing the supplier to work for low, normal levels of profit), or both. The buyer can also normally choose in this power circumstance the type of relationship management style (arm's-length or collaborative) with the supplier that they prefer.

Thus the most effective leverage strategy (ability to record the most significant increases in value from a supplier) for any buyer is the capability to transform the power situation with suppliers from a situation of supplier dominance to one of buyer dominance (Route 1). In these circumstances one would expect the use value and the costs of ownership to improve dramatically in the buyer's favour. As Figure 2.4 indicates, however, there are alternative leverage routes or commercial strategies available for the buyer. In Route 2 (supplier dominance to interdependence) the buyer is also likely to experience improvement in use value and/or costs of ownership but, because the buyer must share some of the value with the supplier in the interdependence scenario, the benefits will be lower than under Route 1.

Under Route 3 (supplier dominance to independence) the gains would be somewhat less for the buyer than under Route 2. This is because the buyer is not able to increase their general share of the market place and, while the supply market becomes more contested, the buyer does not have the ability to influence and leverage supplier behaviour directly. Instead the buyer receives improvements in use value and costs of ownership due to the increased level of contestation taking place in the market place. Under Route 4 (interdependence to buyer dominance) a buyer would expect significant improvements comparable to Route 2. In this scenario the buyer is able to develop a greater share of the market and more dependency for suppliers on the buyer's business, with coincidental increases in leverage for the buyer over the supplier.

In Route 5 (interdependence to independence) the buyer may have the opportunity to reduce the commitment to longer-term collaborative relationships with suppliers in favour of independence power situations. In this scenario the increased contestation in the market place makes it unnecessary for the buyer to develop long-term sharing of value strategies in preference for innovation through market contestation, with more short-term relationship management approaches. In Route 6 (independence to buyer dominance) the buyer achieves much greater leverage through the ability to take a major share of market revenue and this provides the basis for the buyer to expect better value from the supplier.

Supplier dominance may be the worst scenario from which a buyer can appropriate value but it is clearly the most congenial environment for suppliers when they engage in exchange transactions with buyers, as Figure 2.5 demonstrates. This is because in this scenario the supplier can normally determine use value and set pricing so as to achieve above normal returns. If buyers must therefore always ideally seek ways to move out of supplier dominance in the direction of buyer dominance (or other more congenial power scenarios as described above) suppliers also have similar aspirations but in the opposite direction. Suppliers are ideally trying to move away from buyer dominance, because buyer dominance provides the buyer with the capability to leverage improved use value from the supplier, while forcing them to accept only low returns for their efforts. Thus suppliers are always interested in opportunities to leverage more value for themselves (in the form of increased revenue and returns) by moving from buyer dominance in the direction of supplier dominance.

As Figure 2.5 demonstrates, the most effective commercial leverage strategy for any supplier is Route 1 (buyer dominance to supplier dominance). This is because to achieve this movement a supplier would have to be in a position to move out of a highly contested market with a high degree of dependency on the buyer into a situation in which the supplier owned a key isolating mechanism. By possessing such an isolating mechanism the supplier is able to close the market to competitors and reduce their dependency on the buyer, forcing the buyer to become much more dependent on the supplier for any particular use value or exchange costs. At the same time the supplier is in a position to increase revenue share in the market, with above normal returns.

Route 2 (buyer dominance to interdependence) is also desirable for suppliers. In this scenario the supplier is able to reduce the contestation in the market place by developing a longer-term relationship with the buyer and by creating switching costs for the buyer that make it difficult for them to source from alternative sources of supply. In this circumstance the supplier may expect to be able to increase the share of

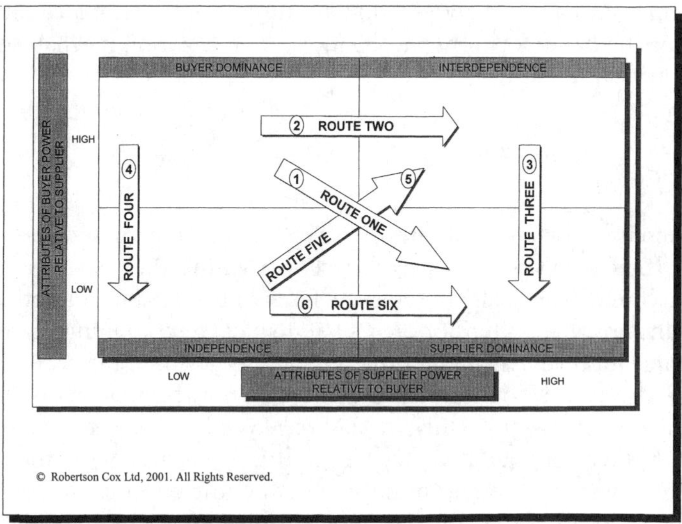

Figure 2.5 Repositioning supplier leverage in the power matrix

revenue and the returns achievable from a particular buyer relationship because the buyer becomes much more dependent on the supplier. This strategy is taken to a higher level under Route 3 (interdependence to supplier dominance) because the supplier is able to increase the sunk and switching costs post-contractually with the buyer to such an extent that a situation of complete lock-in is created that allows the supplier to premium price and achieve above normal returns with guaranteed revenue from the buyer. This route can also be created through the development of an isolating mechanism as indicated under Route 1 above.

Under Route 4 (buyer dominance to independence) the supplier may be able to create a higher level of return by becoming less dependent on a particular buyer by finding ways of working with less powerful buyers with a smaller share of market revenue than dominant buyers. In this situation the relative weakness of smaller buyers may provide opportunities for suppliers to achieve somewhat higher returns in a highly contested market than from a contested market with dominant buyers. Under Route 5 (independence to interdependence) the supplier is able to find ways of offering buyers increases in use value in return for a guaranteed long-term share of the buyer's revenue, with a somewhat higher level of return than achievable from participation in a highly contested market place. Finally, in Route 6 (independence to supplier dominance) the supplier is normally able to use information asymmetry to achieve above normal returns due to ignorance on the part of the buyer, or from the creation of an isolating mechanism as described in Route 1.

2.4 Conclusion

The discussion above indicates two things. First, buyers and suppliers have their own commercial goals, which define their *strategic ends*. These commercial goals or strategic ends are not the same for both parties, and are often in tension. The six individual repositioning strategies available for the buyer and for the supplier in the Power Matrix demonstrate clearly the commercial and strategic tension that exists in all business relationships. Only in the *interdependence* power scenario is there less tension, but as we have seen, this is not necessarily the ideal or best power and leverage position for either the buyer or the supplier to operate from. If the buyer or supplier is operating in a commercially and strategically rational manner they should be striving to move to the buyer dominance power position if they are a buyer, or the supplier dominance position if they are a supplier.

Second, while it is one thing to understand theoretically that there is a power circumstance that has to be managed, it is altogether another to understand the most operationally effective ways for a buyer or a supplier to leverage improvements in their respective commercial goals. Even when buyers and suppliers objectively understand their strategic purposes, they also have to make operational choices about the types of *relationship strategies* to be used with one another, and the *styles of relationship management* that should be adopted, to achieve any particular commercial goal. In other words there are *strategic ends* to which relationships are directed commercially for both buyers and suppliers and there are appropriate *operational means* by which these ends can be achieved.

In the next chapter the *operational means* that buyers and suppliers can select from are outlined. This is achieved by an analysis of the four major *sourcing approaches* available to buyers when they procure supply inputs and the eight major *approaches to customer account management* available to suppliers in their relationships with buyers. Related to this is a discussion of the four major *relationship management styles* that buyers and suppliers can utilise in their relationships with one another.

References

Bensaou, M. (1999) 'Portfolios of buyer–supplier relationships', *Sloan Management Review* (Summer), pp. 35–44.

Cannon, J. and Perreault, W. D. (1999) 'Buyer–supplier relationships in business markets', *Journal of Marketing Research*, vol. 36 (November), pp. 439–60.

Connolly, W. E. (1972) 'On interests in politics', *Politics and Society*, vol. 2, pp. 459–77.

Cox, A. (1997a) *Business Success* (Helpston, UK: Earlsgate Press).

Cox, A. (1997b) 'On power, appropriateness and procurement competence', *Supply Management*, 2 October, pp. 24–7.

Cox, A. (2001a) 'Understanding buyer and supplier power: a framework for procurement and supply competence', *The Journal of Supply Chain Management*, vol. 37, no. 2, pp. 8–15.

Cox, A. (2001b) 'Managing with power: strategies for improving value appropriation from supply relationships', *The Journal of Supply Chain Management*, vol. 37, no. 2, pp. 42–7.

Cox, A. (2005) *The Rules of the Game: How to Capture Value in Business* (Helpston, UK: Earlsgate Press).

Cox, A., Sanderson, J. and Watson, G. (2000) *Power Regimes: Mapping the DNA of Business and Supply Chain Relationships* (Helpston, UK: Earlsgate Press).

Cox, A., Ireland, P., Lonsdale, C., Sanderson, J. and Watson, G. (2002) *Supply Chains, Markets and Power: Mapping Buyer and Supplier Power Regimes* (London: Routledge).

Cox, A., Ireland, P., Lonsdale C., Sanderson, J. and Watson, G. (2003) *Supply Chain Management: A Guide to Best Practice* (London: Financial Times/Prentice Hall).

Gallie, W. B. (1955/6) 'Essentially contested concepts', *Proceedings of the Aristotelian Society*, vol. 56, pp. 167–98.

Hallen, L., Johanson, J. and Seyed-Mohamed, N. (1991) 'Interfirm adaptation in business relationships', *Journal of Marketing*, vol. 55 (April), pp. 29–37.

Low, B. K. H. (1996) 'Long-term relationships in industrial marketing: reality or rhetoric', *Industrial Marketing Management*, vol. 25, pp. 23–35.

Lukes, S. (1977) *Power: A Radical View* (London: Macmillan).

Rumelt, R. P. (1987) 'Theory, strategy and entrepreneurship', in D. Teece (ed.), *The Competitive Challenge: Strategies for Industrial Innovation and Renewal* (New York: Harper & Row), pp. 137–58.

3
The Operational Means for Successful Business Relationship Management

The discussion of operational means that follows is divided into three sections.

- The first section focuses on the *commercial sourcing outcomes* and *operational supplier management approaches* that buyers can select from when they consider how best to achieve power leverage and repositioning.
- The second section focuses on the *commercial customer outcomes* and the *operational account management* approaches that suppliers can select from when they consider how to achieve power leverage and repositioning.
- The final section discusses the range of *relationship management styles* that buyers and suppliers can select from, and which must be aligned with commercial and operational choices, for effective and successful relationship management to occur.

3.1 The commercial and operational sourcing choices of the buyer

When organisations act as buyers and source supply inputs they have to make decisions about the best operational strategy to increase commercial value for money. This normally involves a search for increases in use value and reductions in the total costs of ownership. If this strategic and commercial ideal outcome cannot be achieved a buyer may trade one of these aspects against the other. Thus a buyer might settle for an increase in use value with costs remaining the same, or a reduction in the costs

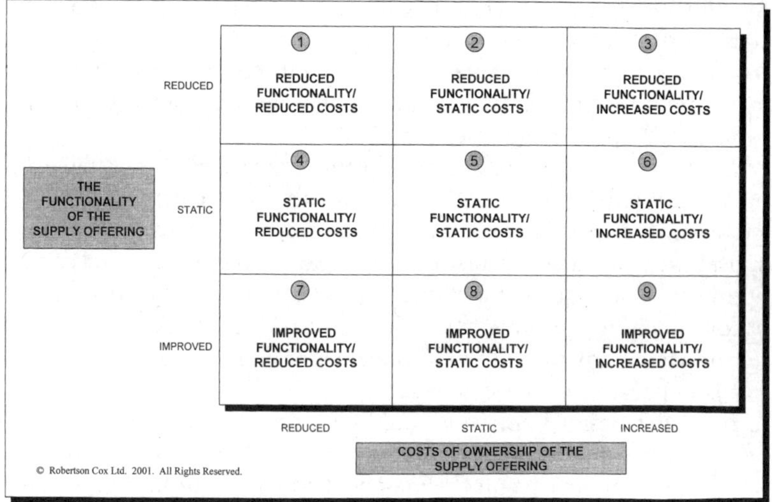

Figure 3.1 Buyer value propositions

of ownership with use value remaining the same. There are a number of permutations that a buyer can accept when they source supply inputs. The value proposition trade-offs between use value (functionality) and the costs of ownership are described in Figure 3.1.

As the diagram demonstrates, buyers have nine basic options when they source supply inputs:

1 Reduction in functionality/reduction in costs
2 Reduction in functionality/static costs
3 Reduction in functionality/increase in costs
4 Static functionality/reduction in costs
5 Static functionality/static costs
6 Static functionality/increase in costs
7 Improvement in functionality/reduction in costs
8 Improvement in functionality/static costs
9 Improvement in functionality/increase in costs

Clearly some of these options may be more or less desirable for a buyer, and some may be undesirable. Thus option 7 (improvement in functionality/reduction in cost) is the ideal that all buyers wish to receive from their suppliers and on a continuous basis. If this cannot be achieved then buyers may be willing to accept other trade-offs. Thus option 1 (reduction in functionality/reduction in costs); option 4 (static functionality/reduction in costs); option 8 (improvement in functionality/static costs); and option 9 (improvement in functionality/increase in costs) may all be better value for money, and acceptable under particular commercial circumstances, even though they are not the ideal value for money improvement of option 7.

The remaining options are not normally particularly desirable for buyers. Option 2 (reduction in functionality/static cost) and option 6 (static functionality/increase in cost) are retrograde steps for the buyer and to be avoided. The worst-case scenario for the buyer is, of course, option 3 (reduction in functionality/increase in cost), with option 5 (static functionality/static cost) merely sustaining the status quo and not providing any improvement in value for money over time.

It is important to stress, however, that under some circumstances all of these less desirable options could be acceptable to a buyer. This is because the value for money of any particular purchase is relative to what others can achieve in the market at any moment in time. Thus it is possible to argue that option 5 (static functionality/static costs) could be highly desirable, especially in situations in which every other buyer in the market is forced to pay more for the same level of functionality. Thus, even option 3 could be desirable in relative terms, especially in circumstances in which the relative reductions in functionality and the relative increases in costs were less than those being experienced by all other buyers in the market. This issue of relativity applies to all of the nine options available to buyers. A good deal for a buyer is, therefore, always relative to what others are receiving in the market place.

Commercially, buyers normally prefer to receive option 7 as their preferred option and option 3 as their least preferred option. Given this, one of the major decisions that buyers have to make is which operational sourcing approach is best able to provide them with continuous increases in value for money, whether through the development of options 1, 4, 8, 7, 9 or relatively superior performance in all of the available commercial options in the market (1 through 9). In making this operational sourcing decision buyers have to be cognisant of two major variables. The first is the internal capabilities they possess to work with suppliers, and the second is the current external power structure that exists with actual or potential suppliers in the market, and how their chosen sourcing approach will impact upon buyer and supplier power in the future.

Given these two major considerations buyers normally have to consider the current competence of suppliers to provide them with particular levels of functionality as well as their congruence, or ability to do

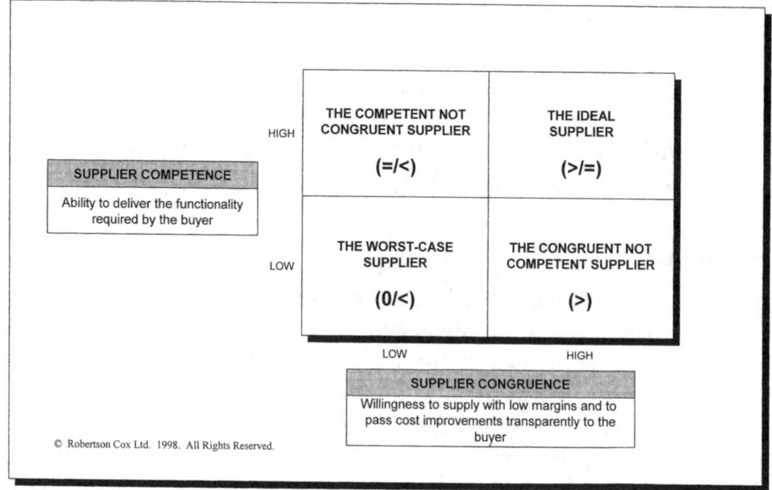

Figure 3.2 The competence and congruence matrix
Source: Adapted from Cox (1999, p. 31).

so with diminishing costs of ownership. How buyers think about this trade-off is demonstrated in Figure 3.2.

The ideal supplier

As the matrix demonstrates, an *ideal supplier* is currently capable of providing high functionality (use value) as well as doing so in a highly congruent manner. This implies that the supplier works transparently for normal returns (low profits) and regularly passes any cost improvements to the buyer in return for regular work and low but guaranteed margins. This situation normally occurs when power situations of either *buyer dominance* or *interdependence* exist in any exchange relationship. The only difference is that in a dominant situation the buyer normally receives relatively more improvement in functionality and reduction in costs of ownership than is possible under interdependence.

The worst-case supplier

A *worst-case* supplier cannot deliver the required functionality or reduce the total costs of ownership and requires above normal returns. This implies that the power situation is one of either *independence* or *supplier dominance,* depending on the levels of returns being achieved by the supplier without any commensurate increase in functionality.

The competent not congruent supplier

A *competent but not congruent* supplier can provide the required functionality but the buyer has to pay above normal returns to obtain it, and cost improvements are not normally automatically passed to the buyer. It is normal that this situation occurs when there is *supplier dominant* power relationship with the buyer.

The congruent not competent supplier

A *congruent but not competent* supplier is willing to work for low returns and to be transparent in the passing of cost improvements to the buyer, but is currently not able to deliver the level of functionality that the buyer desires. This implies that the power situation is likely to be one of *buyer dominance* because the supplier cannot work with the buyer unless the buyer is willing to develop their capabilities for them. If they cannot it is unlikely that a buyer would be interested in working with such a supplier.

It follows from this that while it is obvious that all buyers would prefer ideal suppliers they often operate in supply markets where the ideal does not exist. This means that buyers must strive towards the creation of the ideal from a mixed bunch of potential supply partners – some of whom are competent but not congruent; some of whom are congruent but not currently competent; and some who are neither competent nor congruent. In deciding on which suppliers to work with (and how) buyers have to make complex selection decisions, not only about which suppliers and how many of them, but also about the ways in which they will need to work with them in order to improve the trade-off between functionality and the costs of ownership in the future.

Buyers appear to have four major operational sourcing options that they can choose from when they work with suppliers to achieve continuous improvements in value for money. As Figure 3.3 demonstrates, buyers can act *reactively* or *proactively* when they develop relationships with suppliers. The figure also indicates that buyers must also decide whether they have the capability and resources to undertake *first-tier* relationship management, or work throughout the *supply chain* with suppliers from the first tier through all tiers down to raw-material suppliers.

As Figure 3.3 demonstrates, there are four sourcing options all of which involve the buyer in more or less involvement with particular suppliers (Cox *et al.*, 2003). In what follows, a brief description is provided of what each of the four sourcing options implies for the role of the buyer and the supplier in any relationship.

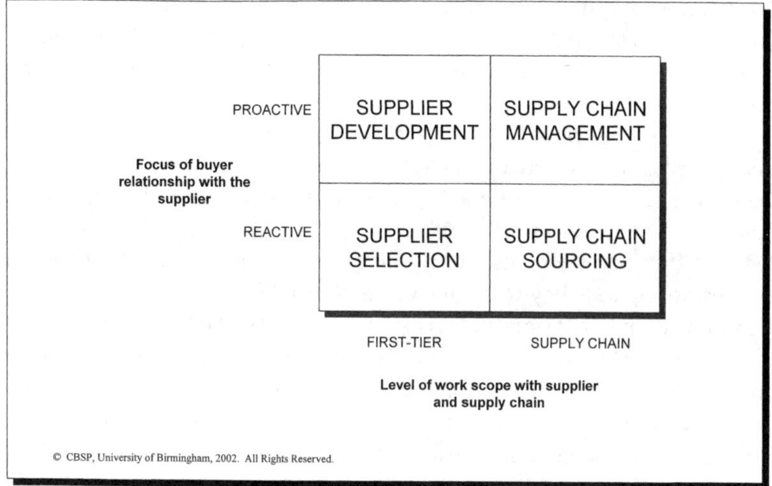

Figure 3.3 The four sourcing options for buyers

Supplier selection

Under supplier selection the role of the buyer is essentially *reactive*. To be reactive implies that the buyer does not posses the internal capabilities and resources to be able to work closely with the supplier to engineer improvements in either functionality or cost reduction. On the contrary, when a buyer has to act reactively this implies that there is no competence currently within the buying organisation to show a supplier how to improve the trade-off between functionality and costs. Relatedly, *proactive* buying is normally not required of a buyer when the supply market within which they are operating is highly contested with many interchangeable suppliers who are consistently competing by improving functionality and/or reducing costs in order to win business from the buyer.

In such circumstances all that the buyer needs to do to achieve constant increases in value for money is develop relatively short-term relationships with suppliers at the first tier of the supply chain, undertake rigorous performance measurement of what is supplied and constantly test the market on a regular basis to allow newly innovating suppliers to replace incumbents. Obviously this can only be achieved if the switching costs between particular suppliers are kept low and no individual supplier can create isolating mechanisms to close the market to competitors. It is also critical that the buyer has access to comprehensive and detailed levels of information about market choices, otherwise suppliers may be able to shift the power in the relationship using information asymmetry.

Clearly there is nothing wrong with behaving reactively as a buyer. In many circumstances buyers do not have either the financial resources or technical know-how to be able to work proactively with suppliers to help them engineer improvements in value for money. In such circumstances the buyer will normally have to rely on the market to drive contestation, and they will have to accept that even when they act professionally they will only ever receive current standard industry pricing and use value from suppliers. Most buyers find themselves confined to the supplier selection role for the vast bulk of their sourcing requirements, and in particular for many of their indirect (non-revenue generating and support) and low value direct (revenue generating) activities.

Supply chain sourcing

Supply chain sourcing is a similar relationship management choice for the buyer but under this scenario the buyer undertakes supplier selection activities of a reactive kind within the total supply chain for the goods and services they require, rather than just at the first tier. Clearly this approach requires relatively more time and effort to be devoted by the buyer to sourcing issues and the development of more sourcing relationships than under supplier selection. The reason for this is that the buyer must search for suppliers throughout the supply chain that services the first-tier supplier, and undertake far more supplier selection and performance measurement exercises than if they simply relied on the first-tier supplier managing these relationships with the supply chain for them. Having said that, the basic principles of relationship management are the same as under supplier selection. The buyer normally develops essentially short-term relationships with the supplier or suppliers and uses market contestation whenever possible to receive currently available improvements in value for money.

Supplier development

Supplier development also operates at the first tier of the supply chain but requires far more dedicated investment by a buyer in the relationship with the supplier than either the supplier selection or the supply chain sourcing options. Under supplier development the role of the buyer is to work directly with the supplier to engineer improvements in value for money – whether in the form of increased functionality and/or reductions in the costs of ownership. It follows that in acting in this way the buyer is taking on a more proactive role in changing the trade-off between functionality and costs than is the case when the buyer merely relies on market contestation to drive innovation. Clearly, under this approach the buyer will normally have to invest considerable financial, technical and personnel resource into the relationship, as well as undertake to make a relatively longer-term commitment to the relationship than would be the case under reactive sourcing approaches.

The major reason why buyers may choose to adopt this proactive approach is because they believe that innovation cannot be driven at the pace they require by market contestation, or they wish to achieve differentiation by having suppliers working for them who are able to provide levels of value for money that are higher than that being provided to their competitors by other suppliers in the market. Once again it is obvious that while this approach may provide an opportunity for buyer-led or joint buyer and supplier-led innovation this option is only available to the buyer if they posses the financial, technical and personnel resources to make it work effectively.

It is also important to recognise that there are also serious potential commercial risks in the development of supplier development relationships operationally. This risk arises because close collaborative relationships can lead to situations in which a 'fundamental transformation' can occur in the power relationship between buyers and suppliers (Williamson, 1985). This occurs because the dedicated investments and relationship-specific adaptations that the buyer and supplier normally have to make can sometimes create sunk and switching costs that make it difficult for the buyer to exit from the relationship post-contractually.

Supply chain management

Supply chain management is something of an essentially contested concept. This is because it has very different meaning for many writers. In the context that it is used here, supply chain management refers to a proactive approach by a buyer to work not just with the first-tier supplier, but also to work with all of the tiers of the supply chain, using a supplier development approach to drive innovations in functionality and costs of ownership throughout the chain as a whole.

Clearly the buyer can drive this approach from the top down or it can be undertaken on a joint basis by all of the parties in the supply chain. It is obvious, however, that whichever of these two styles of management is selected, this approach requires the most extensive and continuous dedication of investments by a buyer when sourcing. For this approach to work the buyer has to be able to provide all of the financial, technical and personnel resource and capabilities to be able to manage supplier development activities throughout an extended network of buyer and supplier exchange relationships. There is little doubt that this cannot be undertaken without long-term commitments to the players in the supply chain.

It follows, therefore, that the risk of the 'fundamental transformation' of power between the buyer and the supplier (that is associated with problems of post-contractual moral hazard commercially) is at its most extreme when buyers undertake supply chain management sourcing strategies. It is also clear that unless the buyer understands how to ensure low switching costs and scope for exit from any relationships, the problem of post-contractual lock-in to supply chain partners will be very high indeed. This, of course, may not be a problem if the partners in the chain are able to drive continuous improvement in value for money relative to the buyer's competitors. Unfortunately, if this benign circumstance does not occur then buyers may find that over time they may be locked into sub-optimal sourcing relationships.

There is a further point that must be made for those wishing to undertake supply chain management, which applies equally to those wishing to pursue supply chain sourcing strategies. It is essential that buyers seeking to develop sourcing strategies within supply chains understand the power structures that exist throughout the supply chain. While it is one thing to recognise that supply chain sourcing, supplier development and supply chain management strategies cannot be pursued in the absence of the necessary financial, technical and personnel resources internally, it can also be argued that this alone is not enough. If the power resources externally are also not conducive to a particular approach then it is unlikely that a buyer's sourcing strategy will be successful (Cox *et al.*, 2003). This implies that buyers must carefully analyse the power regimes that exist within particular supply chain networks before they embark on either supply chain sourcing or supply chain management strategies (Cox *et al.*, 2000, 2002).

It is obvious that buyers must therefore think carefully about their internal capabilities and the external power circumstances they are involved in when they develop a relationship with any particular supplier. At the same time the buyer must also understand clearly what the value proposition is that they are trying to source from a supplier. Thus when assessing their own internal capability to undertake any of the four sourcing options available the buyer must also understand which of the

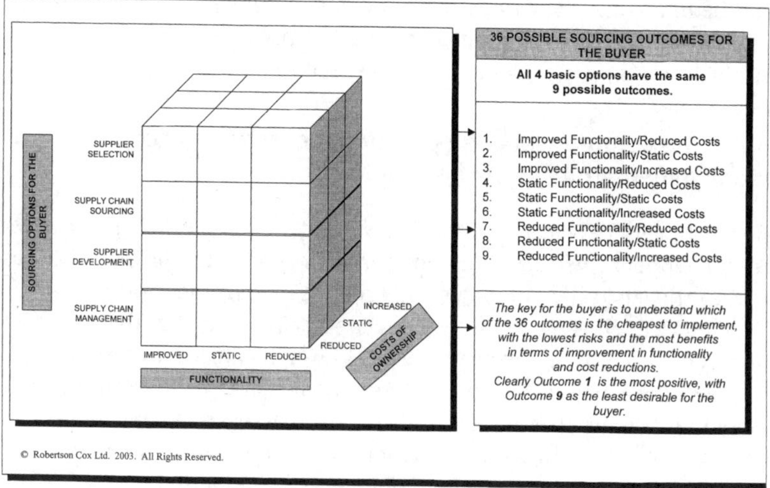

Figure 3.4 The range of sourcing outcomes for the buyer

four options offers the best value for money opportunity – i.e. capability to move the suppliers into the *ideal supplier* position in the competence and congruence matrix. This choice is demonstrated in Figure 3.4

Obviously the 36 choices that are theoretically available to a buyer must be understood in relative terms. Thus the buyer will have to consider the internal risks, as well as the costs and benefits of undertaking any of the available sourcing options, and the relative scale of the cost reductions and functionality improvements that might be achievable. A framework for making this sourcing choice has been provided elsewhere (Cox *et al.*, 2003, chapter 2), but it is imperative that buyers recognise that when they make their own sourcing selection decisions they take into account both the internal as well as the external costs and benefits of any particular sourcing approach.

To focus on the internal costs and benefits is not of course to ignore the importance of the external dimension. Indeed it is one thing for the buyer to understand the potential benefits for themselves of adopting any sourcing approach but they also have to understand that suppliers also have their own commercial goals (ends) and make their own decisions about the best operational means to deliver these. It is clear that many buyers, when they make sourcing decisions, pay scant attention to the fact that their suppliers have their own strategies that may or may not be in alignment with those of the buyer. The operational means by which suppliers develop relationships with buyers to achieve their strategic goals are discussed in the next section.

3.2 The commercial and operational customer/account management choices of the supplier

Just as buyers have value propositions (and sourcing options to deliver these) suppliers also have to consider their own value propositions, as well as the customer outcomes and account management options available to deliver these. Unlike buyers – who focus on the trade-off between use value and exchange costs – suppliers focus on the trade-off between the share of revenue potentially available to them from individual customers (the buyer) and in any market generally (buyers in general), and the returns they can achieve from securing the maximum share of an individual customer's demand requirements.

As Figure 3.5 demonstrates, suppliers have to consider whether working with a customer will lead to an increase or decrease in revenue or returns. Suppliers also face nine basic theoretical trade-off options when they work with any potential customer:

1 Reduced revenue/reduced returns
2 Reduced revenue/static returns

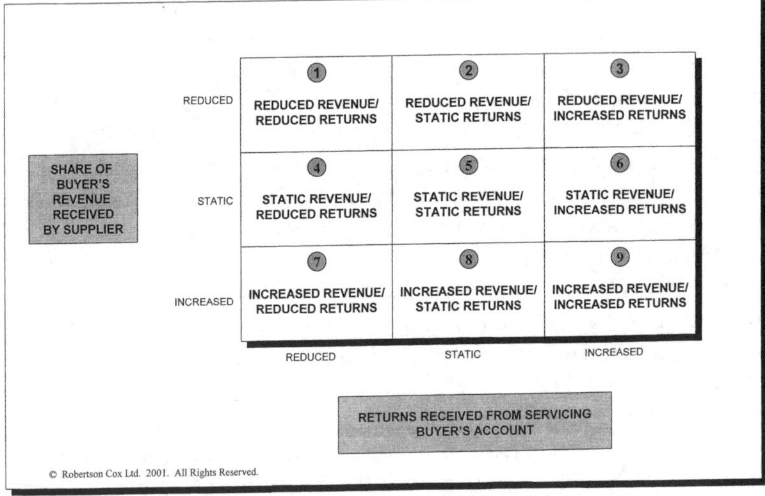

Figure 3.5 Supplier value propositions

3 Reduced revenue/increased returns
4 Static revenue/reduced returns
5 Static revenue/static returns
6 Static revenue/increased returns
7 Increased revenue/reduced returns
8 Increased revenue/static returns
9 Increased revenue/increased returns

Obviously, suppliers normally have preferences concerning these potential trade-offs. Suppliers normally will prefer option 9 to all other options because both market share and revenue are increasing, providing increasing relative and total profitability. Suppliers will also welcome options 6 and 8 if they cannot achieve option 9. This is because, under option 6, revenue is static but profits are increasing relatively, and under option 8 profits are static but revenue is increasing, thereby ensuring a greater total level of profitability. Under option 3 the supplier may be losing total revenue share but is able to increase relative profitability from a declining market share. This is clearly a potentially desirable trade-off for the supplier even if it is not ideal.

Beyond these four relatively benign options the remaining trade-offs are more problematic. Option 5 may or may not be desirable. This is because static revenue and static returns can be desirable if based already on a large market share of revenue and on above normal returns. This is of course less desirable if the current market share is low with only normal levels of profitability. Option 7 could be acceptable if not ideal for a supplier. This option requires the supplier to reduce profit levels in order to achieve increased market share, and is often used by suppliers who wish to use price wars to force competitors out of the market. It can therefore be detrimental to relative returns in the short term, with the intention of increasing returns later when there is less competition in the market place and the survivors have a greater share of total market revenue.

The least desirable options are numbers 1, 2 and 4. Option 1 is clearly the least desired option for a supplier because it involves the supplier reducing returns, while also losing market share. Options 2 and 4 are somewhat less threatening though still not very desirable outcomes for suppliers. Option 2 involves the supplier in sustaining relative returns but with declining market share, undermining total profitability. Option 4 involves the retention of current market share but through reductions in both relative and total profitability.

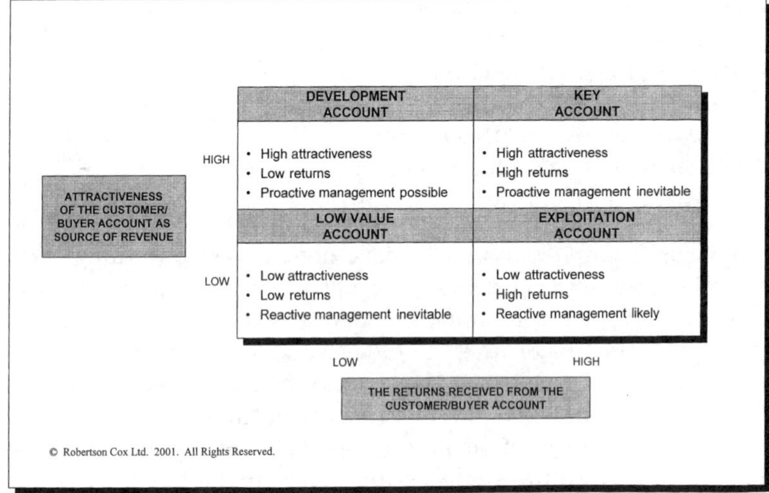

Figure 3.6 The four commercial outcomes for the supplier

Suppliers have to think about the future potential trade-offs between these two commercial variables of revenue and returns but they also have to link them to the current commercial outcomes that occur from having a relationship with any particular customer. When thinking about these current outcomes suppliers will normally consider the attractiveness of a customer's account and the returns that they can achieve from working with them. This trade-off is described in Figure 3.6.

As Figure 3.6 demonstrates, suppliers can experience four broad commercial outcomes from a relationship with any buyer: the development account; the key account; the exploitation account; or the low-value account.

Development account

In a development account the supplier perceives the customer to be highly attractive for the development of future revenue (either from that specific customer or through association with that customer from other potential customers). In return, however, the supplier is not able to currently obtain high returns from the receipt of any given level of revenue, and profits are low.

When a supplier enters into a development account with a customer this implies that the supplier currently does not receive a large share of the buyer's total business revenue. If they do it implies that the customer is not necessarily a major player in the market place but the relationship provides an opportunity for the supplier to create differentiation or brand/reputation effects to allow them to increase their future total market share. In other words, the supplier accepts that they currently do not have the power to leverage high returns from the customer but are entering into the relationship with the intention of using low pricing levels (and low returns) to win market share and/or to develop opportunities to grow their market share with other potential customers.

There may also be an understanding, if the supplier can convince the buyer to work with them proactively to develop relationship-specific adaptations, that there could be an opportunity to lock the buyer into a long-term relationship with high switching costs. In these circumstances the supplier could potentially transform a contested market situation (as indicated by the current ability to generate only low returns) into one in which the relationship is transformed into either a key account (with higher returns) or one in which an exploitation account is created.

This is an important point because buyers have to recognise that the ideal situation for suppliers is to have their customers in the exploitation account and, failing that, to have them in the key account quadrant. The development account can therefore provide opportunities for improvement for the supplier, but there is no certainty that this will occur. In fact buyers are often most happy with suppliers who operate proactively to improve functionality and reduce costs in the development quadrant. This is because they are innovating at low returns – i.e. increasing use value and reducing the total costs of ownership for the buyer in the short term. These are the two variables that the buyer most wishes to see developed, and this implies that a situation of *buyer dominance* normally exists in the power relationship between the buyer and supplier in a development account.

Key account

In a key account the supplier normally has a high share of the buyer's available revenue, and is heavily reliant on it for the operation of the supplier's own business. This ensures that the supplier views the buyer as a highly attractive customer in revenue terms. This combined with the fact that the supplier is able to make high levels of return from the relationship implies that the supplier must ensure that the buyer's account is not lost to other potential competitors, or that the buyer is not in a position to be able to force them to reduce their returns by reducing the costs of ownership.

In this circumstance it is inevitable that a supplier will wish to encourage relationship-specific adaptations by the buyer and by themselves that create a permanent lock-in of both parties. Thus competent suppliers will seek to create tangible and intangible switching costs in the relationship so that the barriers to market entry for competitors are too high for the buyer to countenance in the future. Ways in which this is achieved are through the creation of additional service offerings to existing product and service offerings; by creating difficult to replicate ways of working; or by embedding operational software into customer business processes that are difficult to remove.

The key account quadrant is a highly desirable situation to be in for suppliers but it is not the ideal. The reason for this is because in order to generate high returns the supplier must also undertake dedicated investments and must continue to innovate for the customer. This raises the possibility that other suppliers might be able to enter the market against the supplier if they do not continue to make heavy investments in innovation that provide the customer with continuing improvements in use value and lower costs of ownership than that possible from other suppliers. This can be a challenging business environment to operate in as a supplier, and normally implies some level of *interdependence* in power terms between buyer and supplier.

Exploitation account

In the exploitation account the supplier does not view any particular customer as more attractive than another, but is able to make high returns from working with any or all of them. This must be the ideal situation for suppliers, because in this quadrant the power situation is normally one of *supplier dominance*, and there will normally be many potential customers that can be serviced with low switching costs.

Dominance will also normally be based on the supplier having isolating mechanisms compared with their competitors. These are supplier-owned resources that provide for a better trade-off between use value and exchange costs for the buyer, from the possession of which the supplier can still appropriate above normal returns. Dominance also occurs for suppliers when the buyer is subject to post-contractual moral hazard (lock-in) or information asymmetry that allows the supplier to take advantage of the buyer commercially, even though the market is contested and better deals may be negotiable elsewhere.

The fact that the supplier can make high returns from any relationship with customers, even when they are of low attractiveness to the supplier, means that it is highly unlikely that the supplier will be willing to act proactively towards any specific customer. On the contrary, it is more than likely that dominant suppliers in this situation can fix quality and price standards and impose these on the customers. Furthermore any attempts by customers to work closely with suppliers in these circumstances are likely to be stillborn because the supplier can appropriate any improvements in value from proactive ways of working for themselves. The buyer, therefore, has few opportunities to leverage value from the supplier, who can impose their own terms of trade on the relationship.

Low-value account

In the low-value account the supplier does not view any customer as highly attractive and is unable to make reasonable returns from any relationship. In this situation the power position of buyers and suppliers is likely to be *independent*. This implies that the supplier will normally be operating in a highly contested market, in which the individual customer has insufficient volume of demand to encourage any supplier to make dedicated investments in the relationship. Given this, it is likely that the supplier will operate reactively and instead offer customers a standard product or service at a standard price.

Furthermore, the opportunities to develop proactive approaches with any customer are likely to be countered by the easy replication of any new innovation by all other suppliers in the market, making it difficult for the supplier to countenance any heavy investments in relationship-specific adaptations to create differentiation. This environment also ensures that switching costs for both the buyer and the supplier will be low and that the market is likely to be heavily contested. In such an environment the returns will be low, and there must be a real threat that suppliers will consider exit from such markets rather than the adoption of proactive innovation.

This situation is clearly the least attractive and least profitable for any supplier to operate from. In such circumstances buyers can expect only a basic and relatively arm's-length relationship from any supplier, who may also consider exiting from this type of situation if more congenial revenue and return opportunities can be created elsewhere.

It is clear, therefore, that suppliers receive particular commercial (revenue and reward) outcomes from working with specific customers, and, as we have seen, this will also imply that an objective power situation normally exists between the buyer and the supplier. It is interesting to note that sometimes suppliers will have very different power and leverage situations with specific customers for the same products and services. The marketing tool known as *price dispersion analysis* – which demonstrates the different net prices and costs to serve positions for individual customers buying the same products, but with different levels of volume and attractiveness – clearly indicates this fact (Shapiro *et al.*, 1987).

Whatever the current revenue and returns situation, in thinking about how to leverage improvements in their relationships with buyers, suppliers (like buyers) have to consider how they can change any current power circumstance to their commercial advantage. In other words, just as buyers regularly think about how to move their relationships into the *buyer dominance* and *ideal supplier* quadrants respectively, so suppliers normally consider how they can move them into the *supplier dominance* and *exploitation account* quadrants. In moving into these quadrants, suppliers (like buyers) have to consider what the operational means are to achieve these goals, and how any of the choices available to them will impact upon the trade-off between revenue and return.

There are six basic customer account management approaches that suppliers can choose from when they decide how to work with any buyer. Suppliers, like buyers, can choose to work *reactively* or *proactively* when they develop a relationship with any customer. If a supplier decides to operate *reactively* in a relationship with a customer this implies that they will develop their capabilities internally within the company but develop only arm's-length relationships with their customers, so that any innovations they make in their own business model are only understood and retained internally within the company. Close bonds are not created with any particular customers (and by extension the suppliers in the first-tier supplier's own extended supply chains). The relationship will normally be confined to the sharing of limited product and volume information with the customer.

When a supplier decides to operate *proactively* in any relationship with a customer it is likely that they will engage in developing close collaborative working relationships with them. This may extend to the development of legal, technical and commercial bonds and there will be a high level of sharing of sensitive technical and commercial information, perhaps with dedicated investments being made in relationship-specific adaptations to operational processes and systems and the creation of cooperative norms (Cannon and Perreault, 1999). This highly *collaborative* way of working may also extend beyond the initial first-tier relationship with the customer to include the supplier's own suppliers, throughout their own extended supply chains. In this circumstance the innovations made by the supplier may well be specific to, and highly visible to, the customer.

Suppliers, therefore, think most of all about the trade-off between revenue and return strategically, but operationally they also have think carefully about how much time and effort they must put into a customer relationship in order to create a situation in which they can improve future revenue and returns. This means that, just like buyers, suppliers make short and long-term calculations when they enter into relationships. The willingness of a supplier to be reactive or proactive in any relationship will therefore clearly be a function of their perception of the *attractiveness* of the buyer's account for the development of their own short and long-term strategy around revenue generation, as well as their ability to make high or low levels of *return* in the future.

To speak of attractive buyers in this context implies that the buyer's account provides the supplier with opportunities to generate revenue from the individual customer over time, as well as providing opportunities (by working with the customer) to create differentiation and/or cost leadership for themselves in the market against their direct competitors, in such a way that they can grow their share of the total market in the future.

Customer attractiveness cannot therefore be understood in relation to just the current trading relationship between a supplier and their customer. It must also be understood in terms of the potential that the supplier perceives any customer might bring to them in pursuit of their competitive strategy against other actual or potential suppliers (*competitors*) in the market. Buyers often fail to understand these aspects of attractiveness when they negotiate with suppliers. Suppliers are also often economical with the truth when explaining the relative importance of any customer to their own competitive strategy in the market, because they do not always wish to inform buyers of one of the most important levers they can have in a negotiation – knowledge about the relative importance of the specific relationship to the supplier's overall business strategy.

It follows, therefore, that when suppliers assess a relationship with a buyer they will make two calculations related to attractiveness. The first is related to their ability to lock the relevant customer into a long-term relationship that allows them to receive all of their market demand from working with the customer (both now and in the future). The second is related to the impact that this relationship may have on the ability of the supplier to develop a differentiated brand, or cost leading supply offerings and/or create brand associations that allow it to position in the general market place against competitors and with other potential customers.

As always, the concern for the supplier is, first, about revenue share and levels of return. Use value and the cost of ownership (the concerns of the buyer) are important but secondary considerations. These factors are, however, inextricably combined in the supplier's calculations about any relationship, because while suppliers may be willing to increase use value and reduce price in the short term, this is normally only done in pursuit of longer-term strategic considerations related to revenue and returns.

It follows from this that suppliers will tend to act proactively with buyers when the customer is perceived as highly attractive for the generation of increased revenue and returns. High attractiveness, therefore, involves the ability of a customer to provide the supplier with a constant and/or increasing share of revenue, and/or a capability to differentiate themselves from their competitors (whether by technical or reputational characteristics). Thus suppliers will make dedicated investments in a relationship, and undertake relationship-specific adaptations to their own working practices, whenever there is an opportunity to differentiate or create long-term lock-in over the customer by the creation of high sunk and switching costs.

A supplier will tend, however, not to see any necessity to work proactively with buyers when there are low switching and sunk costs in a relationship and when the customer under consideration has relatively low volume requirements and provides few opportunities for the supplier to differentiate themselves against competitors, or opportunities to use brand and reputation associations to win greater shares of the market. Under these circumstances the supplier will tend to regard the customer as of low attractiveness and provide them, reactively, with the standard product or service offering available to everyone else in the market. This way of working can be described as *arm's-length*. This is because the supplier sees no necessity to develop long-term dedicated investments in the relationship with the buyer.

The supplier – when considering how best to maximise revenue and return – must however not just think about the way that they should work with the customer. The supplier also has to understand how to

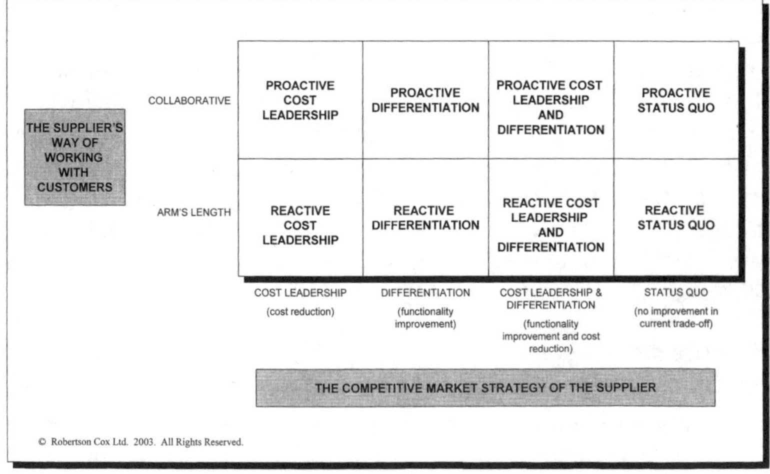

Figure 3.7 Customer and competitor strategies for the supplier

position competitively against other potential suppliers. As is now well known, there are many ways in which a supplier can think about developing their own supply offering strategy, and in general terms there are four broad strategic approaches that can be developed (Porter, 1980; Cox *et al.*, 2003). Suppliers can develop competitive market strategies focused on *cost leadership, differentiation,* or a combination of *differentiation and cost leadership* and they can also decide to leave the trade-off as it is and pursue the *status quo*. These four competitive positioning strategies can also be undertaken by working *collaboratively and proactively*, or at *arms-length and reactively* with customers and the supply chain.

As Figure 3.7 demonstrates, the supplier can choose to operate using the following eight broad customer/competitor strategies.

Proactive cost leadership

Under proactive cost leadership the essential positioning strategy of a company is to become a supplier that is capable of providing reduced costs of ownership to the customer. Clearly there are two choices within this approach. The supplier could choose to reduce the cost and leave the functionality the same, or reduce the functionality and reduce the cost of ownership for the customer. Most customers would normally prefer the first option but some might be prepared to source at a lower quality and at a lower cost of ownership as a result. This implies there are potentially two cost leadership options if the trade-off with functionality is considered.

If a supplier chooses to operate proactively in any customer relationship, it normally implies, as we argued earlier, that the supplier will be prepared to make dedicated investments in the relationship and undertake relationship specific adaptations in order to provide customers with improvements. This would imply both a willingness to undertake long-term collaborative forms of interaction, and also a willingness to engage with customer sourcing strategies of supplier development and/or supply chain management.

Proactive differentiation

Under proactive differentiation the positioning strategy of the supplier is to achieve significant improvements in functionality such that the supplier is able to provide products and services that are superior to others in terms of use value in the market. Once again, however, the improvement in functionality that differentiates the supply offering can involve two relationships, but now with costs. The functionality improvement could occur with costs remaining the same, or with an increase in costs. Clearly, there may be two types of potential customers to target in a market: those who are not prepared to pay more for any increase in functionality, and those who are.

When a supplier decides to operate proactively to create differentiation the same characteristics are likely to be in place as described above. The supplier will be willing to enter into long-term relationships with the customer and will also consider engaging with them in supplier development and/or supply chain management activities. These will necessarily involve close and collaborative working relationships with the buyer, in which dedicated investments are made in the relationship, involving the sharing of technical and commercial information and the creation of relationship-specific adaptations.

Proactive cost leadership and differentiation

Under proactive cost leadership and differentiation the same relationship-specific adaptations and dedicated investments are likely to be made and there will also be a corresponding willingness to engage in supplier development and/or supply chain management activities. Now, however, the focus of the innovation from the supplier will be to offer customers the winning combination of reduced costs of ownership with increased functionality relative to other potential suppliers.

Any supplier able to develop such a double benefit to customers is in a very strong strategic position if other suppliers are unable to do the same.

Reactive cost leadership; reactive differentiation; and reactive cost leadership and differentiation

These three options mirror the basic proactive variants discussed above. The only major difference is in the attitude of the supplier both to the relationship with the customer, and to his or her own suppliers and extended supply chains. In each of these variants the supplier is not willing to accept a close and collaborative relationship upstream or downstream.

As a result, the supplier will not make dedicated investments in the relationship and will seek to retain all knowledge and know-how about the ability to innovate closely within the confines of the company. This unwillingness to share embedded knowledge or develop new knowledge and understanding will also be replicated with a fairly closed and arm's-length approach to suppliers, with a preference for supply chain sourcing and supplier selection relationships with customers and the company's own suppliers and supply chains.

Proactive and reactive status quo

It is sometimes possible for suppliers to enter into relationships in which they have no real intention of providing any improvement in the trade-off between cost and functionality for the customer. In the reactive variant the supplier simply makes their current best supply offering to the customer and expects to deliver this to them throughout the term of the contractual relationship.

The proactive variant is a somewhat more subtle approach because in this variant the supplier may offer the prospect of improvements in either functionality or costs (or both), and undertake to make collaborative relationship-specific adaptations in the relationship but without any real intention of innovating in the future. On the contrary, the real intention of this approach is to lock the buyer into the supplier's business by the creation of high switching costs through the creation of collaborative technical and personal linkages. By doing so the supplier need only provide the same value proposition to the customer while maximising their revenue share and returns overtime.

Given these eight basic options it is self-evident that suppliers, just like buyers, have to make calculations about which operational approach to a relationship they should pursue when they work with any customer. All suppliers would prefer ideally to be in a situation where they could make innovations in the trade-off between functionality and cost, and keep any benefits for themselves, while also closing the market to their customers. Unfortunately, this type of arm's-length approach is not always possible and suppliers always have to make a calculation about what the benefit will be of working proactively and collaboratively, or reactively and at arm's length with their customers.

This calculation always involves complex trade-offs between the ability of the customer to help the supplier to develop their own strategies against competitors, and the impact of this approach on the trade-off between the supplier's future potential opportunities to generate increased revenue and returns. This, as Figure 3.8 demonstrates, will involve them in weighing the relative merits of each relationship management approach in relation to the trade-offs between revenue and returns.

As Figure 3.8 shows, each of the customer and competitor strategies open to suppliers requires an understanding of the relative impact of that option on revenue and return. Clearly suppliers will prefer any of these potential approaches that tends to provide for maximum opportunities to increase revenue or return, or ideally both at the same time.

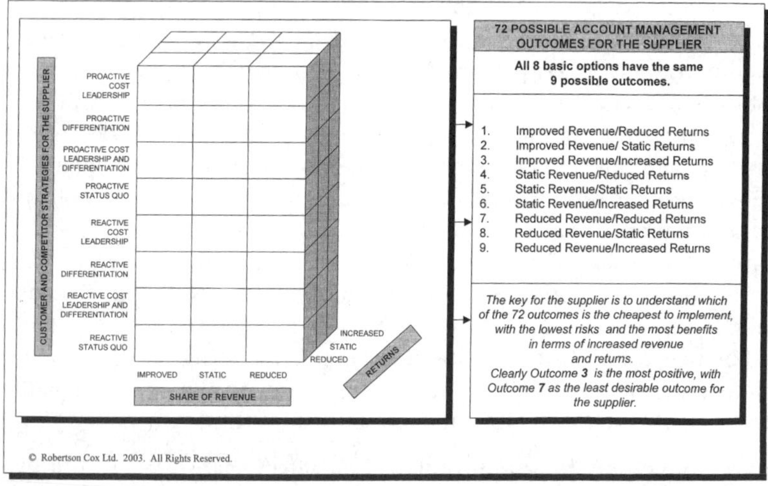

Figure 3.8 The range of account management outcomes for the supplier

3.3 The ideal and the optimal: selecting appropriate relationship management styles

Given these potentially divergent goals on the part of the buyer and the supplier, the key problem for effective external relationship management is clearly the difficulty of aligning the goals of the buyer with those of the supplier. It is self-evident that both the buyer and the supplier will normally be concerned, first, with the development of approaches that favour their own interest rather than those that serve the interests of the other side in any relationship. It is because of this that there is often tension, misalignment and, sometimes, outright conflict in business relationships.

Tension arises in relationships, therefore, because there is an objective conflict of interest between buyers and suppliers due to the fact that *the ideal situation for buyers is normally to operate from the buyer dominance power position*, while *the ideal position for suppliers is to operate from the supplier dominance position*. This means that if buyers and suppliers are seeking to maximise their own goals they will always be involved in tension as each side strives constantly to arrive at the objectively ideal situation for themselves.

This statement does not preclude the possibility, of course, that under some circumstances working together and sharing equally what is created in the relationship can be a desirable situation for both a buyer and supplier. The point here, however, is that when buyers and suppliers enter into such a relationship it is likely that it will be an *optimal* rather than *ideal* outcome for both parties.

By *optimal* one means that while the buyer and supplier both recognise that they would prefer to operate in the *ideal* power position (from which they could leverage benefits for themselves at the expense of the other), the current power resources available to them ensure that neither party has the capability of doing so. As a result, the next best option available to both parties is to work together in an *interdependent* power situation and either to share the value equally or perhaps proportionate to the effort put in by both parties.

All of the research reported here demonstrates that effective business relationship management hinges on the ability of both buyers and suppliers to understand objectively what the current power circumstance between them is, as well as the future opportunities that are available to leverage improvements in the commercially valued goals (*strategic ends*) of both parties to the exchange transaction. One of the most common problems (that will be encountered later in the empirical case studies) is a combined failure by both buyers and suppliers to understand the objective power circumstances operating between them, as well as a subjective failure to understand which levers (*operational means*) must be put in place by both sides to arrive at a mutually acceptable power position in the future. For this to be achieved it is essential that both sides understand and accept the future relative power positions once they have entered into a relationship, and know how to align their internal processes in such a way that external alignment can be achieved.

There is also a need by both buyers and suppliers to understand that if they do intend to move to a new power position they must find suitable partners with whom they can work in an appropriately incentivised manner. This implies that both sides to the exchange relationship must receive something they value from the transaction. This may not always be the maximisation of their position in the relationship. It can be enough for both parties that they receive outcomes that are less than ideal, but which are relatively superior to any other outcome that they might receive from any other potential transactional partner.

As the case studies that follow show, in our experience few practitioners appear to have the requisite level of understanding of these issues to undertake effective business relationship management and alignment. In far too many of the cases analysed it is clear that there is a major competence gap amongst practitioners, whether they are buyers or suppliers. This competence gap is rooted in:

- an inability to understand the tension that exists objectively in all business relationships between buyers and suppliers;
- an inability to understand the objective power circumstances that exist;
- an inability to understand which operational relationship management approaches available to buyers and suppliers work best in particular power circumstances; and,
- an inability to select, align and incentivise exchange partners appropriately in specific power and operational relationship (sourcing and customer and competitor) management approaches.

But there is an additional problem for both buyers and suppliers that militates against the effective management of business relationships. This problem relates to the inability of many practitioners to properly understand the objective purposes of business transactions and the operational *relationship management styles* that must be developed and used to deliver *strategic ends*. In general, although this failure to subjectively understand the commercial purposes of business is evident in companies when they act as buyers and as suppliers, our research and consulting activities have found this problem to be more apparent on the buying side of the relationship than on the supplier side.

This problem is simply explained by reference to the argument that *being non-adversarial* (i.e. through the creation of win-win relationships) is the most efficacious for both parties in an exchange transaction. As we saw in Chapter 1, this argument has been developed most extensively in the relationship management literature on alliancing and partnering and also by the transaction costs economising school (TCE). This topic is discussed in more detail elsewhere but it is worth summarising some key points here (Cox, 2005).

When proponents of the win-win concept argue the case for such outcomes in buyer and supplier exchange relationships they normally claim that relationships do not work well between buyers and suppliers if one side in the relationship is attempting to appropriate the value for themselves at the expense of the other parties to the exchange. The basic argument follows that, if all sides to the exchange would only consider being more open, transparent and trusting in the relationship then it would be possible for more value to be created, and for both sides to maximise their returns from the relationship.

This is a potentially winning argument but on closer reflection it is possible to argue that the argument, while not wholly invalid, has serious weaknesses. The most important weakness in this line of argument is clearly the fact that proponents of the win-win approach do not properly explain what it is that drives the buyer or the supplier to enter into any transaction, and why historically it is that transparency and trust has not always been common in business relationships. Indeed one might argue that if it is so self-evidently beneficial to both parties why do business people not do it more often?

The reason that buyers and suppliers find it difficult to be transparent and trust one another in business relationships is not because they are simple-minded but because there is clearly an objective tension in business transactions. This objective tension has been explained earlier by reference to the fact that buyers, when seeking to maximise their commercial ends, must always strive to operate in the *buyer dominance* quadrant and have suppliers pass increased functionality at lower cost to them. Similarly, if suppliers wish to maximise their commercial goals they must seek to operate in the *supplier dominance* power situation, and force buyers to provide them with the maximum share of revenue possible while appropriating the highest level of returns possible from their control of market offerings superior to those of their competitors.

This fact of objective tension does not, however, deny the possibility (as discussed above) that there will be many circumstances when neither buyers nor suppliers are in a position to be able to achieve their ideal power situation. Given this, there will be situations when being more transparent and trusting is clearly the most appropriate way in which to manage the relationship. It seems clear that when a situation of *interdependence* exists between a buyer and supplier, and there are no current opportunities for either party to shift the power circumstance to their advantage, then a more trusting and transparent approach to relationship management may be appropriate. In such relationships it is also likely that both sides will wish to share commercial returns in proportion to the effort made by each party. This sharing of value may be based on equal shares or it may not be, but in all cases the power structure would normally require *satisficing* rather than *maximising* strategies by both parties.

To argue, however, that *satisficing* is always the most appropriate way to manage all relationships is patently absurd (Simon, 1997). As argued earlier, the *ideal* (best possible) option for a buyer must be to operate from a power situation of *buyer dominance*. In this situation the buyer is provided with the relatively free choice of adopting either a collaborative or arm's-length, long-term or short-term relationship with the supplier. Furthermore the buyer decides on how much value the supplier receives from the relationship. Similarly, the *ideal* situation for a supplier is to be in the *supplier dominance* power situation. In this circumstance the supplier is free to choose whether to work in the short or long term, and collaboratively or at arm's length with any customer. Once again, in this situation, it is the supplier who decides what the trade-off between functionality and cost will be. The supplier can also normally retain control of high levels of revenue and earn above normal returns in this power situation. If achievable, and sustainable, both of these options are clearly superior to *satisficing* alternatives.

Theoretically it can be argued therefore that when buyers and suppliers enter into transactions with one another they have to consider what the purpose of their interaction with the other party is likely to be. They must therefore decide whether they wish to *maximise* or *satisfice*, and when and how it is appropriate to do so. These considerations will force both parties to consider the risks and rewards to the achievement of their own unique *strategic ends* of operating with the other party in particular ways.

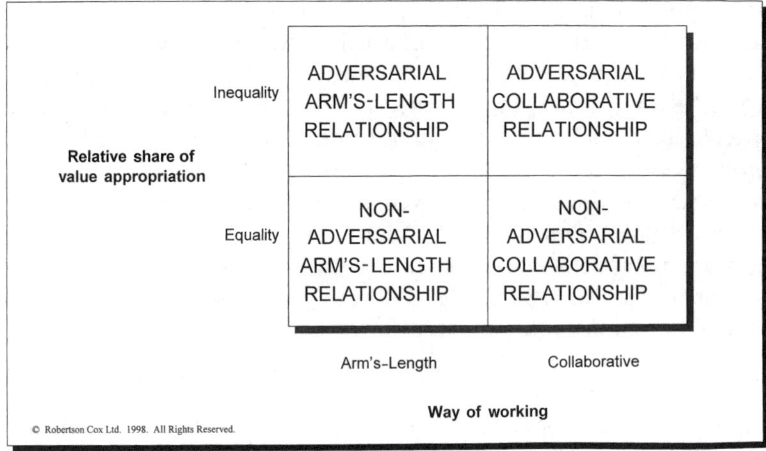

Figure 3.9 The four basic relationship management styles
Source: Cox (1999, p. 23).

On the one hand, both parties may be happy with current power circumstances and may not wish to leverage improvements in their own value propositions by moving to more congenial power circumstances. On the other hand, in modern capitalist economies practitioners are constantly pressurised to improve performance, whether as buyers or suppliers. This implies that practitioners are rarely content with the status quo and are constantly striving to transform power circumstances to their advantage. When doing so both parties have to consider the way they will work with the other party in operational as well as commercial terms. This combination of operational and commercial requirements provides buyers and suppliers with four basic choices about the relationship management style to be adopted when they engage with one another in a business relationship. Each of these four *relationship management styles* is described below, and shown in Figure 3.9.

Adversarial arm's-length relationships

Under an adversarial arm's-length relationship the management style adopted by the buyer or the supplier is one in which one party to the exchange is forced to bear most of the risks (i.e. makes most of the investments) in the creation of value, while the other side enjoys a disproportionate share of the value created.

In this context one would expect there to be few technical bonds or dedicated investments made by either party in the exchange transaction.

This implies that the relationship is likely to be short-term and the sharing of product and process information will be low, with few operational linkages over time and with limited development of cooperative norms in the relationship. Neither side will make many relationship-specific adaptations to create innovation in the development of the products or services provided.

Furthermore the commercial exchange is likely to be one in which the buyer will seek to maximise for themselves improvements in functionality and reductions in the cost of ownership, while attempting to force supplier profit margins (returns) as low as possible without offering any tangible long-term volume commitments in exchange. The buyer's relationship with the supplier will approximate closely to the classical short-term market relationship of *supplier selection*, based on short-term design and specification and volume (and perhaps social) information exchange by the buyer, with short-term product/service, capacity and financial (and perhaps social) information exchange by the supplier.

This type of relationship is best exemplified for the buyer by the use of reverse auction bidding, where price is normally (if not always) the final mechanism of selection after initial bid lists have been approved. This way of operating is the traditional approach used by buyers when they operate in the supplier selection and supply chain sourcing modes. It is often disparagingly referred to as 'three bids and a buy' by those who think it is an ineffective mechanism for improving sourcing leverage.

Suppliers also tend to use this approach when they wish to protect their product and service innovations from buyers who might backward integrate against them, or when they fear that there may be significant risks of sensitive product or service information leaking into the market place if they develop close collaborative relationships with particular buyers. Suppliers will also adopt this approach when they are in a strong competitive position with significant advantages over other suppliers and with a dominant share of the potential volume in the market.

In these circumstances it is likely that the supplier will be fixing price and quality standards in the market and will be able to dictate the terms of trade to buyers. This means that the supplier will set the standards for functionality and costs of ownership and will be able to retain revenue without necessarily passing value in lower costs to the buyer. This will normally allow the supplier to appropriate above normal returns at the expense of higher relative costs to the buyer. The supplier here would be operating with the customer in the *exploitation* account management mode.

There is one other circumstance when suppliers can use this management style, and this occurs when there is serious information asymmetry between the buyer and the supplier, which favours the supplier. Thus, a supplier may be operating in a highly contested market, in which buyers ought to be able to receive increased value from suppliers through contestation in the market place. This would normally be an *independence* power circumstance.

In this situation, if the buyer suffers from high levels of bounded rationality, and is unaware of market conditions, it is possible for the supplier to deny this information to the buyer and achieve higher returns than would be possible if the buyer had the same quality of information that the supplier and other buyers possess. The supplier in this example is using opportunism as a mechanism to achieve higher than normal returns, and creating a de facto position of *supplier dominance* with the uninformed buyer and operating in the *exploitation* account management mode.

This strategy is not, of course, without risks. The supplier has to calculate the potential for the buyer to become better informed and the consequence of this realisation for the relationship in the long term. In general, however, this is not a major consideration since the adversarial arm's-length approach is normally used by suppliers when they recognise that relationships with buyers are likely to be short-term and there are low switching costs in the relationship for both sides, with many other potential buyers and/or suppliers to work with in the future.

Clearly this management style will only be appropriate for buyers and/or suppliers when neither side needs to work closely with the other to achieve their strategic ends. It is likely this will only be possible when the buyer is operating either in the *buyer dominance* or *independence* power circumstances using supplier selection and supply chain sourcing strategies. It will only be possible for suppliers when they are operating in the *supplier dominant* circumstance, using *exploitation* customer account management strategies.

It is obvious that this can be a highly appropriate style of managing relationships for both buyers and suppliers when there is no incentive for either party to work with the other closely to achieve their respective strategic ends. This logic implies, however, that this relationship management style works best (i.e. it is in *alignment*) when the other party in the exchange relationship is not operating in the same way. Thus if there is no reason for a buyer or supplier to develop close collaborative ways of working the ideal alignment of the relationship is for the dominant party to operate in the adversarial arm's-length style and for the weaker party to operate in a non-adversarial arm's-length style.

This is the most aligned approach from the dominant party's perspective and conflict is unlikely to occur, even though there may be some tension in the relationship because the dominant party controls the relationship and the weaker party can be expected to seek ways of reducing dominance, or perhaps even exiting from this situation altogether. Tension of this kind is inevitable, even in aligned relationships, but outright conflict will only occur if relationships are seriously misaligned. Thus, if both parties are involved in a power situation in which there is significant leverage favouring one party, but both sides are pursuing adversarial arm's-length styles, then *misalignment with dysfunctional conflict* is inevitable. In such circumstances it is likely that the dominant party has the wrong partner in the exchange relationship and should look for a more congenial, less adversarial partner.

Similarly, from this perspective it is possible to argue that sometimes in arm's-length relationships the dominant party may misperceive the power circumstance and the appropriate relationship management approach required and pursue sub-optimal strategies. Thus, if, in a dominant situation, the dominant party pursues a non-adversarial management style then they will be forgoing opportunities to appropriate more value than they could if they pursued a more adversarial approach.

Finally, if either party adopts collaborative approaches then it is likely that they will be making investments in the relationship that are inappropriate, of limited value and wasteful of scarce resources. In each of these cases we can argue that relationships are *misaligned and sub-optimal* even though outright dysfunctional conflict is unlikely to occur. There are clearly major opportunities in these situations for the dominant party to realign their relationship style to improve leverage in the future.

Non-adversarial arm's-length relationships

In a non-adversarial arm's-length relationship the way of working is the same as under the adversarial variant. The buyer or supplier operating in this management style does not make dedicated investments in the relationship and does not expect to work in a close and collaborative manner with the other party. On the contrary, all innovations by the buyer or supplier are undertaken independently. In this sense, if there is to be a relationship, both parties have to make their own investments in what it is that they do, without sharing detailed technical and commercial information to allow the other party to develop their requirements more effectively or efficiently.

In this context one would expect the buyer to decide on the design and specification of their requirements independently of the supplier. The supplier would also be expected to develop their supply offerings independently of a close working relationship with the buyer, with limited detailed understanding of the buyer's future design and specification requirements, and without the creation of technical bonds or relationship-specific adaptations between the two parties. The detailed interaction would also be limited to basic tender and supply offering information as under the more adversarial variant discussed above.

The key difference with the more adversarial variant is the fact that the party operating in this style recognises that they do not have the power levers to appropriate more value from the relationship directly. They have to accept that they will only receive the level of commercial return that is proportionate to the level of investment they have made in the relationship, and relative to the power circumstance that exists.

Thus, a non-adversarial buyer could be expected to be a price and quality receiver. This is because the buyer has no power levers to force any supplier to offer better than the current market prices for any given level of functionality required. In such circumstances the supplier may or may not be earning above normal returns, but the buyer has no power resources to be able to force either an increase in functionality and/or reductions in the costs of ownership and/or in the returns that a supplier can earn. In this sense the buyer takes what he can get and is unlikely to develop long-term relationships with any supplier. This is because the buyer is not seeking opportunities for long-term collaboration from the supplier, and is only interested in sourcing from the supplier that, in the future, can offer the best short-term deal.

Obviously non-adversarial arm's-length can be an appropriate way of working for the buyer, especially in power circumstances of *independence* and of *supplier dominance* where there is no scope for the buyer to develop long-term relationships with a supplier. Obviously the relative benefits that a buyer will receive in either situation will be somewhat different. In the *independence* situation the buyer will be a price and quality receiver, but the contested nature of the market provides opportunities for the buyer to switch to the currently lowest-cost and best-quality supplier. The buyer will also, if they are competent, receive the current best trade-off between quality and price in the market which, because of competition, is likely to improve over time. In this sense, in *independence* power circumstances buyers are sometimes seen as the inadvertent beneficiaries of supplier competition – things improve without much effort on their part.

The situation is somewhat different for a non-adversarial arm's-length buyer in a *supplier dominant* situation. In this situation the buyer is a price and quality receiver, but the supplier normally makes above normal returns, and it is the supplier who decides whether there will be any innovation in functionality and the costs of ownership. In this power situation the buyer is normally a supplicant who takes what is given and prays for contestation to increase, or for technological innovation to destroy the supplier's advantages in the market. The buyer will normally use *supplier selection* and *supply chain sourcing* strategies in either of these two situations.

A non-adversarial arm's-length supplier can be characterised as a willing supplicant. A willing supplicant supplier is one who accepts that they are in a highly contested market place with low switching costs, where there is little opportunity for them to create sustainable isolating mechanisms against any of their direct competitors. Given this highly competitive environment, suppliers will normally have to recognise that in order to stay in business they must constantly innovate to reduce costs and improve functionality. They also have to recognise that they will have to pass all of the value they create to their customers, and earn low (normal) returns in return.

This is the way in which suppliers normally have to operate in *independence* and *buyer dominance* power circumstances, when there is no need for both parties to collaborate and arm's-length ways of working are adequate. Clearly both of these are highly beneficial situations for buyers but not necessarily ideal for suppliers, because in *independence* power situations the supplier has to constantly innovate without high returns and without the prospect of any guaranteed future business from the buyer. The normal customer account management strategy of the supplier in this circumstance is the *low value* approach. In a *buyer dominance* situation, the buyer has even more leverage by virtue of their ability to force suppliers to innovate for them with potentially lower returns in return for higher volume orders. In this circumstance the supplier normally operates in the *development* customer account management style.

It is clear that the non-adversarial arm's-length situation provides few leverage opportunities for either the buyer or supplier to use against one another. Despite this, if a buyer or supplier has no alternative other than to operate in this environment, and this is the best deal currently available to them, then it is an appropriate relationship management style to adopt.

In practice it is clear that on occasions buyers and suppliers can misunderstand this power circumstance, and fail to align their relationship management styles appropriately. Thus, if either or both parties to an exchange in the *independence* power situation begin to develop adversarial ways of working, then it is likely that the relationship will be seriously *misaligned with dysfunctional conflict*. Furthermore, the relationship will be *misaligned and sub-optimal* if either party to the exchange begins to undertake dedicated investments of a collaborative kind in such situations. This is because the buyer and supplier would be making dedicated investments that are likely to be wasteful of scarce resources.

Alignment will only occur in relationships involving non-adversarial arm's-length relationship management in circumstances where both the buyer and supplier recognise the power situation and adopt the appropriate relationship management style. Thus, in *independence* the appropriate relationship management style is for both the buyer and supplier to operate non-adversarially and at arm's length. In situations of *buyer dominance*, where there is no benefit to the buyer from collaborative ways of working with any supplier, the appropriate relationship management style is for the buyer to adopt adversarial arm's-length relationship management, while the supplier must adopt a non-adversarial style. Alignment occurs in *supplier dominance* when the supplier, seeing no benefit from collaborating closely with any buyer, adopts the adversarial approach and requires the buyer to operate as a willing supplicant in the non-adversarial arm's-length style.

Adversarial collaboration

When considering collaborative approaches to buyer and supplier relationship management it is clear that the commercial imperatives for the buyer and supplier are the same as under the two arm's-length styles, and what changes is the operational way of working.

Collaborative relationship management styles are very different from arm's-length approaches. Under an arm's-length approach the relationship primarily involves information exchange. The key aspects of information exchanged normally involve tender details by the buyer (volume requirements, scheduling, design and specification and performance measurement requirements) and supply-offering details from the supplier (product/service specifications, logistics capabilities, financial standing, capacity and price).

Under collaborative relationship management ways of working this level of information (and normally even more) will be required to make an initial supplier selection decision, but, after that, since the buyer and supplier are entering into a more long-term exchange relationship the levels of interaction are much more extensive. This is because both parties recognise a considerable advantage to the achievement of their own individual *strategic ends* from participating in a longer-term relationship with the other party. Given this, it is normal that the level of information will be much higher but extend also into the creation of relationship-specific adaptations (Hakansson, 1982; Hallen *et al.*, 1991; Cannon and Perreault, 1999).

These relationship adaptations normally involve mutually beneficial changes to processes, products and procedures that allow the relationship to operate more effectively. Relatedly, collaborative relationships also witness the development of a high-level sharing of proprietary commercially and operationally sensitive information, and the development of cooperative norms in the relationship between the buyer and the supplier. These may include joint product and process development, joint process and supply chain mapping for waste reduction exercises and the development of joint trust building initiatives. Ultimately, this level of close interaction will lead to the development of technical bonds – or the linkage of systems, procedures and routines to facilitate the flow of information and goods and services.

Clearly there are major costs and benefits from any decision to enter into a longer-term collaborative relationship. On the plus side the ability to develop relationship-specific adaptations that allow improvements in the way in which buyers provide robust and timely information to suppliers, and by which suppliers can minimise waste and inefficiency, while maximising product and process innovations that improve the overall supply offering, are to be valued. On the other hand the creation of relationship adaptations is not without its risks to both parties. The major risk is associated with the fungibility and non-fungibility of the relationship adaptations or dedicated investments that both parties brings to the relationship.

The TCE's major contribution to the understanding of buyer and supplier transactions has undoubtedly been the specification of the conditions under which buyers can become locked into post-contractual moral hazard in long-term collaborative relationships (Williamson, 1985). Williamson shows clearly that one of the problems of any dedicated investment is the impact that this may have on the ability of either party to exit easily from the relationship.

Some dedicated investments may create no problems for a buyer or a supplier because they are fungible for both parties. This simply means that both parties to the relationship can easily switch from one party to another, and none of the dedicated investments in the relationship create inordinate costs of switching. On the other hand, if the dedicated investments create problems of switching for both parties then a situation of bilateral dependency has been created. This is not so bad because the bilateral dependency is the same for both parties and neither side should operate opportunistically (at least not in theory) against the other.

Worse is a situation in which the dedicated investments create asymmetric power. This is a situation where the dedicated investment is fungible for one party (they can switch easily) but non-fungible for the other (they cannot switch easily). In this latter circumstance there is a shift in power post-contractually and, as Williamson puts it, a 'fundamental transformation' has occurred in the power relationship between the buyer and the supplier. Now one party to the exchange can move easily out of the relationship but the other is likely to find that post-contractual moral hazard is capable of being used against them to maximise the other side's returns at their expense.

It is clear that many of the problems faced by buyers when they undertake outsourcing decisions arise as a consequence of problems of post-contractual moral hazard under circumstances of close, long-term collaborative buyer and supplier relationship management (Lonsdale and Cox, 1998). Similarly, many suppliers who adopt relationship-specific adaptations to create operational efficiency in the delivery of products and services find that their ability to switch out of these relationships is very difficult once the initial process investments have been made. This is arguably one of the major learning experiences that those suppliers investing in vendor-managed inventory systems for retail supermarkets have discovered. They are locked into dominant buyers with very high sunk and switching costs that provide the buyer with significant levers by which they can improve their appropriation of value from the buyer.

Given the problems it seems clear that while there may be significant advantages for buyers and suppliers from creating long-term collaborative working relationships requiring dedicated investments, there is also the possibility that the advantages are not always mutually beneficial for both parties (Low, 1996). This conclusion raises the theoretical proposition that when buyers and suppliers collaborate together there is the possibility that one side may be able to operate adversarially in relation to the other.

Adversarial collaboration involves, therefore, one party in the relationship trying to create dedicated investments, with the avowed (if unarticulated) intention of locking the other party into the relationship, so that in the long term the short-term costs incurred by them will eventually be more than recompensed by their ability to create dependency by the other party on them. Often this strategy involves accepting a power situation that is disadvantageous in the short term so that a long-term situation of dominance can be created in the long term. This is a classic example of what has been called 'self-seeking interest with guile' (Williamson, 1985).

Clearly, this form of adversarial collaboration can occur under two different power circumstances. Under *buyer dominance* one might expect a buyer to encourage suppliers to make dedicated investments for them with the promise of long-term and high-volume business. In this approach the supplier eventually becomes so dependent on the buyer for their revenue flow, and the switching costs of the dedicated investments made are so high, that it becomes almost impossible for the supplier to diversify their customer base. In such circumstances the buyer is now in a strong position, not only to force the supplier to innovate for them in terms of functionality and the costs of ownership but to insist that (because of transparency over their internal business model) they should only receive a very low margin on any business that the buyer provides.

Obviously a buyer cannot push this too far and force a supplier out of business but it is clear that adversarial collaboration can be an extremely effective way by which buyers can force dependent suppliers to innovate for them and also control their margins. In this circumstance the buyer would normally use *supplier development* or *supply chain management* sourcing strategies and require the supplier to operate in the *development* customer account approach.

Suppliers can also use this approach successfully, especially when they are in the *supplier dominance* power situation. In this circumstance the fact that there is a high level of relationship-specific adaptation by the buyer with the supplier, and assuming that the supplier has the ability to work with other customers and is not heavily dependent on the buyer for their business revenue, it is possible for suppliers to create long-term dependency of the buyer on them.

Once long-term dependency with high switching costs has been achieved – normally by providing short-term improvements in functionality and the costs of ownership – the supplier (over time) can then reduce the level of innovation relative to that currently available in the market place and, by doing so, achieve above normal returns relative to what is happening elsewhere. Obviously the ability of suppliers to adopt this approach will depend on whether or not information asymmetry can be sustained about current market conditions post-contractually, and also on the level of sunk and switching costs in the relationship for the buyer.

There is, however, another variant of this approach that can be adopted by a dominant supplier even when it is clear to everyone that they are dominant. Sometimes buyers with a large volume of business with a dominant supplier will explore the possibilities of working closely with the supplier on operational process improvements. The expectation here is normally that the supplier will share any improvements achieved in the form of increased functionality and/or lower prices. Once the dedicated investments have been made it is possible for the dominant supplier to refuse to provide the levels of improvement originally agreed and retain the bulk of the benefits achieved in the form of higher returns for themselves.

The benefits that a dominant supplier can achieve from this approach can be very large indeed, especially when the collaboration with one customer allows the supplier to make improvements in processes and systems that can be applied equally beneficially to all of its other customer relationships. Normally, when the supplier is dominant in these ways the supplier operates in the *exploitation* customer account quadrant, with the buyer attempting to undertake *supplier development* or *supply chain management* sourcing strategies with them.

These are just some of the ways in which buyers and suppliers can use collaboration in an adversarial manner to appropriate higher returns or better value for money for themselves at the expense of their relationship partners. Obviously *alignment* in adversarial collaborative relationships normally occurs when both parties to the exchange understand objectively the power circumstance they are in and operate accordingly. It follows from the discussion above that *alignment* occurs under conditions of *buyer dominance* when the buyer is able to use an adversarial collaborative approach in which the supplier accepts that they should operate as a willing supplicant in a non-adversarial collaborative manner. Similarly if *supplier dominance* exists then the situation is reversed and *alignment* occurs when the supplier adopts an adversarial collaborative approach with the buyer using non-adversarial collaboration. Non-adversarial collaboration in this situation implies that the buyer or supplier accepts that they should pass the majority of the value to the other party in return either for regular work but with low margins (the supplier) or for only minor improvements in functionality and the costs of ownership (the buyer).

Misalignment with dysfunctional conflict occurs when either the supplicant buyer or supplicant supplier operates in the relationship using an adversarial rather than non-adversarial style. *Misaligned and sub-optimal* relationship management occurs when either party pursues an arm's-length approach when they should be collaborating, or when either or both parties attempts to operate this approach in the *independence* or *interdependence* power situation.

Non-adversarial collaboration

Non-adversarial collaboration has all the characteristics of adversarial collaboration operationally, but it differs in the way in which parties to the exchange deal with one another commercially. In this approach the buyer and supplier accept that they will make dedicated investments in the relationship, but recognise that it is unlikely that either the buyer or the supplier will ever be able to use these relationship-specific adaptations to leverage a dominant position for themselves against the other.

Given this, the most appropriate way to manage the collaborative relationship is to accept that it is likely (other things being equal) to be long-term, and that opportunism is unlikely to be functional in this situation. On the contrary – it is normal that both the buyer and supplier recognise that opportunism is likely to destroy trust, and that they should be more transparent and less opportunistic in their transactions with one another, in the hope that superior performance can be achieved that is mutually beneficial.

It seems that for the many writers who favour partnering or alliancing, non-adversarial collaboration is the holy grail of relationship management. In other words, it is the ideal state to which all buyers and suppliers should be moving. As argued earlier, we do not agree with this viewpoint, although it is clear that non-adversarial collaboration is one of the major relationship management styles available to buyers and suppliers when they engage in exchange transactions. The key question that has to be answered, however, is under which circumstances is this approach the most appropriate one for buyers and supplier to use?

It is clear that non-adversarial collaboration works best in circumstances of *interdependence*. The reason for this should be self-evident. In the interdependence power situation the buyer and supplier both have major levers of power over one another. The buyer will normally have a large share of the available market demand and is a highly attractive potential customer. The supplier on the other hand will normally be one of only a few who could provide the level of functionality and costs of ownership trade-off that the buyer requires.

In these circumstances the buyer has to recognise that if they wish to obtain improvements in the trade-off between functionality and costs of ownership, and if they also want to receive greater benefits than the other buyers in the market, then it will be incumbent upon them to work closely with a preferred supplier or suppliers and not attempt to adopt an adversarial commercial approach. This normally implies that the buyer will have to accept that the supplier will receive above normal returns on a continuous basis in return for improved functionality and reduced total costs of ownership relative to other players in the market.

In such circumstances there is an obvious need for a non-adversarial approach by both parties to the transaction. The buyer must recognise the supplier's right to earn a premium return for the specialist skills they bring to the relationship. The supplier has to accept that they cannot expect to receive the bulk of the buyer's business revenue if they do not constantly provide a better trade-off between functionality and the costs of ownership for them. In creating dedicated investments in the relationship the two parties eventually become mutually interdependent (both operationally and commercially). It is logical, therefore, that the development of operational linkages and cooperative norms in the relationship should be developed in as transparent a manner as possible.

There is one major problem that both parties have to recognise, however, in these types of relationships. If either side becomes complacent, then, as technological and market circumstances change over time, it may be possible that a long-term collaborative relationship will create inertia for one or both parties. Furthermore, there is always the risk that, as circumstances change, one party may stop being non-adversarial and use opportunism as a way of shifting the current relationship from one of *interdependence* to one of *buyer or supplier dominance*.

Despite these potential risks it is clear that non-adversarial collaboration is also a highly appropriate way in which to manage buyer and supplier relationships. This approach is most in *alignment* (works best) in situations of *interdependence* and when both the buyer and the supplier are using non-adversarial relationship management styles. Normally buyers will develop *supplier development* and *supply chain management* sourcing strategies in this situation. Suppliers, on the other hand, will normally operate within the *key* customer account quadrant.

Misalignment with dysfunctional conflict occurs when either party adopts an adversarial style when the other is working non-adversarially. In these circumstances the collaborating party is working with an inappropriate exchange partner. *Misalignment and sub-optimal* relationship management occurs when one party is trying to be collaborative and the other is operating at arm's-length, when the power circumstance is one of *independence*, or when the buyer or supplier attempts to use this approach when one of them is in the *supplier dominance* or *buyer dominance* power situation. In these circumstances the dominant buyer or supplier could achieve more for themselves by using adversarial collaboration.

3.4 Conclusion

This discussion has demonstrated that there are conditions that must be in place for the successful conduct of business relationships. Essentially these conditions are as follows:

- Buyers and suppliers must, first, understand the power circumstances that they are operating in, as well as the future power situation that is the most conducive and attainable for them to work towards. For the relationship to work effectively both sides must accept that they are happy to be operating in the current and future power situation, and that the goal of both sides is to work together to achieve this.
- Buyers and suppliers must also understand the value propositions (strategic ends) they are seeking to achieve by working with one another to create a future power location. These strategic ends must then be aligned internally with the operational capabilities of each party in the exchange.
- This internal alignment requires that the buyer must understand which operational sourcing approach is most appropriate to their needs; while the supplier must understand which customer account management approach is most appropriate to their needs.
- Once the internal alignment of commercial value propositions and operational means is achieved, these approaches must be compatible externally. This means that if the relationship is to work effectively the buyer's sourcing approach must be aligned appropriately with the customer account management approach being adopted by the supplier.
- Only then is it possible for the buyer and supplier to understand which type of relationship management style is the most appropriate for both parties to utilise when working together. If the relationship management styles are appropriate (given the power circumstance envisaged and operational needs of the relationship), then a situation of relationship alignment will occur.
- Misalignment in relationships can take two forms. The first form is the most difficult to rectify, and is referred to as *misalignment with dysfunctional conflict*. This occurs because the commercial drivers of

the parties in the exchange are not aligned and this implies that the parties cannot work together successfully. The second form is referred to as *misalignment with sub-optimal relationship management*. This implies that there is a lack of operational not commercial alignment. It is possible that these types of relationship misalignment can be rectified if both parties in the exchange are prepared to make the effort.

The discussion above is quite complex and, in order to assist the reader, the next short chapter provides a way of thinking about the effective alignment of business relationships in different power circumstances. The discussion that follows is supported by reference to six ideal-typical cases of alignment of business relationships as a guide to best practice.

Having outlined these ideal-typical examples of best practice the discussion turns in the second part of this volume to an analysis of real-life empirical cases of business relationship management in practice. These case studies have been drawn from the academic and consulting work of the authors and provide examples of *alignment, misalignment with dysfunctional conflict* and *misalignment with sub-optimal relationship management*. As the cases demonstrate, there are many practitioners who intuitively understand how to align relationships, but there are also a large number of managers who do not.

References

Cannon, J. P. and Perreault, W. D. (1999) 'Buyer–seller relationships in business markets', *Journal of Marketing Research*, vol. 36 (November), pp. 439–60.

Cox, A. (1999) 'Improving procurement and supply competence', in R. Lamming and A. Cox (eds), *Strategic Procurement Management: Concepts and Cases* (Helpston, UK: Earlsgate Press).

Cox, A. (2005), *The Rules of the Game: How to Capture Value in Business* (Helpston, UK: Earlsgate Press).

Cox, A., Sanderson, J. and Watson, G. (2000) *Power Regimes: Mapping the DNA of Business and Supply Chain Relationships* (Helpston, UK: Earlsgate Press).

Cox, A., Ireland, P., Lonsdale, C., Sanderson, J. and Watson, G. (2002) *Supply Chains, Markets and Power: Mapping Buyer and Supplier Power Regimes* (London: Routledge).

Cox, A., Ireland, P., Lonsdale, C., Sanderson, J. and Watson, G. (2003) *Supply Chain Management: A Guide to Best Practice* (London: Financial Times/Prentice Hall).

Hakansson, H. (ed.) (1982) *International Marketing and Purchasing of Industrial Goods* (Chichester: John Wiley).

Hallen, L., Johanson, J. and Seyed-Mohamed, N. (1991) 'Interfirm adaptations in business relationships', *Journal of Marketing*, vol. 55 (April), pp. 29–37.

Lonsdale, C. and Cox, A. (1998) *Outsourcing: A Business Guide to Risk Management Tools and Techniques* (Helpston, UK: Earlsgate Press).

Low, B. K. H. (1996) 'Long-term relationships in industrial marketing', *Industrial Marketing Management*, vol. 25, pp. 23–35.

Porter, M. E. (1980) *Competitive Strategy* (New York: Free Press).

Shapiro, B. P., Kasturi Rangan, V., Moriarty, R. T. and Ross, E. B. (1987) 'Manage customers for profit (not just sales)', *Harvard Business Review*, (September–October), pp. 101–8.

Simon, H. A. (1997) *Administrative Behavior* (New York: Free Press).

Williamson, O. E. (1985) *The Economic Institutions of Capitalism* (New York: Free Press).

4

A Framework for the Alignment of Buyer and Supplier Relationships

In this chapter a framework is provided to allow managers to understand how to align business relationships between buyers and suppliers under different power circumstances. The chapter is divided in two sections:

- The first section provides a brief summary of the six *value appropriation outcomes* that can occur between a buyer and supplier in any relationship.
- The second section provides, for each of the six theoretically possible *value appropriation outcomes*, a template to allow managers (whether they act as buyers or suppliers) to understand how to align their *strategic ends* with *operational means*. The aim is to indicate how both parties to the exchange should align their respective commercial goals, given the current and future power balance between the buyer and supplier.

4.1 Value appropriation outcomes in buyer and supplier exchange

In previous chapters the range of commercial goals (*strategic ends*) that buyers and suppliers can choose from was described, as well as the theoretically possible power situations that both parties to an exchange transaction might operate within. We have also demonstrated the range of *operational means* available to the buyer and supplier when they decide how to work with one another in particular power situations, and in order to move into more congenial power circumstances. In managing any relationship we have also argued that there is a range of *relationship management styles* that both parties can utilise to achieve their intended goals.

This discussion may have given some readers the impression that buyers and suppliers can choose to utilise any *operational means* with any *strategic ends*, in pursuit of any power circumstance, that they would prefer. This is, of course, far from true. In fact it is evident, both theoretically and from the research and consulting activities that we have conducted, that some types of *operational means* and some *relationship management styles* have to be aligned closely together under particular power situations for successful business relationship alignment and the delivery of desired *strategic ends* (commercial goals). In other words, if managers wish to be successful in business relationship management they have to recognise that there are preferable choices to be made about *operational means* for both the buyer and the supplier within specific power circumstances.

Figure 4.1 takes a first step towards summarising how ideal-typical relationship management approaches can be constructed. In this figure the types of *relationship management styles* that are the most appropriate for the effective achievement of particular *value appropriation outcomes* in specific power situations are outlined.

The six-box matrix provided is created by bringing together three major variables. The first variable is the way in which buyers and suppliers can choose to work together operationally in any transaction. As we argued earlier, particular relationships may require arm's-length working relationships, while other types of relationships may require much more collaborative approaches. This necessary operational way of working is then contrasted with a second variable. This variable focuses on which of the two parties to the exchange is the major beneficiary in terms of their relative ability to achieve their preferred commercial goals (*strategic ends*) in the form of appropriating value from the relationship. Whether or not any party to the exchange can achieve more than another commercially will, of course, be dependent on a third variable. This is the balance of power between the buyer and supplier in the transaction, now and in the future.

A buyer would be seen to achieve the most value appropriation in a circumstance where the buyer was able to receive continuous improvement in functionality and reductions in the cost of ownership, but the supplier was forced to work constantly for very low returns. This would create a *relationship that favours the buyer*. Or to put the matter another way (as we discussed in Chapter 1) the relationship would exist but with *tension for the supplier*. This would equate to a transaction in which *buyer dominance* occurs.

THE WAY OF WORKING	BUYER DOMINANT	BUYER-SUPPLIER RECIPROCITY	SUPPLIER DOMINANCE
ARM'S-LENGTH	**BUYER DOMINANT ARM'S-LENGTH RELATIONSHIP** • Short-term operational relationship, with limited close working between buyer and supplier • Buyer adversarially appropriates most of the commercial value created and sets price and quality trade-offs • Supplier is non-adversarial commercially and a willing supplicant, accepting work rather than high margins/profitability from the relationship • ***Buyer Dominance power situation (>)***	**BUYER–SUPPLIER RECIPROCAL ARM'S-LENGTH RELATIONSHIP** • Short-term operational relationship, with limited close working between buyer and supplier • Buyer accepts current market price and quality trade-offs • Supplier accepts normal (low) market returns • Both buyer and supplier operate adversarially commercially whenever possible, but normally have few leverage opportunities • ***Independence power situation (o)***	**SUPPLIER DOMINANT ARM'S-LENGTH RELATIONSHIP** • Short-term operational relationship, with limited close working between buyer and supplier • Supplier adversarially appropriates most of the commercial value created and sets price and quality trade-offs • Buyer is non-adversarial commercially and a willing supplicant, paying whatever is required to receive given quality standards • ***Supplier Dominance power situation (<)***
COLLABORATIVE	**BUYER DOMINANT COLLABORATIVE RELATIONSHIP** • Long-term operational relationship, with extensive and close working between buyer and supplier • Buyer adversarially appropriates most of the commercial value created and sets price and quality trade-offs • Supplier is a non-adversarial supplicant commercially, and accepts work rather than high margins/ profitability from the relationship • ***Buyer Dominance power situation (>)***	**BUYER–SUPPLIER RECIPROCAL COLLABORATIVE RELATIONSHIP** • Long-term operational relationship, with extensive and close working between buyer and supplier • Buyer and supplier share relatively equally the commercial value created • Buyer and supplier agree price and quality trade-offs, with supplier making more than normal returns • Both buyer and supplier operate non-adversarially commercially • ***Interdependence power situation (=)***	**SUPPLIER DOMINANT COLLABORATIVE RELATIONSHIP** • Long-term operational relationship, with extensive and close working between buyer and supplier • Supplier adversarially appropriates most of the commercial value created and sets price and quality trade-offs • Buyer is a non-adversarial supplicant commercially, and pays whatever is required to receive given quality standards • ***Supplier Dominance power situation (<)***

WHO APPROPRIATES VALUE FROM THE RELATIONSHIP?

Figure 4.1 Value appropriation, power and relationship management styles

On the other hand, if a supplier was able to achieve complete control of the revenue of the buyer, and also receive very high (above normal) returns, without having to improve the functionality or reduce the costs of ownership of what is supplied to the buyer, then this would create a relationship that *favours the supplier*. This type of value appropriation outcome creates a relationship that has *tension for the buyer*. This would equate to a transaction in which *supplier dominance* occurs.

When both sides achieve only some of their commercially desired *strategic ends* then a situation of *buyer and supplier reciprocity* exists in the relationship from a value appropriation point of view. In this case neither side is able to dominate in the achievement of their commercial goals and each party has to allow the other side to achieve a reasonable commercial return as well. This closely approximates to *satisficing* behaviour by both parties in a transaction (Simon, 1997).

Given this basic analysis it is now possible to begin to predict under which power circumstances these outcomes are most likely to occur for both the buyer and the supplier. The matrix in Figure 4.1 indicates that, under different power circumstances, six alternative *value appropriation outcomes* are most likely to occur for buyers and suppliers when they engage in business transactions together. It is interesting to note that whenever previous writers have addressed the issue of relationship outcomes by matching or mapping buyer and supplier strategies, even though this has normally been undertaken from a one-dimensional perspective focused on either the buyer or suppliers interests, they have also tended to arrive at six potential relational outcomes. The major problem with these approaches is, however, that they deal with only one side of the relationship and therefore fail to properly understand how to align the operational and commercial goals of both parties (Campbell, 1985; Krapfel *et al.*, 1991; Olsen and Ellram, 1997). In what follows we describe the appropriate alignment of both the buyer's and the supplier's relationship management strategies in particular circumstances of power and leverage.

The buyer-dominant arm's-length relationships

When the *buyer dominance* power situation exists and the parties to the exchange must operate at arm's-length it is likely that the buyer will be in a strong position to dominate value appropriation from the relationship with the supplier. This occurs because the buyer has power levers over the supplier. These levers allow the buyer to use revenue (volume) and regular work as a key lever to force the supplier to pass value to them in the form of increased functionality and lower total costs of ownership. Since the supplier operates in a highly contested market place with low switching costs they will normally have to do the bidding of the buyer, and accept low returns for constant innovation, or lose business.

It is likely in this relationship that the buyer will be a price and quality fixer rather than receiver. This implies that it is the buyer who will adversarially set the 'stretch' improvement targets in functionality and costs reductions that prospective suppliers will have to achieve if they we wish to win business from the dominant buyer. The buyer will be *commercially adversarial* and *operationally arm's-length*, while the supplier will be *non-adversarial commercially* but also *arm's-length operationally*.

The buyer–supplier reciprocal arm's-length relationship

In a power situation of *independence* neither party to the exchange relationship has many levers of power to use against the other party. In such an environment the supplier's main concern is with the ability to stay in business against many other competitors in the market, who are all equally well endowed to provide the current trade-off between functionality and costs of ownership. In such a highly contested market suppliers must constantly innovate just to stay in business. It is inevitable in this circumstance that unless they find some form of differentiation that is sustainable against their competitors, they must constantly pass value to buyers and earn low returns.

The buyer in this relationship has only limited volume to use and cannot offer the supplier a significantly large volume of revenue to make the relationship attractive either now or in the future. Given this, the buyer simply buys as effectively and efficiently as possible by constantly monitoring the market for the supplier with the currently best available trade-off between functionality and cost, without making any long-term commitment to the relationship with any one supplier. The buyer receives the currently available functionality and cost trade-off but only at the same level as achieved by all other similar buyers in the market.

As a result, an *inadvertent* reciprocal relationship is created in the sense that neither the buyer nor supplier can maximize their leverage over the other party and must accept the terms of trade currently operating in the market. The buyer obtains a constantly improved supply offering but with no benefits over and above what other similar buyers can achieve. The supplier receives enough revenue and return to stay in business but is on a treadmill of constant innovation with limited control of revenue and returns.

In this circumstance both parties have to accept the terms of trade operating in the market. This means that the neither the buyer nor the supplier see any value in close working relationships and neither have the power resources to leverage the other party in the exchange. Given this, both parties will be aligned if they both operate *non-adversarially commercially* and *arm's-length operationally*.

The supplier-dominant arm's-length relationship

In power situations of *supplier dominance* it is likely that it will be the supplier that fixes price and quality standards rather than the buyer. Thus when there is no need for the supplier to work closely with the buyer in order to close markets to competitors, the supplier will have no need to share any of the value they can appropriate from the relationship with the buyer.

Thus, if the supplier has a number of isolating mechanisms this will allow them to differentiate themselves from the competition and provide a superior trade-off between functionality and costs of ownership, while at the same time controlling all of the business revenue of the buyer and making higher then normal returns. In these situations it is the supplier who determines what level of innovation in functionality and costs of ownership will be provided to the buyer.

Innovation is normally only provided to the buyer by the supplier when other competitors threaten to catch up to the current trade-off in functionality and costs of ownership. This dilemma forces the currently dominant supplier to bring forward new products with a superior functionality and cost trade-off, but, since they are the only suppliers capable of providing it, they can still control revenue and premium price to make above normal returns. This approach partly explains the historic competitive success of Intel in the microprocessor market place (Grove, 1998).

In this circumstance the ideal relationship alignment is for the supplier to operate *adversarially commercially* and at *arm's-length operationally*. The buyer in this case must operate *non-adversarially commercially* but also at *arm's-length operationally*.

Buyer-dominant collaborative relationships

The fourth value appropriation outcome is similar to the first in terms of the power situation, but very different in the way in which the buyer interacts with the supplier operationally. As in the first outcome the power situation is one of *buyer dominance*. Once again it is the buyer who is in a position to fix price and quality standards now, and the 'stretch' targets of the future.

The major difference with this approach is not the commercial outcome but that the operational relationship with suppliers is not short-term and arm's-length but long-term and collaborative. This operational approach is necessary when the buyer recognises that the innovation in functionality and the costs of ownership required from suppliers is only possible when they have some guaranteed commitments to a relationship and volumes of work, with guaranteed margins. By providing these sureties the buyer is providing the supplier with the confidence that they should make long-term dedicated investments in the relationship in order that innovation in functionality and cost reduction can occur over time.

It is clear that this is the approach to continuous sourcing improvement most commonly adopted by successful exponents of supply chain management, especially those emanating from the Japanese car industry – Toyota, in particular (Cox, 1997; Bensaou, 1999). The logic of this approach is to force the supplier into a long-term dependent position through collaboration, with the buyer providing a minimum guarantee for the supplier (volume and low margins) in return for constant innovation.

It can be argued that most sourcing best practice is undertaken by managers that are exceptionally good at understanding how, in a highly contested supply market when the buyer has dominance, collaboration can be used as a much more powerful leverage tool than short-term arm's-length relationship management. This adversarial approach to collaboration can, of course, be a win-win relationship for both the buyer and the supplier. The buyer is still dominant, however, because they obtain continuous improvement in functionality and costs of ownership at guaranteed low margins.

The supplier, on the other hand, cannot normally earn above normal returns but they can sometimes achieve a better outcome by accepting this deal rather than the next best alternative currently available to them. Thus while the supplier has to accept dependency on the buyer, if regularity of volumes and low (but guaranteed) margins are a better alternative for the supplier than being left to the mercy of a highly contested market place with adversarial buyers using arm's-length strategies with no guarantees, then this is a better deal.

In this power scenario, therefore, the buyer dominates and pursues an *adversarial commercial* strategy with *collaboration operationally*. The supplier, on the other hand, has to accept a *non-adversarial commercial* strategy, but must accept *collaboration operationally* at the dictat of the buyer.

The buyer–supplier reciprocal collaborative relationship

This is the approach that is most appropriate for the buyer and supplier to utilise when they operate in the *interdependence* power situation. It is also the approach that most proponents of partnering, alliancing and supply chain management prefer. As Figure 4.1 indicates, when operating in this circumstance the buyer and supplier need to work together to achieve improvements in their respective commercial goals. This is normally a function of a limited number of current and potential buyers who satisfy the customer requirements of the supplier, and there are also a limited number of suppliers with the capability to provide the current and future functionality and costs of ownership trade-offs that the buyer needs.

In order to improve the functionality and cost trade-off for the buyer both parties have to work closely together to create the long-term cultural and technical bonds (dedicated investments) that allow for trust in one another to be developed so that transparency over sensitive commercial and technical information can be shared. Only by sharing this level of information and working together on functionality improvement and cost reduction strategies is it possible for both parties to achieve their commercial goals.

Since neither side can dominate commercially due to limitations on their power capabilities with one another it is imperative that the two parties agree to *satisfice* one another's commercial goals. Thus the buyer will receive constant innovation from the supplier in functionality and the costs of ownership, but the supplier will only continue to do this if they are allowed to receive above normal returns and a large share of the buyer's revenue.

In this power scenario, therefore, the buyer and supplier normally both agree to work together *non-adversarially commercially* but with extensive *collaboration operationally*.

The supplier-dominant collaborative relationship

The supplier-dominant collaborative relationship is similar to the buyer-dominant collaborative relationship except that it is the supplier who controls the trade-off in functionality and costs of ownership for the buyer, as well as being able to make above normal returns. This situation can only occur, however, when the dominant supplier must work with the buyer to sustain differentiation against its competitors.

This requirement to collaborate on the part of the supplier arises when only by constantly working with the buyer can the supplier refresh their own supply offering, so as to sustain the supplier's current relative superiority in functionality and costs of ownership. In some circumstances it is only through the supplier's ability to understand the changing needs of the buyer and the buyer's own direct customers that the supplier can understand the need for future product and service innovations. This may also arise because the buyer is involved in constant technological or service innovation that the supplier must also be aware of.

In such a circumstance the supplier must work closely with the buyer and establish the same types of dedicated investments as found under buyer-dominant or interdependent forms of collaboration. This time, however, while the buyer may receive the benefits of collaboration (in the form of innovation in functionality and costs of ownership) the relationship is hardly reciprocal. The reason for this is because the supplier will only bring new innovations to market if they are threatened by superior innovation from their competitors.

It is not, therefore, the collaboration that drives innovation in functionality and costs of ownership *per se*, but the fear by the supplier of catch-up by other potential suppliers in the market (Grove, 1998). In this sense, collaboration is a defensive mechanism and the supplier will only pass improvements in functionality and costs of ownership to the buyer if they are also able to premium price their own product offerings. The supplier, in other words, uses collaboration for their own benefits rather than for the benefit of the buyer. If the buyer receives a benefit this is an incidental by-product of perceived competitive threats not the consequence of a commitment to reciprocity in the collaborative exchange. Furthermore, in supplier dominance the buyer will always have to pay for the innovation through above normal returns for the supplier.

In this power scenario the supplier operates *adversarially commercially* but *collaborates operationally*. The buyer has to be *non-adversarial commercially* but *operationally collaborative*.

4.2 Six ideal-typical frameworks for the successful alignment of buyer and supplier relationships

It is clear, therefore, that in the 'real world' inhabited by managers there are different *value appropriation outcomes* that can be achieved if buyers and suppliers understand how to appropriately align power circumstances and relationship management styles. This leads to the inevitable conclusion that for business relationship management to be successful there must be an appropriate alignment of buyer and supplier *strategic ends* with *operational means*. Given this, it is now possible to specify the *ideal-typical* alignments of buyer and supplier *strategic ends* and *operational means* that provide for successful business relationship management under specific power circumstances.

The ideal alignment of buyer and supplier relationships in arm's-length buyer-dominated power circumstances

Figure 4.2 demonstrates how buyer and supplier relationships should be aligned ideally for a successful relationship outcome for both parties when there is a power situation of *buyer dominance* (now or in the future), and when there is no need for either the buyer or the supplier to work together operationally on a collaborative basis for either side to achieve their commercial goals.

As the figure demonstrates, both parties to the exchange have to recognise that the current and future power situation will remain *buyer dominance*. This means that the buyer will be providing a large share of the supplier's total business revenue, and there are many potential suppliers who can provide the current and future trade-off between functionality and costs of ownership. In this situation the buyer recognises that all of the major power levers are at their disposal and the supplier recognises that they do not have many now, nor will they in the future.

Given this scenario it is self-evident that the best position for the supplier is to be a 'willing supplicant'. This implies that the buyer is now in a position to demand from the supplier improvements in functionality and reductions in the costs of ownership. Every supplier has to recognise that, given the 'stretch' value proposition set by the buyer, they can only expect to retain their share of the buyer's business revenue if they delight the customer by constantly innovating internally within their own business. By doing so the supplier can become the *ideal supplier* from the buyer's perspective – i.e. someone who passes all value (*improvements in functionality and reduced costs of ownership*) to the buyer. Obviously, if it is not technically possible for the supply market to make improvements in all areas then the buyer may have to settle for *improved functionality with static costs* or *static functionality with reduced costs*.

The buyer's approach, given that there is no need to work collaboratively to drive improvements in functionality and costs of ownership, is normally to rely on reactive, short-term adversarial market testing, so that business is awarded only to the supplier or suppliers who are able to offer the best value for money in the future. This approach – referred to here as *arm's-length adversarial relationship management* – is commonly the most appropriate to use with *supplier selection* and/or *supply chain*

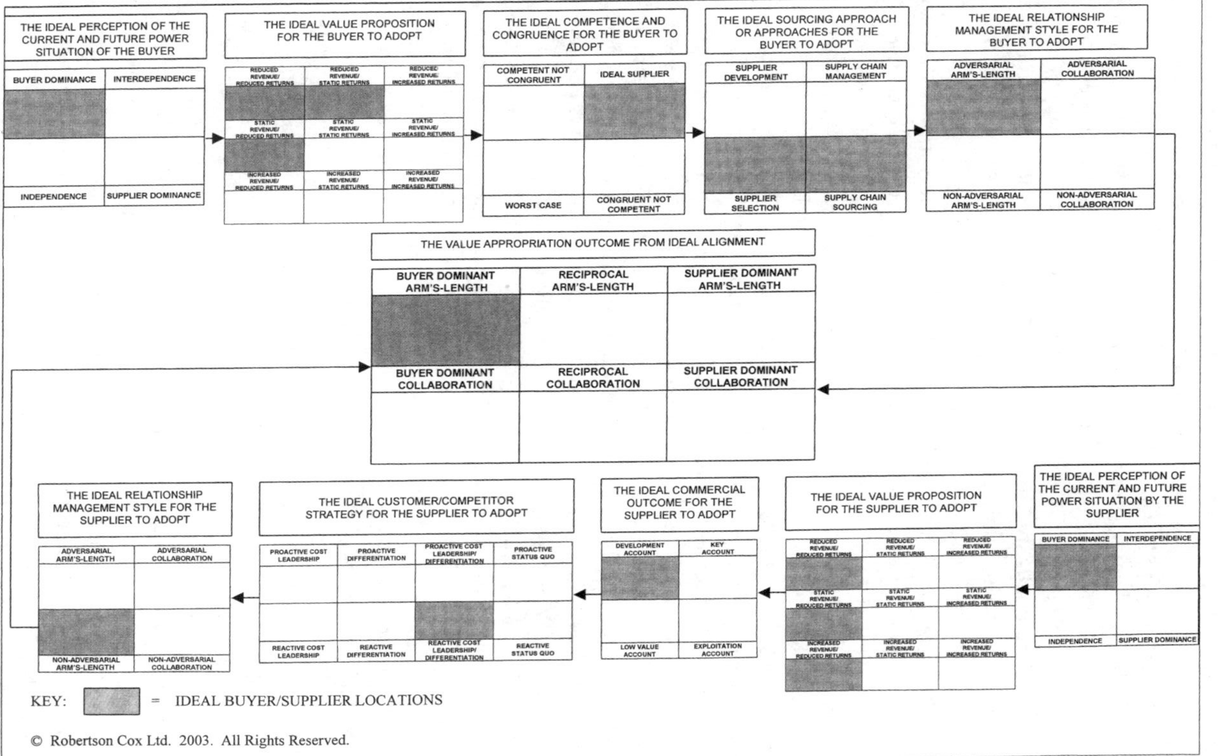

Figure 4.2 The ideal alignment of buyer and supplier in arm's-length buyer dominance

sourcing approaches. As will be clear, because there is no benefit from collaboration the buyer's preferred sourcing approach is to react to the level of contestation in the market place.

Buyers can always undertake *supplier selection* in any power circumstance – it is a default option for all buyers, even those who are not competent but still buy things. Whether or not a buyer can use *supply chain sourcing* depends, however, on whether or not the power regimes in the supply chain for the goods/services they are sourcing are conducive or not to this approach. How a buyer can decide on whether this is possible or not is explained elsewhere (Cox *et al.*, 2003).

Having recognised the dominance of the buyer, the supplier's most aligned customer positioning approach is to work in the *development account* quadrant for commercial outcomes. This means that they will work best with a customer who is attractive to them (i.e. can give them the volume they require to operate effectively) but with whom they will not be seeking to leverage high profit margins. This situation is improved for the buyer if the value proposition that the supplier faces is one in which they are increasing their revenue share with the buyer, because this means that there is a good chance that they will be more dependent on the buyer's demand for their business revenue. In this circumstance of increased revenue dependency on the buyer the supplier is normally willing, as a result, to work for lower returns. *Increased revenue and reduced returns* may be the ideal situation for the buyer but other trade-offs are potentially acceptable such as *static or reduced revenue*, but both with *reduced returns*. This general situation of supplier dependency/buyer dominance is also most effectively aligned if the supplier's customer and competitor strategy is also to pursue reactive *cost leadership and differentiation,* while also working in a *non-adversarial arm's-length* relationship management style with the buyer.

Clearly, if a buyer can find a supplier who fulfils all of these characteristics, and can align their own internal commercial and operational approaches satisfactorily, then an ideally aligned business relationship can be created. A buyer in this circumstance would receive constant innovation in functionality and the costs of ownership, and would be able to switch easily to any supplier in the future who might be able to bring more innovation to the relationship than the current incumbent. On the other hand, the supplier would recognise that they are not in a position to leverage improved value from the relationship and that they can only survive in business by operating as an innovator working for low margins. This means accepting the role of a 'willing supplicant' to a dominant buyer.

Even though this would be an ideally aligned *buyer-dominated arm's-length relationship*, such relationships are not without tension. The reason for this – as we discussed earlier – is that all business relationships contain objective conflicts of interest and, therefore, tensions even when they are aligned, because while the buyer may be the dominant party in this relationship this situation will only persist as long as the buyer can command a significant share of total revenue either in the market as a whole, or in relation to the revenue required by any particular supplicant supplier.

If the buyer loses this lever over the supplier it is unlikely that any supplier would continue to be a willing supplicant, unless of course the buyer could offer some other form of attractiveness (maybe brand and reputation so that the supplier can use their association with the buyer's name to leverage business revenue elsewhere). The reason for this is that most suppliers would prefer not to be in this dependent situation if they can find more congenial circumstances from which to operate their business model. If the buyer is no longer dominant then it is obvious that the supplier will change their value proposition and their customer and competitor strategy in an attempt to move to a more congenial commercial outcome.

The buyer also faces another potential risk or tension associated with the highly contested nature of the market place. If the supplier they are working with is in a position to provide some form of innovation in functionality and/or costs of ownership (or both together) that cannot be replicated easily by other suppliers, then the supplier would have achieved a sustainable competitive advantage over its competitors. If this occurred then the power situation would be immediately transformed and the buyer would now have a dominant supplier to contend with.

In the short term this might be desirable because the dominant supplier would be providing the current best trade-off between functionality and cost in the market. Over time, however, the dominant supplier would eventually be able to use this position to create a situation in which costs are not fully reduced and perhaps the latest innovations are not introduced unless the buyer is prepared to allow the supplier to make above normal returns. In this way the supplier controls functionality and cost trade-offs over time and sustains above normal returns.

As long as the market remains contested and replication is easy for all market players then this dilemma will not come into play and the buyer will drive innovation through short-term contracting and reap most of the rewards from any supplier relationship. In this circumstance buyers ideally need willing supplicants as suppliers, who understand their situation and accept that any relationship is likely to be short-term if they cannot deliver value for money for the buyer. When this occurs there is a successful and perfectly aligned buyer and supplier relationship.

The ideal alignment of buyer and supplier relationships in reciprocal arm's-length relationships

In this case, as Figure 4.3 demonstrates, the ideal situation is relatively simple to understand and can be clearly specified for both parties due to their relatively equal levels of powerlessness in the relationship. In an *independence* power situation, while the buyer may desire an increase in functionality and a reduction in the costs of ownership it is much more likely, due to their lack of leverage in the market or with any individual supplier, that they will have to accept *static functionality and static costs of ownership*.

This does not mean that functionality and costs will not necessarily improve for them over time, but rather that (given the relatively lack of power of the buyer at any moment that they enter the market) the buyer will only be able to achieve, at best, the currently available trade-off between functionality and costs of ownership in the market. The buyer must, however, keep future options open because as soon as a supplier provides an improvement in functionality or cost of ownership (or both) the buyer will wish to move to them immediately.

The assumption here is that the market is highly contested and that suppliers must constantly innovate. Even so, the buyer is always a price and quality receiver at the moment they enter the market, and it is unrealistic for them to expect that they can achieve any significant improvement in the current generally available trade-off between functionality and cost. In this sense it is also true that, from the perspective of the buyer, all of the available companies they can source from will be *ideal suppliers* – or at least all of those who can match the best value for money deals in the market.

Given this, the buyer must adopt a *non-adversarial arm's-length* relationship management style. This also implies short-term *supplier selection* sourcing strategies, in which the supplier currently providing the best value for money deal is awarded a short-term contract. The reason for this is that, because the market is highly contested, the buyer must keep future options open. Assuming of course that the buyer knows how to undertake a professional tender and negotiation process the buyer ought to receive the currently best value for money trade-off available in the market. Due to their relative lack of power the buyer cannot, however, expect the supplier to provide them with better than current standard market functionality and costs of ownership.

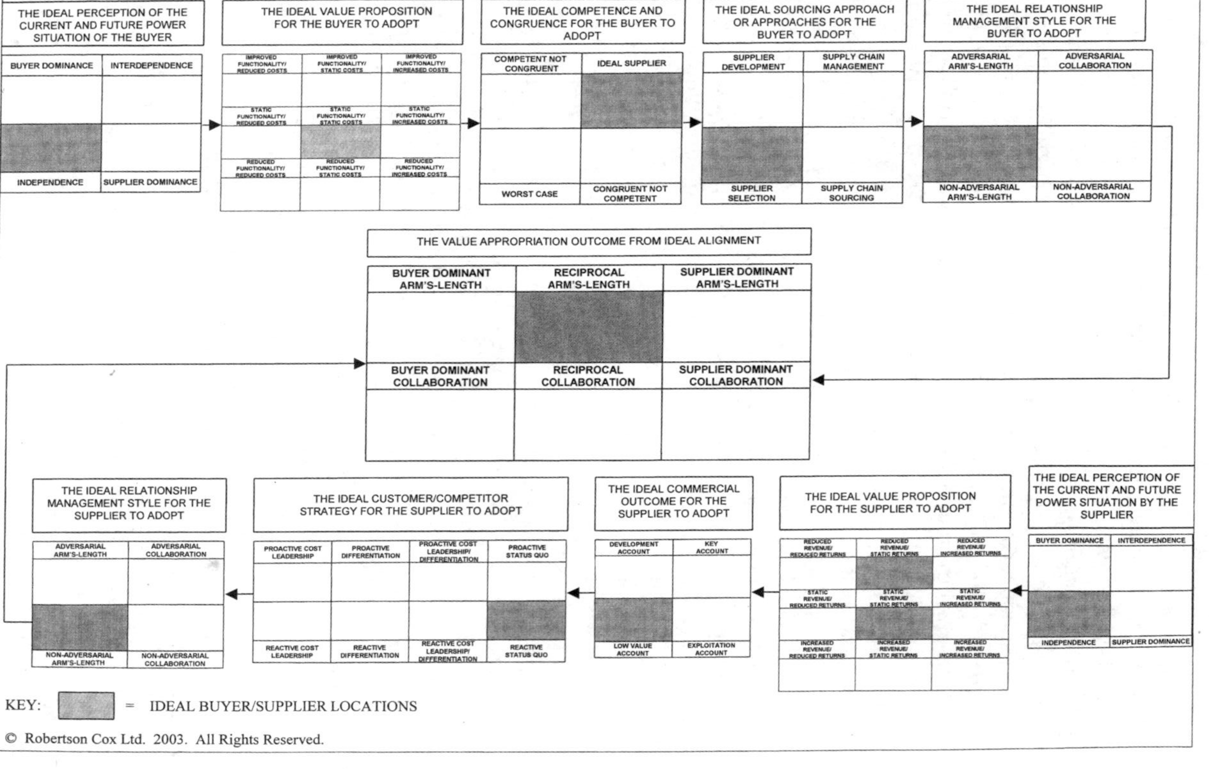

Figure 4.3 The ideal alignment of buyer and supplier in arm's-length reciprocity

The supplier in an *independence* power situation has to accept that the customers they are working with cannot provide them with increasing revenue because the buyer is always a relatively small player in the market. At the same time the supplier must recognise that, because the market is highly contested and the buyer could switch easily from one supplier to another using short-term contracts, the scope for increasing returns will be limited. The primary reason is that in a highly contested market the supplier can only survive by passing value to the buyer. This means that ideally the supplier should accept *static revenue and static returns* from the buyer; at worst they may have to accept *reduced revenue and static returns* if the buyer decides to give some of their current market demand to other suppliers.

In such circumstances all customers will normally fall into the *low value account* for the supplier when they consider the commercial outcome of the relationship. The appropriate customer and competitor strategy for a supplier operating in this situation is to adopt a *reactive status quo* approach. This type of approach fits most appropriately with a *non-adversarial arm's-length* relationship management style. The supplier accepts that they cannot increase the attractiveness of the customer's account and simply provides them with the latest available trade- off between functionality and cost, while hoping to retain the business in the future.

There are of course tensions for the buyer and supplier in this relationship. The most significant of these normally relate to the problem of information asymmetry. These types of *reciprocal independence* relationships work successfully when both parties have no power levers to act in any other way than non-adversarially with one another. The problem with this type of relationship is that, objectively, it normally favours the buyer more than the supplier, because, while the buyer has very few levers that allow them to operate opportunistically, contestation normally forces value to be passed to the buyer over time, even though all buyers do nothing very much to earn this benefit. The market drives innovation. On the other hand the supplier definitely does have levers to behave opportunistically against the buyer.

The key lever a buyer might use is to promise increased volume to a supplier in the future in anticipation of receiving a better deal from the supplier now. This can work, but if the promised increased volume does not eventually arrive then the supplier will quickly understand that the buyer was behaving opportunistically. The supplier, however, has many more opportunities to behave opportunistically because the buyer normally does not have the time and resources to be able to understand what is the best deal in the market.

This occurs because buyers in *independence* power situations, with limited volumes, normally do not invest the resources necessary in search and negotiation to enable them to undertake a thorough analysis of the best value for money deals available. This results in a situation of information asymmetry between the buyer and the supplier, which a supplier can utilise for their own benefit. By being economical with the truth about the current best value for money deals available in the market the supplier can sometimes shift the power structure in a contested market to one which is in fact supplier-dominant – at least in the sense that the supplier can make above normal returns when a more competent buyer might force them to pass these returns to the buyer in the form of lower costs of ownership.

It is clear, however, that while there are opportunities for buyers and suppliers to behave opportunistically in *independence* power situations, the ideal alignment, which allows both sides to obtain their just rewards given the power situation prevailing, is one which emphasises reciprocal short-term, non-adversarial and reactive relationship management approaches by both parties to the transaction.

The ideal alignment of buyer and supplier relationships in arm's-length supplier-dominant power circumstances

Figure 4.4 demonstrates that the ideal alignment of the buyer and supplier in power situations of *supplier dominance,* where the supplier does not need to work with the buyer to sustain their current and future competitive advantage in the market, is one in which the buyer acts non-adversarially and the supplier is adversarial. This is the polar opposite of the ideal alignment for buyer-dominant arm's-length relationship management.

In *supplier dominance* power situations the buyer is normally a price and quality receiver. This implies that the buyer cannot hope to receive improvements in functionality and the costs of ownership because contestation is not forcing the supplier to pass value to the customer. It is unrealistic, therefore, for the buyer to expect to receive this value proposition. The best that a buyer can hope to receive is the current prevailing functionality and cost trade-off, but they may also have to accept *increased costs, reduced functionality* or a combination of both of these. Indeed from the supplier's point of view *reduced functionality and increased costs* is likely to be the preferred value proposition that they would wish to force the buyer to accept. Failing that, *static functionality and static costs* may be the least that a dominant supplier could aspire to force on their customers.

Given this dependency by the buyer on the supplier it is likely that the buyer will have to accept that they are working with a highly

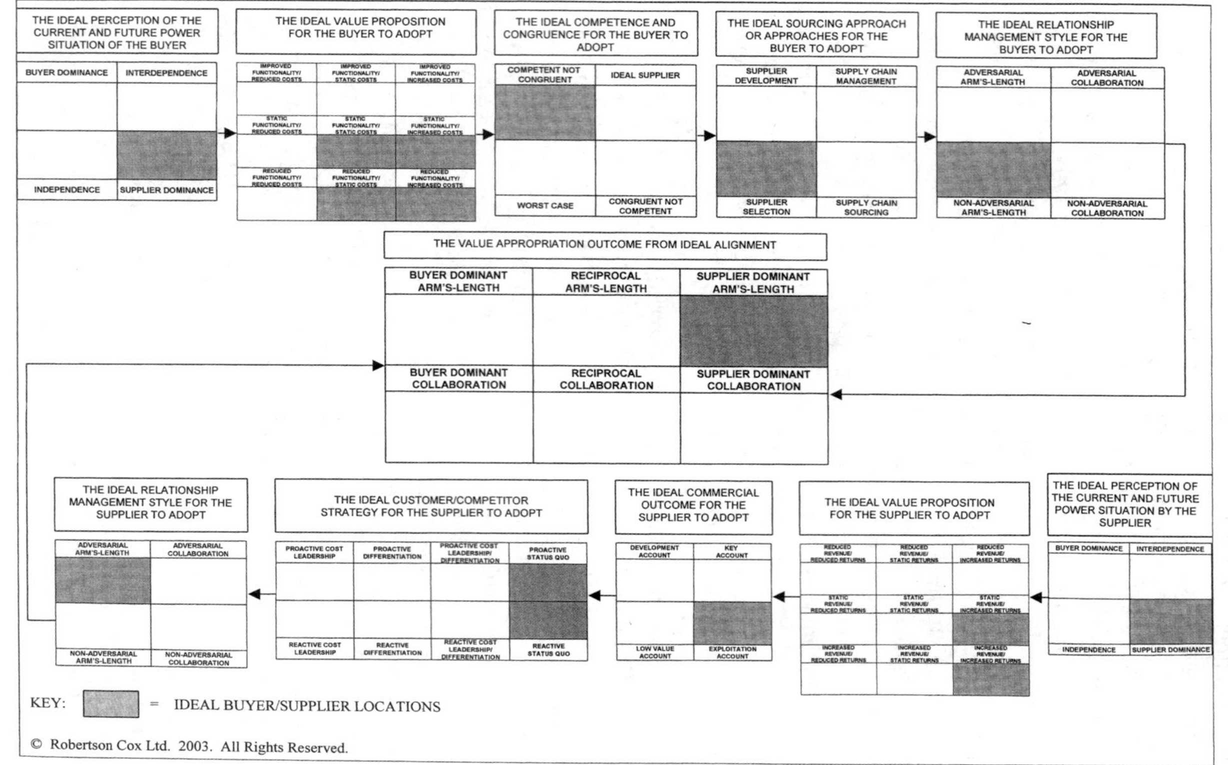

Figure 4.4 The ideal alignment of buyer and supplier in arm's-length supplier dominance

competent but not congruent supplier. This means that the supplier is normally able to provide the currently best available trade-off between functionality and costs of ownership in the market, but is not prepared to do so with continuous improvement in functionality, and certainly not for low returns. The buyer may believe that they should adopt a *supplier selection* sourcing approach but in these circumstances the supplier is normally selecting the buyer, because if the buyer attempts to be adversarial in the relationship the supplier can react by refusing to supply the required product/service to the buyer. In such situations the only logical approach for the buyer is to operate in a *non-adversarial arm's-length* relationship management style, because the supplier has no need to work closely with the buyer in order to sustain market dominance, and collaboration is unnecessary.

From the supplier' s perspective the best that they can hope for from this type of relationship with any customer is that, although they may currently have the majority of the buyer's volume requirements, the buyer may be increasing their supply requirements in the future due to growth in their own business. In this circumstance the supplier may anticipate *increasing revenue and increasing or static returns*. Failing this, if the customer's business is unlikely to grow, then the best that a supplier can aspire to is *static revenue with increasing returns*. The worst that can be expected for a truly dominant supplier is *reduced revenue with increased returns*. This occurs because, although the supplier cannot always control exactly the amount of revenue they will receive from any customer, the competitive advantage that the supplier holds over most other suppliers in the market allows them to control the costs of ownership and, therefore, their own returns.

When a supplier finds themselves in this power situation it also normally means that no one customer is relatively more important than any other customer and, since the supplier is able to make above normal returns from any and all customers, they all fall into the *exploitation account* for the supplier. In such circumstances the appropriate customer and competitor strategy for the supplier is *reactive status quo*. This is because the supplier only has to continue providing the currently best available trade-off in functionality and cost to achieve above normal returns. In this situation it is clear that the relationship management style adopted by the supplier is *adversarial arm's-length*.

There are tensions in this type of relationship. The buyer may be satisfied with the relationship because the supplier is providing them with the currently best value for money supply option available in the market. Despite this, if the buyer is under constant pressure to find better value for money deals, and understands that the supplier earns above normal returns, then the buyer seeks all means by which to reduce the costs of ownership and increase functionality. In such circumstances the buyer has to find ways to encourage increased competition in the market.

On the supplier's side there is also the risk of complacency that comes from dominance. If the supplier simply persists in offering the buyer the status quo, and is not cognisant of the potential by other suppliers (or even customers) to contest the market, then the supplier may quickly find that dominance has disappeared. Thus it is always incumbent on dominant suppliers who wish to stay ahead of the competition to constantly innovate around functionality and costs of ownership. The trick for the clever strategist is, however, to achieve higher levels of innovation in functionality and costs of ownership, but only to pass these improvements to the buyer when competitors catch up to the previous standard in the market.

That said, it is clear that *arm's-length supplier dominance* is an appropriate way to manage relationships. This relational approach is ideally aligned when the buyer accepts that they must operate reactively and non-adversarially and be willing to accept the role of price and quality receiver. The supplier in this scenario is then able to operate adversarially and maximise their appropriation of value, while continuously controlling the current trade-off between functionality and costs. The buyer may not see this as an ideal arrangement from their own perspective but for the relationship to work well they must accept that they are effectively supplicants, just as suppliers have to be willing supplicants in buyer-dominant power situations.

The ideal alignment of buyer and supplier relationships in collaborative buyer-dominant power circumstances

Figure 4.5 demonstrates that in *buyer-dominant collaboration* the buyer controls the current and future trade-offs between functionality and costs of ownership. In such a situation of *buyer dominance* the most appropriate relationship partner for the buyer is a supplier who is a willing supplicant, and who accepts that the buyer will only work with a supplier who constantly innovates and provides *improved functionality with reduced costs of ownership*. Only suppliers who operate in this manner can expect to be an *ideal supplier* in competence and congruence terms. If, however, the collaboration between both parties is unable to create improvement in both elements, the buyer will sometimes accept *static functionality with reduced costs* or *improved functionality with static costs*.

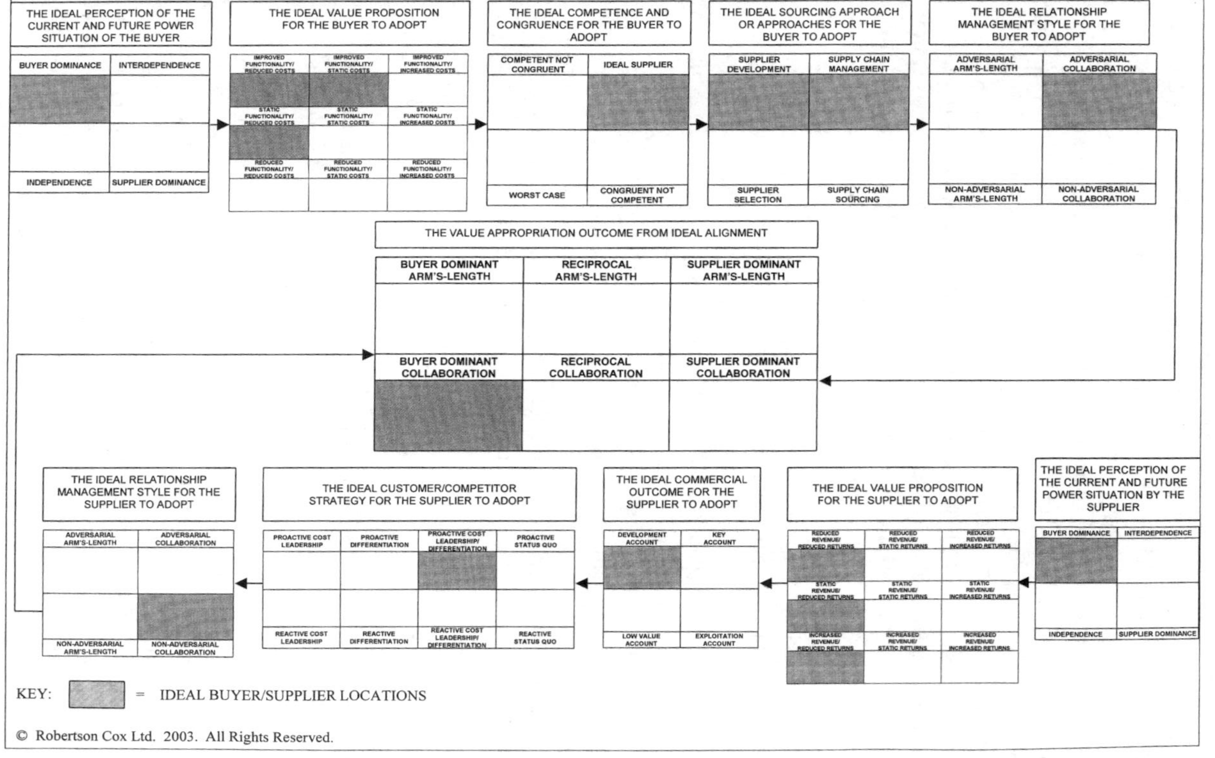

Figure 4.5 The ideal alignment of buyer and supplier in collaborative buyer-dominant collaboration

When a buyer is in such a position they will normally control either a substantial share of the total market demand for the goods or services required, or will be a significant (if not the major) customer to the supplier. *Buyer dominance* is also assisted in such situations by the supplier having to operate in highly contested supply markets (with low margins) and with low switching costs for the buyer if they decide to work with another supplier. In such circumstances the buyer can operate adversarially with the supplier commercially, and force them to accept constant innovation with low returns as the price of having guaranteed work.

In this case, which bears many of the hallmarks of *adversarial arm's-length buyer dominance*, there is however a major difference. This is that both the buyer and supplier need, operationally, to create dedicated investments in the relationship in order for the supplier to make the necessary improvements in functionality and cost. Given this, even though the buyer is prepared to build cultural and technical bonds with the supplier, and share sensitive commercial and technical information, the buyer needs to know what the effective boundary between them and the supplier should be. This means that major investments and risks are normally borne by the supplier, while the buyer seeks to retain the maximum capability to exit from the relationship in the future, even though this may cause commercial problems for the dependent supplier. But the buyer promises to provide the supplier with continuity of work at a guaranteed but low margin in return for the supplier making dedicated investments in support of whatever the buyer needs. This is *adversarial collaboration.*

The supplier in this relationship is normally most aligned with the buyer when they accept that they will become increasingly dependent on the buyer's business. This means that the supplier accepts that the power situation will remain buyer-dominant now, and in the future, and that the buyer would normally prefer that the supplier does not have too much reliance on other customers but is a willing supplicant who is dependent on the buyer. This implies that the value proposition of the supplier is ideal when their *revenue is increased and returns are reduced,* because the supplier is becoming more dependent on the buyer's business and working for lower returns. Obviously the relationship can still work if the supplier has *static* or *declining revenue,* but in both cases the situation is most ideal for the buyer when returns are also being *reduced* (as this is a cost that is borne by the buyer irrespective of the share of revenue the supplier achieves in the market as a whole).

Relatedly the relationship works best if the supplier operates in the *development account* quadrant of commercial outcomes and is committed to a *proactive cost leadership and differentiation* approach in its customer and competitor strategy. If these two approaches are properly integrated the supplier will be operating in a *non-adversarial collaborative relationship management style* with the buyer. To operate in this way indicates that the supplier is an ideal-typical willing supplicant. This means they are prepared to innovate proactively for the buyer, undertake dedicated investments in support of the relationship and pass all value to the buyer in return for guaranteed work at low (and preferably diminishing) returns.

The win-win situation for the supplier in this relationship is that this is a better deal than one without any long-term commitment from any buyer in an arm's-length and highly contested market place. At least by making dedicated investments the supplier is, in this variant, being given some guarantees about regularity and scale of work and fixed (if low) margins by the buyer. This form of relationship management approach will be familiar to all of those who understand the historic Japanese business model – especially as operated in the auto industry (Shimizu, 1996).

This type of relationship is not, however, without tensions. The problem for the buyer is that in forcing the supplier to make dedicated investments in support of the innovation required in functionality and costs of ownership there is always a risk of post-contractual moral hazard. This risk – which can over time transform the power situation post-contractually from *buyer dominance* to *interdependence* and, in the worst cases, *supplier dominance* – has been well documented by writers on transaction cost economics and IT outsourcing (Williamson, 1985; Lacity *et al.*, 1995). This makes it imperative that when buyers engage in these types of collaborative relationship with suppliers they pay close attention to their ability to exit from the relationship and that the external supply market also remains contested.

The supplier also faces tensions from the fact that the ideal scenario for the buyer in the relationship is that the supplier remains highly dependent on them. This may be fine for the buyer but it often conflicts with the avowed intention of most suppliers to achieve a growing business with above normal returns. It is often, therefore, the case that if suppliers accept this approach they will be accepting a level of performance that is sub-optimal from their shareholders' point of view. This means that the supplier may look for all opportunities to use the collaborative relationship as only a short-term mechanism to achieve competitive advantage. This works for the supplier through the development of their own relative competence in the market, allowing them eventually to offer themselves as relatively superior suppliers to the direct competitors of their original buying partner. In this way the buyer can face the loss to their competitors of valuable intellectual property and know-how in which they have invested scarce time and resources. Buyers, therefore, have to be very careful that they do not push their dominance too far (especially in Western culture) so that it generates a counter-response that undermines their competitive position.

There is also the further problem that if the buyer pushes too far and expects the supplier to be overly dependent on them for their business revenue that this may itself be counter-productive. This occurs because the supplier has to cover fixed and marginal costs of operation in pricing its goods and services. If the supplier is so dependent on the buyer that the buyer has to fund all of the fixed and marginal costs of operation this may be more costly for the buyer than if the supplier has a diversified customer base, all of whom are contributing to the fixed costs of operations. In this situation a dominant buyer (who still has the lion's share of the supplier's business demand) can pass some of these costs to other less powerful buyers in the form of lower marginal costs for themselves.

This problem also exists in the buyer-dominant arm's-length variant discussed earlier. This also helps to explain why sometimes there is a better trade-off for the buyer with either *static or reduced revenue and reduced returns* value propositions on the part of the supplier than with *increased revenue with reduced returns* value propositions in both the arm's-length and collaborative variants of buyer dominance.

Despite these caveats it is clear that *buyer-dominant collaboration* can be a highly appropriate way to manage buyer and supplier business relationships. While the buyer may be in control of the relationship it can still be argued that a form of win-win can occur for the supplier in this approach. The most ideal alignment is, however, when the collaboration occurs with the supplier as a proactive and 'willing supplicant' of the buyer's desire for improved functionality and cost reductions.

The ideal alignment of buyer and supplier relationships in reciprocal collaborative power circumstances

Figure 4.6 outlines the ideal arrangement for the buyer and supplier in circumstances of *interdependence*, when both parties can only achieve their commercial goals through close and transparent operational collaboration. As the figure demonstrates, both the buyer and supplier in this scenario must accept that the power structure now, and in the future, will remain in *interdependence* and that, as a result, both parties

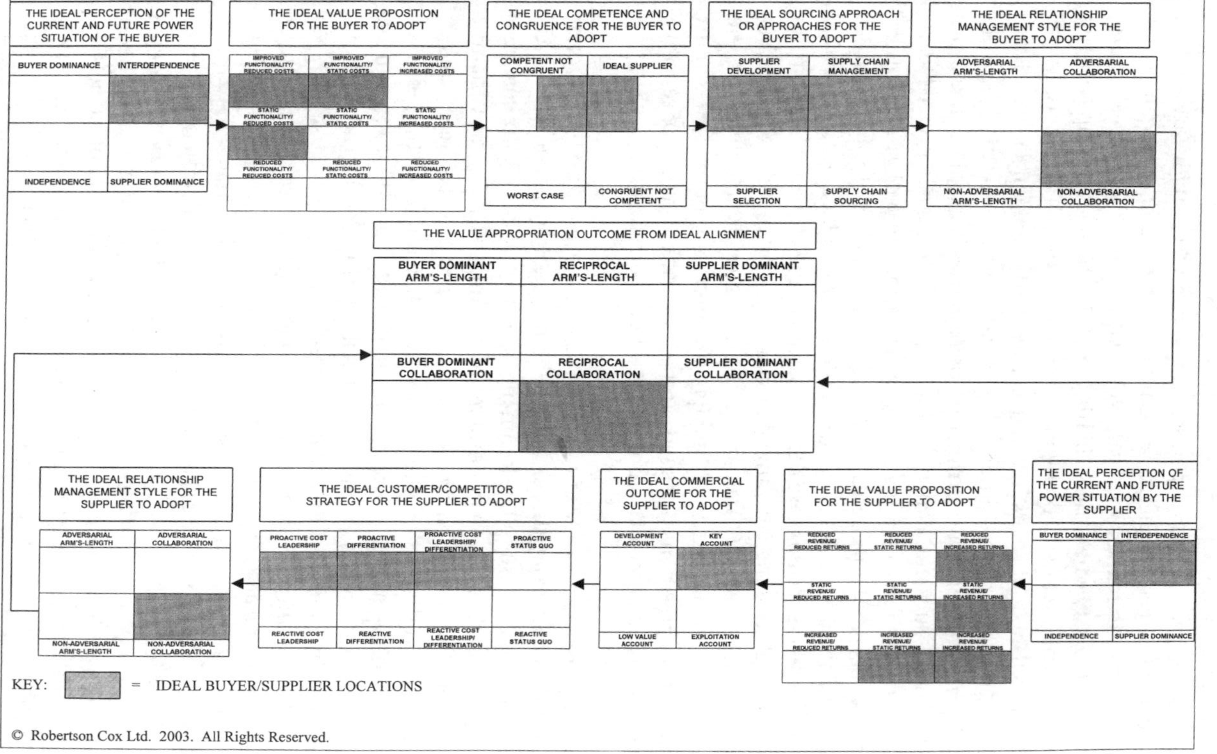

Figure 4.6 The ideal alignment of buyer and supplier in reciprocal collaboration

must work with one another on the basis of *negotiated* or *non-adversarial collaboration*.

Interdependence power circumstances occur when there are limited numbers of buyers in the market and a limited number of competent suppliers in the market who can work with them. This power circumstance also exists when the switching costs in the relationship between the two parties tends to be high for both sides once a relationship has been established. This ensures that neither party can, currently at least, impose their will on the other. In these circumstances relationships are based on *reciprocity*. This means that both parties must allow the other to achieve a substantial part of their commercial goals because each party cannot succeed commercially or operationally without the other.

It is important to recognise that *reciprocity* can occur for both parties either at arm's-length (as discussed earlier) or through close collaborative ways of working. In this case the two parties to the exchange relationship can only achieve their commercial goals by working closely together and creating close cultural and technical operational bonds in the relationship (dedicated investments). Furthermore, both parties must create trusting relationship based on the transparent sharing of sensitive technical and commercial information about current, and future, business plans.

Clearly the operational forms of collaboration used by both parties are no different from those that might be required under the buyer-dominant and/or supplier-dominant forms of relationship management, but there is one major difference commercially. In this variant it is unlikely that either party can impose most of the risks and costs of dedicated investments on the other party while appropriating most of the value for themselves. Both parties are equally locked into their need to make dedicated investments and relationship-specific adaptations that create high levels of switching costs.

For this variant to work well it is self-evident therefore that the buyer will operate ideally with a value proposition that seeks to achieve *improved functionality and reduced costs*. If one of these trade-offs cannot currently be achieved by collaboration with the supplier then the buyer may have to accept *improved functionality with static costs* or *static functionality with reduced costs*. Whether buyers in this power situation will be able to achieve the same levels of reduction in costs of ownership when compared to the *buyer-dominant collaborative* approach is of course open to question. This is because buyers cannot leverage the supplier's margins as effectively in this variant but, nevertheless, buyers will still seek to achieve this benign outcome for themselves if they can.

The buyer will also normally have to accept that the supplier will be *competent but not fully congruent*. This means that the supplier is able to achieve higher levels of returns than the buyer would ideally prefer if they could operate with them in the *buyer dominance* power situation. Nevertheless the buyer will still have the benefit of working with a highly competent supplier, who can deliver on functionality improvement and, perhaps, some degree of cost reduction. In this sense the buyer may have a supplier who is *partially in the competent but not congruent quadrant* and *partially in the ideal quadrant*. To this end it is likely that, if the external power circumstances are conducive (Cox *et al.*, 2003), the buyer will need to work proactively with the supplier to develop their long-term competence and congruence through *supplier development* and/or *supply chain management* sourcing approaches. To make this approach work well in this power circumstance it is imperative that the buyer adopts a negotiated or *non-adversarial collaborative relationship management style*.

The supplier must adopt a similar *non-adversarial collaborative* approach if they also recognise that they are in *interdependence*. The supplier is able to do this because the buyer has to accept that the supplier will only innovate for them if the supplier can pursue their own commercial goals of *increasing revenue and returns*. The supplier has to accept, however, that their ability to maximise returns will also be restrained by their need not to push returns (and therefore costs for the buyer) as high as they might be able to if they were operating in a *supplier dominance* position.

Clearly, although *increased revenue and returns* are the ideal, because the supplier is becoming more dependent on the buyer's business and, thereby, more reciprocally interdependent, the relationship can still work under a number of value proposition trade-offs. Thus, the supplier might be prepared to work with a non-adversarial and highly collaborative buyer if the value proposition on offer was only *static revenue and increased returns, reduced revenue with increased returns* or *reduced revenue with static returns*.

When working with their customers, suppliers who need to collaborate in order to develop their own cost leadership and differentiation strategies in the market will normally operate in the *key account* customer outcome quadrant, and ideally will be pursuing *proactive differentiation and cost leadership* customer and competitor strategies. It is possible, however, that the buyer will not be able to ensure that the supplier focuses always on both differentiation and cost leadership. This will (because of the power symmetry between the two sides) have to be negotiated and the supplier may choose only to operate proactively to reduce costs, or only to improve functionality.

There are also tensions in this relationship. Both the buyer and the supplier in *reciprocal collaboration* may seek ways to lock each other into the relationship by using information asymmetry about future business plans and capabilities. By doing this, one party hopes to make the other party undertake more extensive dedicated investments than they would do if they were in possession of more robust and accurate information about the other party's intentions. A buyer can achieve this if they encourage the supplier to build plant and facilities on the spurious promise of more volume in the future. A supplier can achieve the same result by not explaining the fungibility of the assets they are creating for themselves when they will clearly be non-fungible for the buyer.

This type of use of information asymmetry is what Williamson has termed 'self-seeking interest with guile', and he believes that these types of relationships may require both parties to post hostages against opportunism to guarantee that neither party will take advantage of the other in the future (Williamson, 1985). The major reason for this is because, as Williamson has persuasively argued, in these types of relationships (where it is impossible to predict all future contingencies) comprehensive forms of contracting are not possible, and only 'general clause contracting' between the two parties can operate. Under these conditions the scope for opportunism based on information asymmetry and bounded rationality is very high indeed, and especially when both sides have technical and commercial expertise that the other party lacks. If either party can use this to lever an advantage over the other then *interdependence* can quickly shift to *dominance* for either the buyer or the supplier.

Despite these inherent risks it is clear that *reciprocal collaboration* is an appropriate way to manage relationships under *interdependence* power circumstances. Some writers clearly believe that it is, in fact, the ideal relationship management approach. Our analysis demonstrates that this is not the case. On the contrary it is ideal but only in circumstances of *interdependence* where collaboration is required operationally by both sides to achieve their commercial goals. This is because both the buyer and supplier have superior relationship management choices under different power circumstances.

The ideal alignment of buyer and supplier relationships in supplier-dominated collaborative power circumstances

The sixth and final ideal-type of business relationship management approach is that which occurs under power circumstances of *supplier dominance* when the both the buyer and the supplier must operationally work together to achieve their commercial goals. This is *supplier-dominated collaboration* and is described in outline form in Figure 4.7.

The *supplier dominance* power situation occurs normally when there is one or only a few suppliers in the market who can provide the customer with the currently available trade-off between functionality and costs of ownership. If there is only one supplier then that supplier can normally set the prevailing price and quality trade-off in the market. If there are a few suppliers then they may be interested less in competition and rather more in setting standard industry pricing for a given level of functionality and limiting competition to peripheral areas, like brand association.

While the buyer may believe that this is a benign state of affairs it may not be if one considers the impact of *supplier dominance* on supplier revenue and returns. If there is a dominant supplier (or one of a few that the buyer prefers) then that supplier will normally control all of the buyer's revenue for this product or service and their returns will be correspondingly high and above normal. This is a most benign situation for the supplier if, at the same time, they can innovate faster than others but not pass this innovation in functionality and costs of ownership to the buyers in the market until their direct competitors catch up. In this way dominant suppliers deny their customers potential supply benefits and control the pace and cost of innovation.

Sometimes this situation is created not just by the supplier operating independently of others and innovating internally within their own company, but by the ability of the supplier to develop close and collaborative working relationships with the customer. By creating close technical and commercial bonds the supplier locks themselves into the customer's business and finds ways to offer additional products and services, which create additional switching costs for the buyer if they ever decide to exit from the initial relationship. At the same time, by working in close cooperation with the buyer, the supplier is able to understand the nature of the customer's product and service requirement. If the supplier is proactive this also provides opportunities for the supplier to innovate around functionality and the costs of ownership in ways that will be beneficial not only for the customer they are working for, but also for the customer's competitors and anyone else who might be interested in the supplier's product or service.

This is a situation of *supplier-dominant collaboration* in which the supplier is using collaboration to understand the customer's needs and wants, so as to protect their ability to close markets to other suppliers, control the pace of innovation, and ensure control over revenue with

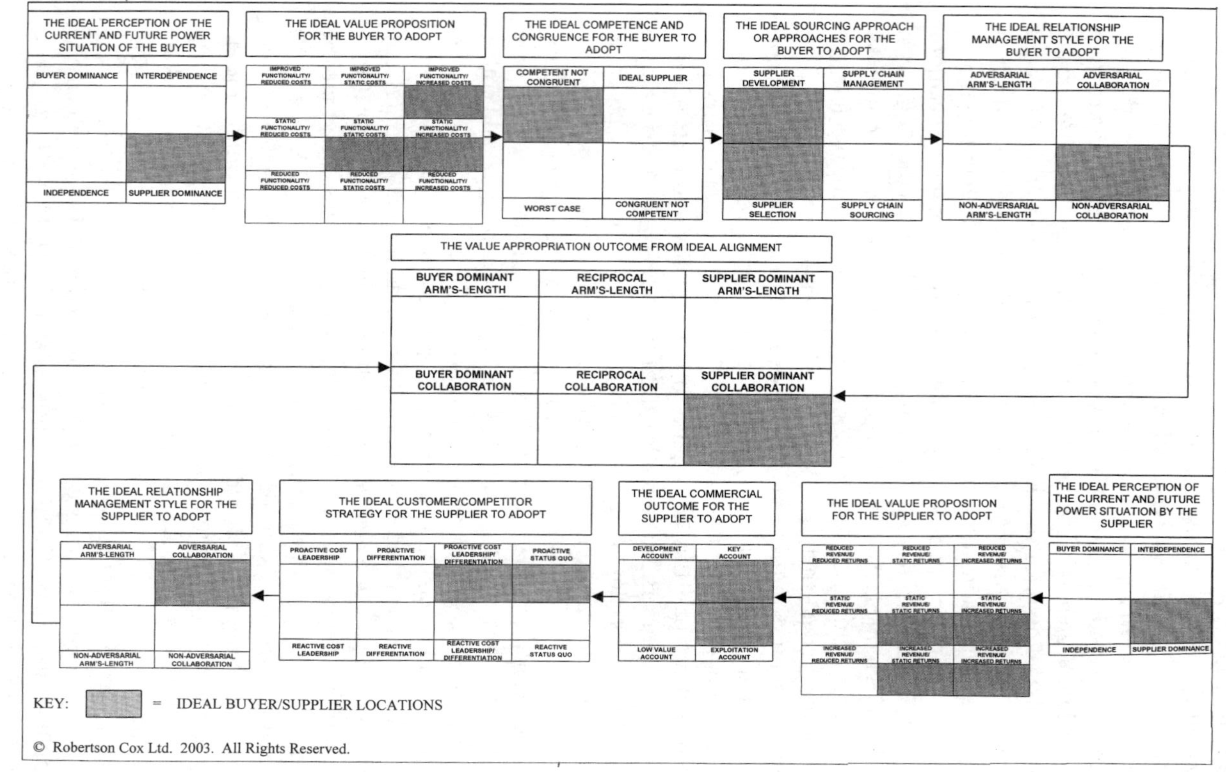

Figure 4.7 The ideal alignment of buyer and supplier in supplier-dominant collaboration

high levels of returns. For this relationship to work effectively it is clear that both the buyer and supplier have to accept that the power structure will remain one of *supplier dominance*. The buyer will also normally have to be content with the current trade-off with functionality and costs of ownership (*static functionality with static or increased costs*), or until the supplier brings forward an increase in functionality, for which, ideally, the supplier would prefer the buyer to be prepared to pay more for any given increase in functionality (*improved functionality with increased costs*).

The buyer in this relationship may believe that they are undertaking *supplier selection* activities but in fact the supplier is normally selecting the customers with whom they wish to have long-term collaborative relationships. Even when the collaboration takes on a more close working relationship, in which joint discussions are held about product development, this is not *supplier development* as understood under *buyer dominance or interdependence* relationship management approaches.

On the contrary, *supplier development* is taking place but it is rarely the supplier being developed by the buyer. Rather, it is nearly always the supplier using the buyer's knowledge in order to develop the supplier's own isolating mechanisms against their direct competitors in the supply market. This is not normally about increasing general competence and contestation in the market but about providing opportunities for the supplier to retain continuing control over an already restricted supply market. In this circumstance it helps the supplier's cause tremendously if the buyer is prepared to operate with them using a *non-adversarial collaborative relationship management style*.

The supplier, as indicated above, is not actually interested in providing improved value for the customer, unless they are forced to do so by other competitors entering the market. It follows, therefore, that the supplier will be most concerned with a value proposition that allows them to *increase revenue and returns*, or, if not, achieve *static revenue with increased returns*, or, at worst, *static revenue with increased* or *static* (but still high) *returns*, and they will always seek to operate in the *key account* customer outcome quadrant. This is because the supplier is likely to find some customers to be relatively more attractive than others to work closely and collaboratively with. This is normally those customers who have a large demand for the supplier's products and services, and those who have technical or commercial differentiation in their own markets, which the supplier needs to understand to stay abreast of new product and service requirements in the future. When the supplier works with these types of customers the aim is not to pass value to them, unless they must; rather, it is to appropriate as much know-how as they can, in order to differentiate themselves in the market from their own competitors.

So sometimes the collaborative dominant supplier will provide a *proactive status quo* offering to the customer and sometimes a *proactive cost leadership and differentiation offering*. This is because the dominant supplier only has to provide what is currently state of the art to their customers – until, that is, competitors catch up, at which point the supplier will either have to pass more value to the buyer or face the profit pressures that arise when real contestation occurs in the market place. It is sensible, therefore, for dominant suppliers to always stay at the cutting edge of product and service innovation and to pursue *proactive differentiation and cost leadership* strategies with their customers, even though they will not pass any improvement in value to them until they are forced to do so by others. This explains why the ideal relationship management style used by dominant suppliers using collaboration is always *adversarially collaborative*.

There are, as with the other ideal-types discussed here, tensions with this relationship management approach. Perhaps the major tension for the supplier is the probability that uninformed buyers may become informed buyers and realise the business model of their dominant suppliers. This is not always apparent to buyers when there is limited competition in the market place and they are currently receiving the best available trade-off between functionality and costs. The business model of the supplier does, however, become transparent when catch-up is achieved in the supply market and new levels of functionality are suddenly offered by other suppliers to customers with whom the supplier has been working for many years. It is also made apparent to buyers when suppliers constantly achieve above normal returns. When any of these events occur it is possible for buyers to begin to consort together and/or to develop strategies to introduce more competition into the market.

On the supplier side another tension in this relationship management approach is complacency. Often dominant suppliers believe that they can do no wrong and that what has allowed them to be successful in the past will allow them to be successful in the future. Unfortunately this is not often the case, and new technological innovations have a way of eventually challenging even the most entrenched and successful business models (Schumpeter, 1939; Christensen, 1997). There is a further problem that can occur with complacent suppliers. Sometimes close collaborative ways of working can provide customers with the opportunity to understand the business model and technical and commercial competencies of the supplier. When this occurs there is always the threat that the complacent supplier may be providing mechanisms for backward integration by the buyer.

Despite these tensions it is clear that supplier-dominant collaboration is an appropriate way for buyers and suppliers to conduct their relationships together. In this relationship management approach the buyer at least achieves the benefits of the currently available best trade-off between functionality and costs of ownership, and may also achieve some additional advantage from working more closely with the supplier than other customers. This decision – to pass a little more value to the buyer – will, however, be in the gift of the supplier not the buyer, and there is a risk that collaborating buyers may not receive any benefit even though they have worked closely with a supplier. This is because whether or not the customer receives more or less value from the collaboration is in the hands if the supplier rather than the buyer in this type of relationship.

4.3 Conclusion: using ideal-typical frameworks to understand and correct relationship misalignments

What is the purpose of describing these ideal-typical examples of business relationship alignment? By addressing the three key variables (*the operational way of working; the power circumstance*; and, *commercial value appropriation*) it is possible to recognise that from an idealised point of view there can only be six basic relationship management approaches available for the effective alignment of buyer and supplier transactions. Furthermore, if buyers and suppliers wish to achieve successful relationship management outcomes then the ideal-types discussed above indicate clearly what is required of the buyer and supplier to make relationships work effectively in particular power circumstances.

The problem for managers is, however, that business life is not as simple as this. The first problem that managers face is that they do not always understand what is the ideal alignment of power, value propositions, relationship outcomes, operational approaches and relationship management styles. More importantly, they are sometimes required to undertake relationships with others who also do not understand this ideal alignment. Unfortunately, even when they do jointly understand the ideal alignment sometimes one or both of the parties are actually trying to achieve something that is unachievable given the power circumstances and relationship management strategies that can be adopted by both sides now and in the future.

This is just another way of saying that most relationships fail to achieve their intended effects because the buyer and supplier have divergent goals that are either commercially non-commensurable, or operationally inappropriate, given the power circumstances achievable by both parties in the transaction. This outcome – *relationship misalignment* – is the state of affairs for most of the buyer and supplier transactions that we have analysed when undertaking academic and consulting assignments. *Relationship alignment* is, in our view, more the exception than the rule. The rule is that most business relationships fail because the parties to the exchange do not understand the power circumstances that are in play; do not understand the appropriate relationship management strategies to adopt given these circumstances; and often have unrealistic and unachievable expectations as a result.

This may seem a depressing conclusion and, at one level, it is. This is because less than 10 per cent of the relationship management approaches that we have studied in the last ten years of academic and consulting activity have been properly aligned. That said, this must mean that there is a massive opportunity for improvement in business relationship management. If up to 90 per cent of all relationships are poorly aligned then the scope for significant bottom-line improvement in most companies is immense.

How can this improvement be brought about? It is our view that the first step, which we have commenced in our discussion above, is to begin the process of properly codifying the ideal-typical relationship circumstances towards which buyers and suppliers should be aligning themselves when they operate in different power circumstances. Our view is that there are six basic ideal-types of buyer and supplier power and relationship management circumstances. In each of these it is essential that buyer and supplier relationships be aligned appropriately for the relationship to work effectively. This does not mean, of course, that both sides in each circumstance must always achieve equal commercial benefit from participating in the relationship. As we have argued at length, for any of the ideal-typical relationships to work effectively all that is required is that each party to the transaction understands objectively the circumstance they are in, and how to manage the relationship choices within it appropriately.

When buyers and suppliers do not understand the power and leverage circumstance they are in, or they do understand but are trying to work towards a different goal from that of their current relationship partner, it is clear that the relationship will break down and that conflicts will appear between the two parties. Given this, it will be possible, if we compare the current approaches of a buyer and a supplier in any relationship against the six ideal-types outlined here, to identify why that particular relationship is either aligned or misaligned. Once this has been achieved it is also possible to indicate whether the breakdown in the relationship is due to fundamental causes that are irreconcilable (because of non-commensurable commercial and power aspirations) or that are reconcilable (because one or both parties has a basic operational misunderstanding about appropriate behaviour, without a fundamental conflict of interest over commercial and power circumstances). This approach is similar to that adopted by Williamson in his discussion of whether problems in transactions are 'remediable' (Williamson, 1996).

Given this, in Figure 4.8 we describe the three basic outcomes that can occur when relationships between buyers and suppliers are analysed in relation to the six ideal-typical aligned relationships.

Relationships can be *aligned*. This means that both the buyer and supplier fully understand the power circumstance they are in now, and what it is likely to be in the future. Both parties accept that this is the best that can be achieved and agree to work together operationally in an appropriate manner given these power circumstances. The commercial benefits each side achieves are also accepted to be a direct function of the relative balance of power, and both parties are satisfied that this is currently the best commercial and operational agreement that they can enter into. The major opportunities and risks in this situation are

	RELATIONSHIP OUTCOME	CAUSES OF ALIGNMENT/MISALIGNMENT	OPPORTUNITIES AND THREATS TO RELATIONSHIP EFFECTIVENESS
1	ALIGNED	Ideal operational and commercial alignment of buyer and supplier, with joint acceptance of the power situation and of appropriate relationship management strategies and styles.	Inertia, and complacency and/or myopia and opportunism over time.
2	MISALIGNED AND SUB-OPTIMAL	Buyer and supplier pursuing the required commercial outcomes, but one or both using inappropriate operational relationship management strategies and styles.	Alignment possible if both sides are prepared to behave objectively and eradicate subjective misperceptions.
3	MISALIGNED WITH DYSFUNCTIONAL CONFLICT	Buyer and supplier pursuing non-commensurable commercial and operational goals, one or both parties seeking alternative commercial and power outcomes.	Limited scope for relationship alignment. Both parties may need to find different relationship partners.

Figure 4.8 The causes of alignment and misalignment in business relationships

that there may be changes that allow one side to be opportunistic against the other, or that one or both parties become complacent and inertia enters into the relationship, such that better value for money deals are missed by one or both parties.

Relationships can be *misaligned and sub-optimal*. This means that the buyer and supplier may accept the current and future power circumstance and understand that the current commercial arrangements are the best that both sides can achieve. Misalignment is therefore not caused by these considerations but by a failure by one or by both parties to understand operationally how to align their own relationship management strategies internally and/or with one another externally. If this is the cause of the misalignment, then, because both parties agree commercially, it ought to be possible for both parties to align themselves if they are prepared to understand objectively the current operational misalignments and eradicate them. This implies that the relationship is 'remediable'.

Relationships can be *misaligned with dysfunctional conflict*. This occurs when there is a basic disagreement between the two parties about the current balance of power and its commercial outcomes, either now or in the future, and one or both parties are behaving opportunistically against the other. In such circumstances there will almost certainly also be operational misalignments as well. It is, however, the commercial and power related conflict that is the cause of the breakdown in the relationship. Obviously if both parties have a commercial and power disagreement then the more conflictual the relationship will be, but it can still break down completely if one party seeks to pursue a commercial and power strategy at variance with the current power circumstance. This implies that the buyer and supplier have the wrong partner and must seek out alternative partners to work with because there is little chance of aligning the relationship with current parties.

It should be clear from this brief discussion of alignment and misalignment what the benefits of using the six ideal-typical relationship frameworks are for the improvement of business relationship management. By comparing current operational practices and commercial goals against the ideal-typical and aligned relationship management approach for any particular power circumstance it is possible for managers to understand how to align their relationships appropriately. This is possible whether the manager is acting as a buyer or a supplier.

How this works in practice is explained in the remainder of the book, where real-life examples of aligned and misaligned relationship management strategies are discussed. While the names of the companies involved have been omitted for commercial and confidentiality reasons the three chapters demonstrate how, in the 'real world', relationship management strategies can be fully *aligned* (Chapter 5), *misaligned and sub-optimal* (Chapter 6) and *misaligned with dysfunctional conflict* (Chapter 7).

References

Bensaou, M. (1999) 'Portfolios of buyer–supplier relationships', *Sloan Management Review*, (Summer), pp. 35–44.

Campbell, N. C. G. (1985) 'An interaction approach to organizational buying behavior', *Journal of Business Research*, vol. 13, pp. 35–48.

Christensen, C. M. (1997) *The Innovators Dilemma: When New Technologies Cause Great Firms to Fail* (Boston: Harvard Business School Press).

Cox, A. (1997) *Business Success* (Helpston: Earlsgate Press).

Cox, A., Ireland, P., Lonsdale, C., Sanderson, J. and Watson, G. (2003) *Supply Chain Management: A Guide to Best Practice* (London: Financial Times/Prentice Hall).

Grove, A. S. (1998) *Only the Paranoid Survive: How to Exploit the Crisis Points that Challenge Every Company and Career* (London: HarperCollins)

Krapfel, R. E., Salmond, D. and Spekman, R. (1991) 'A strategic approach to managing buyer–supplier relationships', *European Journal of Marketing*, vol. 25, no. 9, pp. 22–37.

Lacity, M. E., Wilcocks, L. and Feeny, D. (1995) 'IT outsourcing: maximize flexibility and control', *Harvard Business Review*, (May–June).

Olsen, R. F. and Ellram, L. M. (1997) 'A portfolio approach to supplier relationships', *Industrial Marketing Management*, vol. 26, pp. 101–13.

Schumpeter, J. A. (1939) *Business Cycles: A Theoretical, Historical and Statistical Analysis of the Capitalist Process, Vols I and II* (New York: McGraw-Hill).

Shimizu, I. (1996) *The Dark Side of Japanese Business* (New York: M. E. Sharpe).

Simon, H. A. (1997) *Administrative Behavior* (New York: Free Press).

Williamson, O. E. (1985) *The Economic Institutions of Capitalism* (New York: Free Press).

Williamson, O. E. (1996) *The Mechanisms of Governance* (Oxford: Oxford University Press).

Part II

Alignment and Misalignment in Business Relationship Management

5

Cases in Aligned Buyer and Supplier Relationship Management

In this chapter six cases are presented of aligned buyer and supplier relationship management. Each case is drawn from the six ideal-types discussed in Chapter 4 and demonstrates how the buyer and supplier relationship was commercially and operationally appropriate, even though tensions still existed in the relationship.

5.1 Aligned arm's-length buyer dominance: the closures case

This case demonstrates that buyers and suppliers can work together effectively even though there is no need for close collaborative ways of working, and the buyer is essentially dominant in the relationship. In this case the supplier recognised that the buyer was, and would remain, dominant in the future, and that to win a large share of the buyer's business they would have to accept all of the demands currently being made by the buyer in return for lower commercial returns, but with a growing share of business revenue. The supplier thus accepted that they would have to accept an arm's-length non-adversarial relationship style, with the buyer operating in a commercially adversarial but operationally arm's-length manner.

The context of the case

This case concerns the relationship between a drinks manufacturer operating in a highly contested market place, but where there is some scope for brand differentiation for the producer of the final product. Historically the buying company insourced the production of the beverage and the bottle closures (bottle tops/caps), with bottles, labelling and packaging being bought in from third-party suppliers. In the recent past the company had rationalised its own expensive headcount by outsourcing the production of the closures to the supply market, while retaining in-house the final assembly process.

The buyer was one of the major players in the market, with defensible brand differentiation and a major share of the national market. This meant that it had a high volume requirement for closures from any potential supplier. The supply market for this product was highly contested, with many suppliers willing and able to undertake the production of the closures required by the buyer. The buyer undertook most of the research and development of innovations in closure design, even though production was undertaken by suppliers externally. The supply market was widely dispersed logistically and, although logistics costs were not determinant in any sourcing decision, any suppliers with the available capacity and located close to the buyer's manufacturing facilities had an advantage over suppliers located further away.

Given that the buyer retained all intellectual property in the design and specification of the closure designs it wished to source, and given that its also owned the machine tools for production, it is clear that the switching costs for the buyer were relatively low in this relationship, even when a supplier had a locational advantage. The supplier selected by the buyer in this case was a small company for which the level of demand offered by the buyer represented over 80 per cent of their total business revenue. This revenue guaranteed the fixed cost base of the company and allowed them to operate their production capacity highly effectively and efficiently.

To win the business, the supplier had to accept that it would receive only a short-term contract (that was renewable if the buyer was happy with performance), and that its prices would be lower than the currently benchmarked average prices in the industry. The supplier also had to agree to work with the buyer to improve the functionality of the product, without any long-term guarantees of future work, and also agree that all intellectual property in the innovations would pass to the buyer. Furthermore, the buyer expected an open-book relationship and had forced the supplier to accept that any cost improvements achieved through the life-time of the contract would be passed to the buyer. The buyer also reserved the right to review the supply chain input costs of the supplier and to force them to use any supply input sources that the buyer thought were better than those currently used, and to pass the improved cost benefits to the buyer in the form of lower prices.

Alignment of the buyer and supplier relationship

As Figure 5.1 demonstrates, there was a perfect alignment of buyer and supplier relationship strategies in this case. First of all the buyer and the

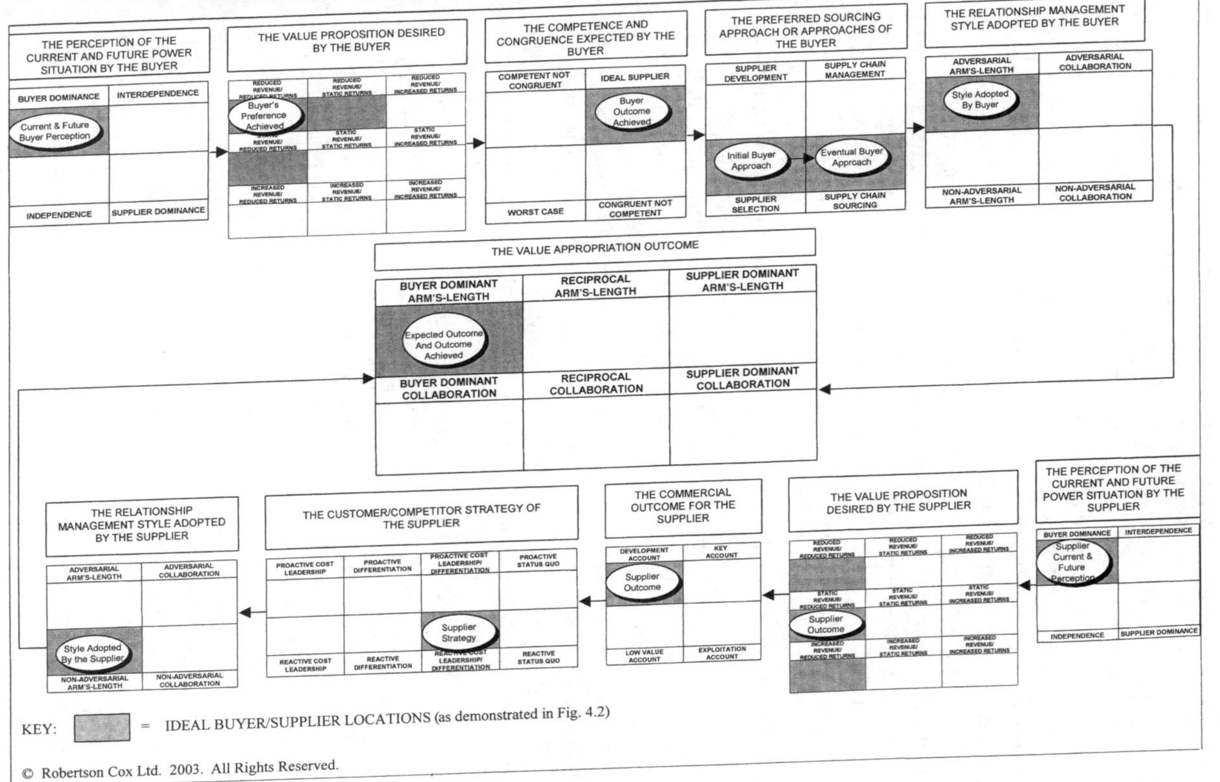

Figure 5.1 Aligned arm's-length buyer dominance in the closures case

supplier both understood that the power circumstance was one of *buyer dominance* and that it would remain so in the future. This was because the buyer had a dominant share of the local and national markets for closures, with relatively low switching costs between suppliers, and the selected supplier had few alternative local customers with the same level of demand, either locally or nationally.

The buyer selected the supplier on the basis that it would be a willing supplicant to the buyer's desire to achieve better than average prices, and with increased functionality improvement. Over the term of the relationship – which had lasted for many years on a short-term contractual basis – the buyer had received year-on-year cost reductions, with continuing improvements in functionality. This indicated that the buyer received the value proposition required, and the supplier was in the *ideal competence and congruence* quadrant.

The buyer was able to achieve these gains, however, without undertaking extensive collaborative interaction with the supplier. The buyer merely operated in the *supplier selection* and, eventually, in the *supply chain sourcing* modes, and retained control internally of all innovation in design and specification, forcing the supplier to undertake all innovations that the buyer required if they wished to win an annual contract renewal. The buyer was clearly operating in the *adversarial arm's-length* relationship style and making few long-term dedicated commitments to the supplier.

The supplier was happy to accept this state of affairs primarily because they had few alternatives. The buyer was their single most important customer, on whom they were heavily dependent for the survival of their business. This ensured that the supplier recognised the power of the buyer in the relationship. The uncertainty induced by the buyer's decision to retain control of design and specification and the ownership of machine tools ensured also that while the supplier would highly value the retention of the contract this would only be possible if they reduced the costs for the buyer and increased functionality whenever required to do so.

This meant that the supplier accepted that the best they could achieve was a value proposition of *static revenue and reduced returns*, and that they would have to operate in the *development customer account* position, with low margins. This was because they found the buyer highly attractive but were unable to achieve high returns due to the open-book approach forced upon them by the buyer. The supplier's strategy in this case was to react to the buyer's desire for functionality and cost improvement (*reactive differentiation and cost leadership*). The relationship management style of the supplier was therefore non-adversarial arm's-length (willing supplicancy). Both parties accepted that they were operating in the *arm's-length buyer dominance* situation.

Sources of continuing tension in the relationship

Despite the fact that the two parties were reasonably content with this relationship arrangement, and it had been in operation for many years, there were a number of inherent tensions in the relationship. As might be accepted, most of these tensions came from the supplier's side of the relationship.

The major problem for the supplier was that while the dominance of the buyer was acceptable at one level – it gave the company guaranteed volumes and ensured their survival – the company recognised that it was highly dependent for its survival on the buyer's business. While the buying company was very successful, and likely to be so in the future, the supplier was aware that if the buyer was able to find alternative sources of supply (with lower costs and improved functionality) its arm's-length and short-term commitment might be withdrawn. This meant that the supplier was always in a state of permanent uncertainty about the viability of the commitment it had entered into. The supplier needed the buyer more than the buyer needed the supplier. As a result, the supplier was actively considering alternative ways of managing its business and looking to diversify its customer base in order to reduce its dependency on the buyer.

In so far as the supplier was able to diversify its customer base the buyer would then face the problem that the supplier might become less willing to innovate and accept the dictates of the buyer. The buying company was aware of the supplier's strategy and was actively monitoring the market to ascertain whether, if the supplier became less interested in working with them, they could source from alternative suppliers at the same or lower costs. The major tension for the buyer was complacency. Because the buying company had achieved what it believed to be best in class pricing and control over the supplier there was only a limited concern in the company about the need to find alternative suppliers. Complacency can sometimes cause problems if the buying company does not keep up with developments in the supply market. Despite these tensions the relationship was clearly aligned and provided both parties with a win-win. The buyer obtained best in class sourcing and the supplier had regular and high-volume work that allowed them to survive in business and at an acceptable (if only very low) return.

5.2 Aligned arm's-length reciprocity: the consumables case

This case is about a buyer and supplier relationship in the *independence* power situation, where neither the buyer nor the supplier had the power capabilities to leverage the other side but agreed to work together to achieve some of their commercial goals without being able to maximise them. This is therefore a case of aligned *non-adversarial arm's-length* relationship management.

The context of the case

The case concerns the sourcing of consumable items by a globally based fast-moving consumer goods company. Consumable items in this case included those standard products associated with office supplies (pencils, envelopes, paper, post-it notes, paper-clips, marker pens, folders, etc.). These were necessary but hardly critical items of spend for the buying company. The major problem for the buying company was that the items were historically sourced in a highly fragmented manner, with no control by the purchasing function over the process or the sources of supply. The result was that the company had over a hundred separate suppliers, with individual buyers at all levels in the company (from secretaries to senior managers) all sourcing from many different suppliers, and paying a wide range of prices for the same types of products.

The existing process was extremely inefficient and had created a complex and costly administrative buying process, which was heavily dependent on paper-based authorisation processes. The purchasing department wanted to obtain more control over the internal process to consolidate the spend and to end 'maverick purchasing' by all and sundry in the business. The hope was that this would significantly reduce internal transaction costs, while also providing for more leveraged pricing over time.

The problem for the buyer was that there is always considerable difficulty in controlling internal processes, and even if this is achieved successfully (and internal transaction costs are reduced) there is only limited leverage for the buyer in the supply market. This is because the buying company, even if it consolidates its spend, is still only a very small fraction of the total demand for these items in the local, national and global markets that exist for consumable office supplies. Given this, and the fact that the buyer was unlikely to be able to find any major supplier who would be heavily dependent on their business, the best that the buyer could hope for was that they would be able to achieve some limited volume leverage, while significantly reducing the internal costs of ownership.

The supplier faced a different problem. There are many potential suppliers who could be used for this purpose, and who would be prepared to give some price reductions for large-volume commitments, especially if there was some prospect of a longer-term relationship. The major problem for the supplier was that the switching costs in this type of relationship are relatively low for buyers. Thus, even if they offer special deals there is no real opportunity for the supplier to create long-term lock-in of the buyer's business. This means that many suppliers are wary of giving exceptional deals because they cannot be sure that the buyer will stay with them if someone offers even lower prices in the future.

The continuous development of such price wars is recognised by suppliers in this market place as an endemic problem, but one that they try to resist if they can. One way of doing this is by trading on the fact that the buyer will not normally devote much time to the analysis of this activity because it is low-value and non-critical. This provides some opportunities for the use of information asymmetry against an uninformed buyer. In this way suppliers are sometimes able to make better than normal returns because the buyer does not have the time or resources to undertake the analysis of the market that would allow them to source the best deals available at any moment in time.

To avoid this problem the buying company decided that the best way to reduce the total costs of ownership was not to focus on constant market testing with potentially opportunistic suppliers, but to focus instead on reducing internal transaction costs by developing a potential longer-term relationship with one consumables supplier. The rationale for this approach was that the buyer was mainly interested in maximising the company's ability to reduce the internal costs of owning a highly fragmented and highly costly paper-based process.

To this end, the buying company achieved internal buy-in. All sourcing of consumable items would no longer be paper-based, and all future consumable sourcing would take place through a computer and internet-based catalogue ordering system, operated by a chosen single source preferred supplier. The beauty of this arrangement for the purchasing function was that it immediately eradicated the paper-based process and made it extremely difficult (if not impossible) for individual managers in the company to source from multiple suppliers. By selecting one catalogue-based supplier it was also possible for the buying company to agree a framework agreement approach with the supplier that provided discounts for agreed volumes. This significantly reduced the internal and external costs of ownership for the buyer.

The supplier was also in a better position because they had the opportunity of a long-term relationship with the buying company and the opportunity to create switching costs against other suppliers. This was achieved by the buying company staff becoming familiar with their on-line ordering catalogue system. The buying company recognised these potential switching costs, but did not believe them to be particularly onerous because many other suppliers offer similar catalogue systems, which can be accessed relatively easily.

The sting in the tail for the supplier was that the buyer insisted that the relationship would only be long-term if the supplier was able to demonstrate that it was providing best in class pricing. The buyer also reserved the right to benchmark the price and delivery performance of the supplier against other suppliers in the industry, and the supplier agreed to provide discounts if there was evidence of lower prices and better performance from other suppliers. The buyer also told the supplier that if they did not match the best in class performance available elsewhere then they would terminate the relationship immediately.

Alignment of the buyer and supplier relationship

There is little doubt that, although this was an essentially arm's-length relationship, both parties were able to achieve some of their commercial goals without being able to dominate the other party in the exchange relationship. The relationship was arm's-length because the buyer did not become involved in the supplier's business in any way at all. The only interaction was to allow the supplier to provide a semi-permanent access for the buyer's staff to the supplier's on-line catalogue. The supplier was then responsible for the on-time delivery of ordered items to the buyer's office locations. The buyer then performance-measured delivery and benchmarked prices against other suppliers in the market.

As Figure 5.2 shows, both the buyer and the supplier recognised that this was, and would remain, an *independence* power situation. The buyer was, however, able to achieve an initial *improvement in functionality and reduce the costs of ownership*. This was because the original approach of the buying company had been seriously sub-optimal. The company was paying inflated prices and had very high internal transaction costs with poor delivery performance.

Once the relationship developed with the supplier the ability of the buyer to leverage continuous improvements in functionality and cost reduction declined. This was because the buyer had achieved the initial improvement and was eventually receiving the best in class pricing and delivery that it should have been achieving given its scale and volume requirements in the market. This meant that eventually the buying company found that it was achieving *static functionality and static costs*, in the sense that they were not able to obtain better than best in class delivery and prices currently prevailing for similar types of buyers in the market.

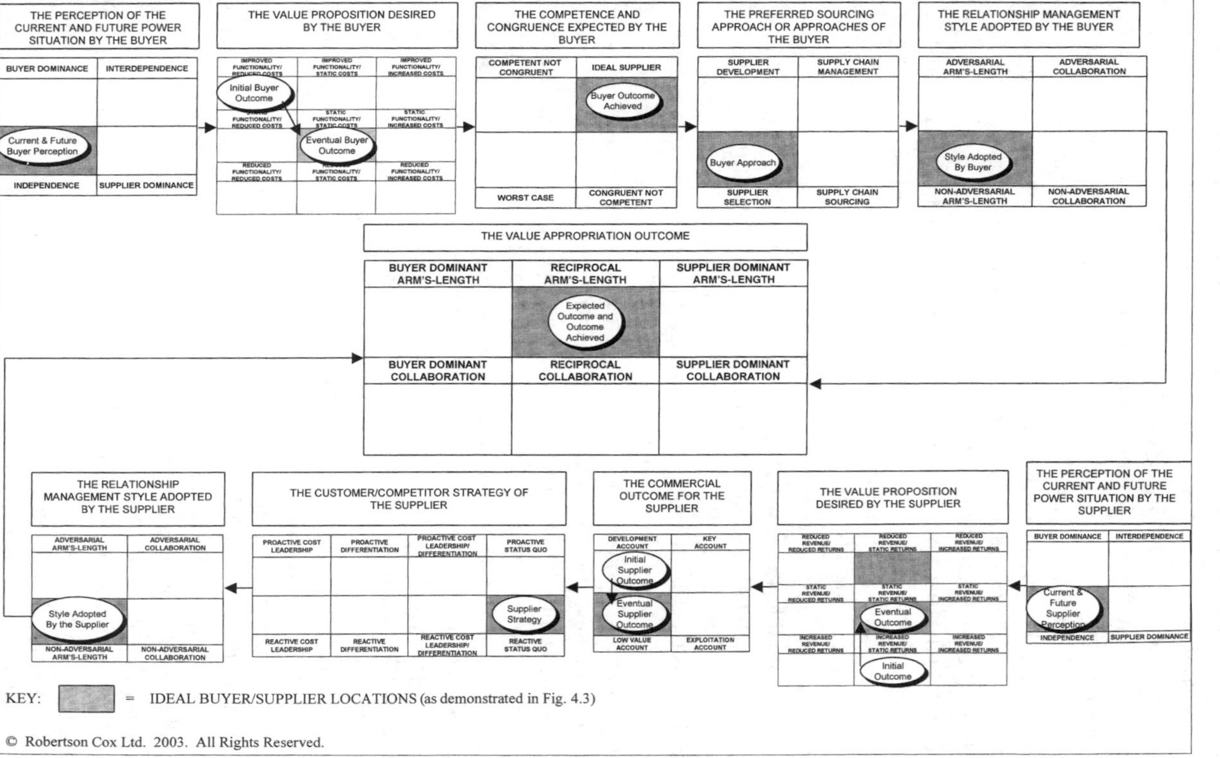

Figure 5.2 Aligned arm's-length reciprocity in the consumables case

Despite this, from the buyer's perspective the supplier was *ideal* (given the power and leverage position that was feasible for a buyer in the *independence* power situation). The buyer was, however, not operating proactively but merely undertaking professional reactive purchasing, using a highly competent *supplier selection* sourcing strategy, with a *non-adversarial arm's-length* relationship management style. The style was non-adversarial because although the buyer was prepared to switch to alternative suppliers if the incumbent failed to deliver, if they did deliver then the buyer was prepared for them to make low returns, but receive all of the company's revenue.

The supplier accepted the prevailing power situation, and that a *reciprocal arm's-length* outcome would provide the best opportunity for it to achieve its initial value proposition. At first the supplier wanted to increase its revenue with the buying company, but had to recognise that because of the approach developed by the buyer it would have to provide consumable items without attempting to leverage higher returns than those generally prevailing in the market place. Over time, of course, once the buying company had provided it with all of their demand it was impossible for the supplier to achieve a value proposition better than *static revenue, with static returns*.

The supplier initially operated in the *development customer account* position, because the account was highly attractive to the supplier since it offered to provide opportunities for a large share of the buyer's volumes, with the prospect of creating some switching costs and barriers to entry against other suppliers. Unfortunately, over time, the supplier realised that the buyer's competence in performance measurement and benchmarking ensured that they would not receive the higher returns hoped for. This was because they had already received all of the buyer's business revenue and there was nothing more to be gained.

Although it was worthwhile having the buyer's account, it was not that significant for the supplier. This eventually meant that the customer account management approach moved into the *low value* quadrant. The supplier wanted to keep the account but was eventually content to service the customer in the same way as many of its other customers. The supplier's competitive market strategy was to provide a *reactive status quo* approach. This was because the supplier was a distributor who provided other suppliers' core products to customers. The supplier was not in any way involved in product development and simply provided the best products available at the best current prices possible.

Overall, however, although the customer was in the low-value customer account box the supplier did not try to commercially leverage the buyer, since the account provided regular volume even if it did not provide many opportunities for significant commercial margin improvement. This was because of the relative ease with which the buyer could switch if they discovered evidence of opportunism. The supplier, like the buyer, therefore operated with a *non-adversarial arm's-length* relationship management style.

Sources of continuing tension in the relationship

There were clearly some tensions in the relationship. The buying company initially achieved most of what had been intended. It was able to end 'maverick purchasing' substantially and was able to leverage its consumable spend effectively, and this provided initial cost reduction and functionality improvement. The problem for the buyer eventually was that it was not in a position to significantly improve leverage over the supplier to achieve better than best in class pricing or delivery over other customers with similar levels of volume. This was because the buyer was operating in the *independence* power situation, where professional buying skills normally can only ever achieve the same market prices as all other competent buyers with similar demand profiles.

The buyer also had to constantly monitor the supplier's performance through market benchmarking, which caused them resource issues. Benchmarking was necessary because, in the absence of being able to undertake this work, the scope for the supplier to be opportunistic if the buyer did not regularly market-test the service would be high.

The supplier on the other hand faced the uncertainty that the buyer would switch to alternative suppliers if they discovered opportunistic behaviour. The supplier was therefore unable to behave opportunistically to raise margins, even when the buyer was not able to discover the best current market prices. The problem for the supplier was that if they behaved opportunistically in the short term, and the buyer found out later, then they would certainly lose their preferred supplier relationship. This meant that, over time, the buyer became something of a low-value account because the scope for higher returns was not available to the supplier. Despite this, both parties had achieved a degree of alignment in what is normally a market place characterised by considerable market volatility, contestation and switching.

5.3 Aligned arm's-length supplier dominance: the decision-control case

This case demonstrates that both the buyer and the supplier can see a dominant supplier situation as a win-win. The case focuses on the purchase of a decision-control software system by a chemical processing company. The case demonstrates that sometimes functionality improvement is far more important to a buyer than cost reduction. In return for an initially improved and then static functionality the buyer in this case was more than willing to accept post-contractual lock-in to the supplier and annual increases in costs to achieve a better operational performance.

The context of the case

Historically the chemical processing company in this case had tried to develop its own software to control and monitor the operational performance of its manufacturing facilities. Over the years the buying company had come to understand that its ability to continually upgrade and develop their in-house decision-control software systems was not leading-edge. The problem for the company was that software development was not its core competence and the decision-control software they had developed was not as effective as that currently available from third-party suppliers.

Given this, the company decided, after much soul-searching about being permanently locked into a supplier's software processes and systems, to tender the requirement and select the most appropriate and current state-of-the-art decision-control software. The company eventually selected a leading multinational supplier specialising in decision-control software and introduced the company's software into all of its manufacturing facilities. By standardising on the supplier's software systems the company committed itself to long-term dependency on the supplier.

The buying company's rationale was that the supplier had wide experience in many kinds of process manufacturing industry in implementing decision-control systems, and the supplier was therefore more capable than they were. The supplier could keep abreast of the latest thinking and developments, and was also able to re-engineer existing software on a regular basis to provide cutting-edge technology and performance. The buying company also expected to achieve initial internal performance improvement and a reduction in internal transaction costs from the fact that their own operational process management staff would be using a common software system.

The buying company initially achieved the functionality improvement they expected, but obviously at an increased cost due to the need to replace their own in-house software with that of the supplier's. Operational performance in general increased and continued to perform at the newly developed levels after the contract was signed. The supplier obviously also achieved significant benefits from the relationship. First, they achieved almost complete post-contractual lock-in and market closure against both other potential suppliers and against insourcing by the buying company. This was because there were very high tangible and intangible switching costs for the buyer if they decided to replace the supplier's software or take it back in-house. This enabled the supplier to look forward to a long-term ability to charge annual licence fees, with future upgrades being limited to general developments elsewhere in the industry, or from their own R&D activities designed to keep ahead of their direct competitors.

Alignment of the buyer and supplier in the relationship

As Figure 5.3 demonstrates, alignment occurred in this case because the buyer was not price sensitive if the supplier could provide a significant improvement in operational performance. The buyer accepted that the power situation would be one of *supplier dominance* as soon as the contract was signed and that, commercially, they would have to keep paying annual licence fees (that would almost certainly increase over time) to the supplier. The buyer was therefore able to achieve *increased functionality with increased costs* initially.

Over time, the operational performance became a *static functionality with increased costs*, because the major benefit for the buyer was the shift to a more effective decision-control software. Once the software was in place any improvements in functionality were incremental and more limited, although software costs tended to increase with inflation, and any new upgrades had to be paid for at prices largely determined by the supplier. The buyer clearly accepted that the supplier operationally was highly *competent but not congruent* commercially. The buyer's approach was essentially arm's-length and reactive. This was demonstrated by its use of a *supplier selection* sourcing approach and a *non-adversarial arm's-length* relationship management style.

The supplier achieved a *supplier dominant arm's-length* outcome post-contractually. This position was readily accepted by the buyer in return for improved operational performance. As a result, once all of the buying company's business revenue had been won, a situation of relatively *static revenue with increased returns* was achieved by the supplier. This increase in returns was achieved due to the buyer having to pay annual licence fee increases and system software upgrade costs.

This meant that, over time, given the size of the supplier's global business and the relatively low level of attractiveness of the buyer's account, the supplier would be managing in the *exploitation customer account management* position. The supplier in this case was able to operate a *reactive status quo* competitive market strategy, because, having locked in

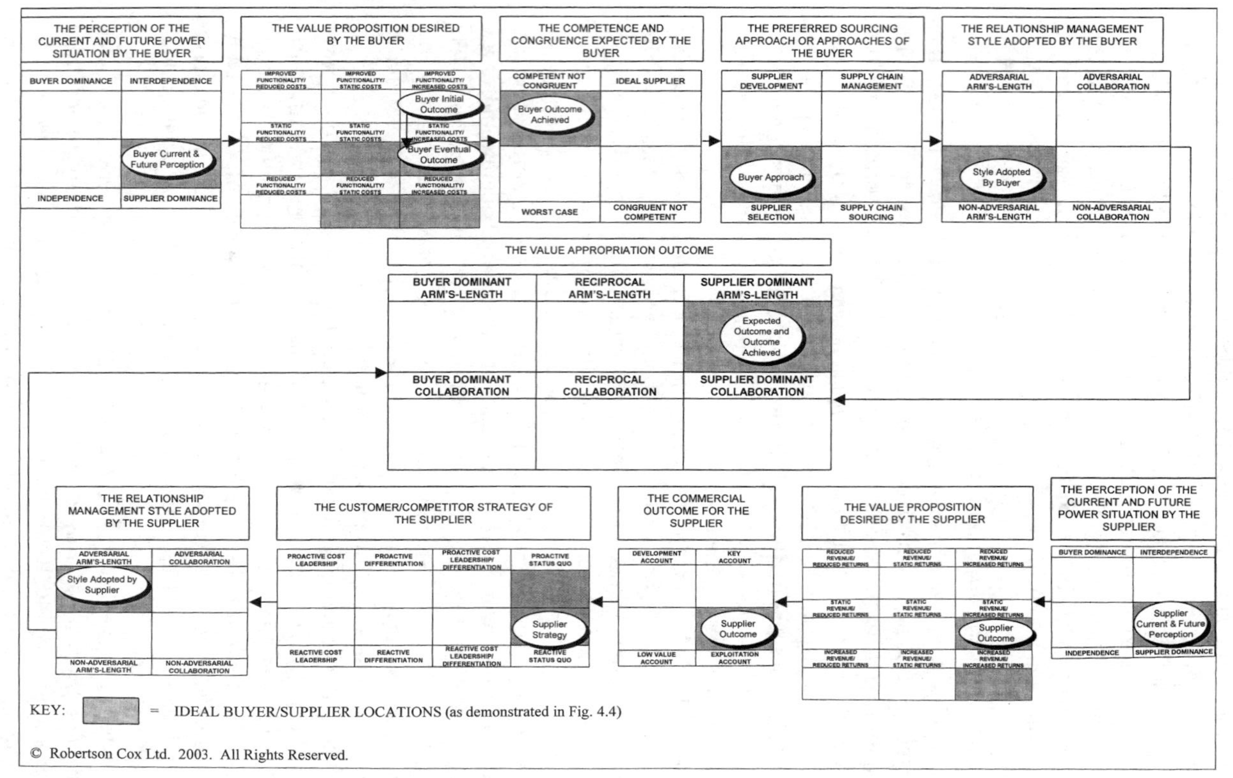

Figure 5.3 Aligned arm's-length supplier dominance in the decision-control case

the buyer to the software offering, the supplier did not need to provide any increased functionality unless forced to do so by competitive pressures elsewhere in the market.

Sources of continuing tension in the relationship

The supplier was clearly in control of the exchange relationship post-contractually but, despite this, the buyer was generally happy to accept the commercial dominance of the supplier. The improvement in operational performance was perceived to far outweigh any increase in costs. It is fair to say, however, that there were a number of tensions for the buyer in this relationship. The first problem for the buyer was that once the initial performance improvement occurred operationally, there was no way in which to engineer continuous improvement operationally on the same scale.

A second tension in the relationship was that much of the learning from what the software provided operationally was acquired mainly by the supplier, who was able to upgrade the generic software at the expense of the buyer. The supplier was also then in a position to sell this learning, not only to the buyer who had indirectly assisted with the process, but also to others – including the buyer's direct competitors. This implied that outsourcing decision-control software systems to third-party suppliers may improve performance in the short term but does not necessarily provide the basis for competitive advantage over time – especially when direct competitors are using the same system supplier's decision support software.

There were far fewer tensions on the supplier's side. The supplier had almost total lock-in of the buyer, with very high barriers to market entry for other suppliers. The major problem here was the switching cost to the buyer in changing software that was responsible for running the company's primary revenue-generating operational processes and manufacturing systems. To switch out would involve significant learning (which means downtime) and a threat to the buyer's revenue-generating capabilities. The only major tensions for the supplier were complacency in the face of superior innovation from its direct competitors and the fear that the buyer might begin to understand how to undertake its own software development projects using outsourced third-party software programmers.

5.4 Aligned buyer-dominant collaboration: the sub-assembly outsourcing case

This case demonstrates that buyer-dominant power circumstances can also be a win-win for the supplier when there is a need for both parties to work closely and collaboratively together to achieve a buyer's value proposition. In this case the buyer undertook a *supplier development* approach with the supplier on a highly collaborative basis, but demonstrated competence by ensuring that the switching costs in the relationship were kept to a minimum. This ensured that the power circumstance remained buyer dominant, with the supplier acting as a 'willing supplicant' throughout the term of the collaborative relationship.

The context of the case

The case concerns a high-technology company operating in a highly innovative and contested market place. The buying company was involved in developing testing equipment for high-technology applications and was a leading global player, facing competition from six other major multinational companies. The key problem for the buyer was the need to operate in a highly innovative manner. Technology changed every six months and responsiveness and agility were critical requirements for staying ahead of the competition. There was the further problem that competitors were able to reverse-engineer most technological innovation quite quickly.

Given this, historically, the company had insourced a high proportion of its testing equipment R&D, configuration, testing, PCB boards and assembly production. The problem for the company was that its own headcount costs were increasingly seen as a competitive impediment when compared with the more outsourced model being used by some of its competitors. This forced the buying company to review its insourcing approach and assess the scope for outsourcing some of its manufacturing processes to external suppliers.

The case demonstrates how the buying company developed a long-term relationship with a sub-assembly supplier. The buying company created a long-term collaborative commitment to the supplier through the creation of technical bonds, dedicated investments, cooperative norms and relationship-specific investments. In doing so the buyer ensured that it retained absolute control over the power situation post-contractually. The buyer retained control over switching costs and had transparency over the supplier's commercial business model. This forced the supplier to operate as a non-adversarial 'willing supplicant' who continually passed value, in the form of increased functionality and lower costs of ownership, to the buyer.

Alignment of the buyer and supplier relationship

The buying company in this case decided, after extensive analysis of the risks of outsourcing, that it was possible to outsource many of the PCB boards and the sub-assembly of the major parts of the testing equipment to suppliers. The company decided, however, to keep in-house all R&D, configuration, testing and the manufacture of one critical PCB board that provided the killer applications that the company used for differentiation purposes. Final assembly and testing was therefore retained in-house. The company's main problem was not in finding suppliers of commodity PCB boards but finding a competent sub-assembler who could put the commodity materials together for them before final assembly.

The buyer's problem was that they were located in a region were there was no tradition of sub-assembly and few potential suppliers available. This meant either developing a local supplier, encouraging a global player to enter the area, or moving the buyer's business closer to existing sub-assembly suppliers. After considerable analysis the buying company decided that it was not sensible to move their established business closer to sub-assemblers and they were wary of encouraging a global sub-assembly company to work with them. They only had low-volume demand, and felt they would be an insignificant source of revenue to such companies, and would not receive the innovative capabilities required to compete in this market place.

Given this, the company decided that it was perfectly feasible for them to develop a local supplier who had little existing competence in this area. The company already knew how to sub-assemble the product, and, in any case, it wanted to find jobs for the in-house staff it needed to outsource to reduce the total costs of ownership. This meant that the buying company had the know-how to work closely with a supplier in order to develop their competence. The main problem was finding a willing supplicant supplier.

Eventually the buying company decided that its current fabrication supplier, who was extremely innovative and located close to the buyer's business, would be the ideal choice. The power situation between the buyer and supplier was one of buyer dominance, because the fabrication company was already heavily dependent on the buyer for over 60 per cent of its business revenue. Furthermore, the buyer knew that the supplier had under-utilised factory room that provided more than enough room in which to relocate the outsourced sub-assembly processes and personnel.

The buyer therefore made the fabrication supplier an offer they could not refuse. They offered them all of the sub-assembly work on a long-term basis but on condition that the supplier provided open-book costings, agreed to work for a fixed margin of 3 per cent on all volumes, and met stretch functionality improvement and cost reduction targets. If the supplier refused to accept the deal the implied threat was that the buyer would take away the fabrication work on which the supplier earned 6 per cent margins.

Clearly, as Figure 5.4 demonstrates, the power situation was one of *buyer dominance*, and both the buyer and supplier accepted that this would continue in the future, since the companies operated in an area of declining employment with reduced opportunities for the supplier to find alternative sources of revenue. This meant that the buyer would remain the number-one customer for the supplier in fabrication and the supplier could not afford to lose the work. The buyer knew this and understood that this gave them considerable leverage.

The buyer's value proposition was clearly to *increase functionality and reduce the costs of ownership*. This was achieved remarkably easily. First the company was able to outsource its expensive headcount and relocate them at lower cost in the new sub-assembly company. The new supplier was an enthusiastic participant in the buyer's *supplier development* programme and quickly began to suggest significant process and cost-cutting improvements that allowed the creation of synergies between fabrication and sub-assembly processes. These all contributed to cost reduction and functionality improvement for the buyer. The buyer had clearly created an *ideal* supplier, even though the overall approach was to be commercially *adversarial*, while operationally highly *collaborative*, in turning the fabricator into a sub-assembler.

From the supplier's point of view this was also a win-win. The major reason was that the supplier did not want to lose the fabrication work that was core to its business survival, and it recognised that it would have to be a 'willing supplicant' to retain the business. The supplier also recognised that the company could use its own capital assets more effectively if it became a sub-assembler, even though this might mean *increased revenue, with reduced returns*. The supplier was, however, happy to accept the opportunity to work in the *development customer account* position and to commit to a *proactive cost leadership and differentiation* strategy, based on a *non-adversarial collaborative* style of relationship management. The reason for this was that *buyer dominance collaboration* was the best deal that the supplier could currently achieve given the declining opportunities in the local market and their over-dependence on the buyer's work for their own business survival.

Sources of continuing tension in the relationship

Clearly, in many ways the supplier was leveraged by the buyer in this relationship, but on the other hand the supplier was able to improve its own financial position and create some guarantees for itself about its

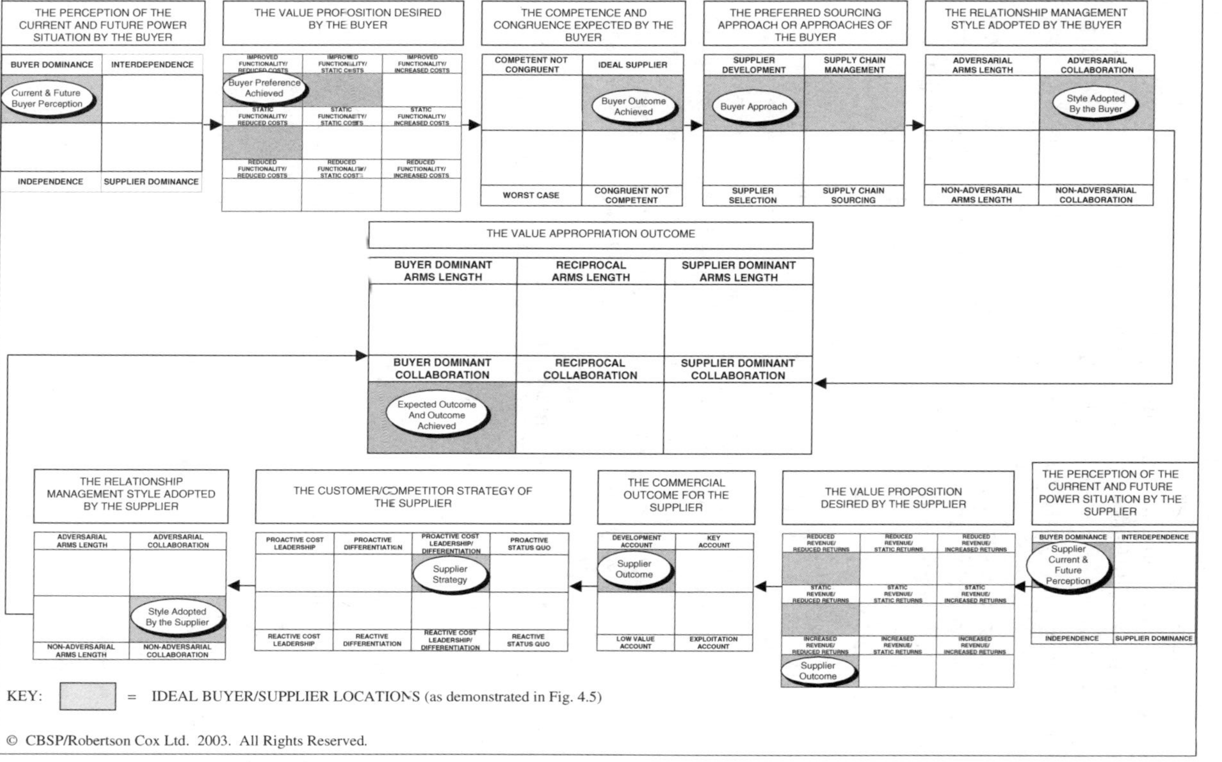

Figure 5.4 Aligned buyer-dominant collaboration in the sub-assembly outsourcing case

core fabrication business. Despite this there were still tensions in the relationship. On the buyer's side the company was concerned that the supplier might learn too much about the technology that differentiated their product from their competitors', and because the company was part of a larger multinational conglomerate there was always the fear of backward integration. This is why the buying company decided to retain final assembly in-house and to locate the sub-assembly work away from their R&D and specialist manufacturing work.

The supplier faced other tensions. The most important was the fear that if they decided not meet the exacting stretch improvement performance targets set by the buyer they might lose not only their sub-assembly but also their fabrication work. This meant that despite the very congenial working relationship between the two companies operationally, the supplier was constantly attempting to diversify its customer base. The supplier had additional land available to extend its facilities, and if it was able to expand its business on the back of its twin capabilities in fabrication and sub-assembly it would have the scope to retain its current work with the buying company and service other customers. Unfortunately, given the declining business prospects in the area, and their distance from other potential customer markets, there was little success for the supplier in this regard. So the buyer and supplier were reasonably content in the *buyer dominant collaborative* relationship they had created, but the supplier was clearly under more uncertainty and tension than the buyer.

5.5 Aligned reciprocal collaboration: the fan cowl doors case

This case demonstrates that buyers and suppliers can work together amicably to increase the functionality and reduce costs for the buyer, while at the same time allowing the supplier to sustain, and potentially increase, their share of revenue and returns. In this case the buyer and the supplier recognised that they were operating in the *interdependence* power situation. As a result, both parties achieved commercial and operational alignment by accepting that *non-adversarial collaboration* was the best way to work together.

The context of the case

This case concerns the relationship between the assembler of an engine and a supplier of the fan cowl door that provides cowling and access to the engine. The buyer was one of only three major assemblers of these types of engines, operating in a fiercely competitive customer market place in which increased functionality is essential, with a constant desire for reduced costs of ownership in all components of the final assembled product. The demand requirement was stable for many years in the future but only for a relatively low number (20 units) annually.

Given the relatively low volumes required it made no sense for the buyer to work with many suppliers, and a single source relationship has been created with the fan cowl door supplier. The buyer was keen to increase the speed with which it assembled engines and was also interested in improving the reliability of all the components used. The buyer was not interested in the after-sales market place and was prepared to allow the supplier to manage this element of the business.

The supply market was restricted because there were only a limited number of suppliers who could meet the buyer's expectations, and there were high switching costs for the buyer, because of the lengthy lead times and rigorous certification processes required to replace any supplier. This created post-contractual lock-in for the buyer. On the other hand the switching costs for the supplier were also high, because the supplier had to make dedicated investments in tooling for the buyer and long-term commitments were required to support the relationship contractually.

Alignment of the buyer and supplier in the relationship

As Figure 5.5 demonstrates, both the buyer and supplier recognised in this case that the power situation between them was one of *interdependence*. Even though the buyer could have selected from a number of suppliers pre-contractually once this decision was made there was a mutual post-contractual lock-in in the relationship. Given this, the buyer took the view that by working closely with one supplier it was possible for the two parties to work cooperatively and non-adversarially on the functionality and cost of ownership issues that needed to be addressed. This meant that the buyer was keen to encourage *supplier development* and, eventually, *supply chain management*.

Reciprocally the supplier accepted this power scenario and recognised that they were operating in the *key account* situation. This required them, proactively but non-adversarially, to increase functionality and reduce the costs of ownership for the buyer, while defending their own revenue stream and returns. Obviously the supplier's first preference was for their *revenue and returns to increase*, but they would still accept either *increased revenue and static returns* or *static revenue and increased returns*.

Initially when the relationship commenced the buyer discovered that the fan cowl doors were not meeting customer expectations with respect to in-service performance. In the spirit of *non-adversarial collaboration*

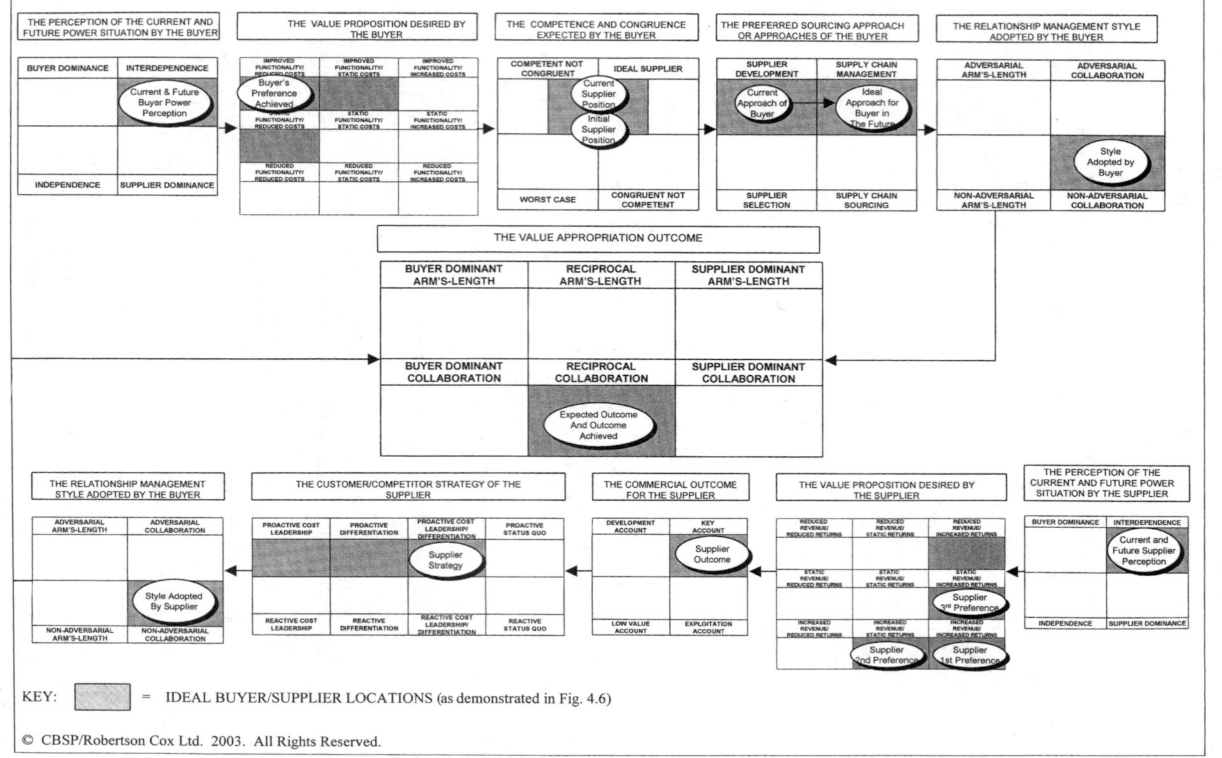

Figure 5.5 Aligned reciprocal collaboration in the fan cowl doors case

that existed between the two parties both sides worked closely together to seek ways of resolving this problem. The result of the close collaborative working relationship was that the buyer and supplier acknowledged that they could only resolve the problem by undertaking a joint redesign of the fan cowl door. In undertaking this redesign it proved possible to use cheaper materials as well as a more automated production process. By doing so it was also possible to reduce the amount of manual labour required. Both of these innovations significantly reduced the costs of the finished product while improving the functionality required.

In this way the buyer was able to increase the use value from the supplier, while also reducing the total costs of ownership – the ideal outcome for the buyer. The supplier on the other hand was able to retain their share of the buyer's revenue flow over the long term and retain their control of a valuable after-sales market, while also providing opportunities for the buyer to sell their supply offering more cheaply in the future. This provided the supplier with the potential opportunity to grow their business revenue in the future alongside that of the buyer. Also, because the buyer was not particularly interested in leveraging the supplier's profit margins down to normal or low levels it also allowed the supplier to operate with the scope for relatively high returns.

Sources of continuing tension in the relationship

Despite the fact that both parties operated in a spirit of *reciprocity*, in this case there was still a source of tension in the relationship. This arose because of the desire by the buyer to leverage continuing improvements in functionality and costs of ownership. This would require the supplier to work with the supplier on a *supply chain management* rather than the current *supplier development* approach.

The problem with this for the buyer was that while there was obvious benefit for them from the adoption of this approach this may not be the case for the supplier. This was because of the buyer's relatively low volume requirements, and their decision not to continue with the sourcing of fan cowl doors in new engines and to allow others to source this for them. This significantly reduced the attractiveness of *supply chain management* for the supplier, because *supply chain management* approaches required a continuous effort by the buyer and supplier to leverage improvements in functionality and costs throughout the supply chain for the fan cowl door.

The problem for the supplier in this case was that, given that they had no future growth potential outside the existing engine relationship, their willingness to commit the time and effort to further improvement beyond those already achieved was limited. They did not have the necessary incentives of increasing revenue and/or returns to encourage them to be as proactive as the buyer would prefer.

Despite this, it is clear that when a buyer and supplier are in the *interdependence* power situation it is imperative that they recognise that they should work together in a non-adversarial collaborative manner. In this relationship management style it is then possible for the buyer to move the supplier into the ideal competence and congruence situation, where the supplier provides increased functionality and lower costs of ownership to the buyer, while still retaining their revenue stream with reasonable returns.

The final tension in this relationship was that the buyer could not reduce the returns of the supplier to normal levels because of the post-contractual lock-in that made exit difficult for them. This was witnessed by the unwillingness of the supplier to accept open-book costing as the buyer desired. In this way a further source of relationship tension existed because of the level of returns achieved by the supplier. As was argued earlier, above normal returns are always unacceptable additional costs for the buyer that they would ideally prefer not to pay – and which they would not if they were operating in *buyer dominance*. Having to accept above normal returns is, however, the price that the buyer sometimes has to pay when they operate in *interdependence*.

5.6 Aligned supplier-dominant collaboration: the flow management case

This case demonstrates that a buyer and supplier can jointly collaborate even in a situation of *supplier dominance*. In this situation the supplier determines the trade-off between functionality and the costs of ownership, and is able to control the buyer's revenue stream and earn above normal returns. Despite this the buyer accepts the situation because the use value they receive from the supplier far outweighs any benefits they currently believe they might receive from leveraging cost reductions and supplier returns aggressively.

The context of the case

This case is about the relationship between a manufacturing company working very closely and collaboratively with a supplier of flow management technology in a final assembly production process, which is critical to the corporate success of the buying company's business. The manufacturing company makes products that can be easily replicated by others and faces fierce global competition from seven major competitors, all of whom rely on flow management technology for the operational effectiveness and efficiency of their final assembly processes. All of these buying companies compete on scale and all use the same supplier for their flow management requirements.

The supplier in this case provided a suction-based technology that allows components to be lifted and transferred from one assembly stage to another, and at a critical stage of the production and assembly process. The supplier was an extremely well-managed company that had developed leading-edge technologies and recently acquired its major competitor, with its own leading alternative technology product. There were other suppliers in the market place but none of them could approach the operational performance of the leading company in the supply market.

Given this, and given also that the buyer in this case recognised that competitive advantage came not from squeezing the margins of the supplier but through working with them to develop leading-edge technology solutions to their own internal (and often unique) operational assembly processes, the buyer had historically accepted *supplier dominance* and worked in a highly collaborative manner with the supplier. Collaboration took the form of the development of extremely close working relations in which commercially and operationally sensitive future market and demand information was shared with the supplier so that the supplier could minimise disruptions to the assembly process, while also maximising their own technological improvements for the buyer's unique assembly production processes.

The buyer's willingness to accept *supplier dominance* in this case was undoubtedly due to the fact that the supplier's costs were infinitesimal relative to the overall costs incurred by the buyer in the assembly process, but what they offered technologically was critical to the buyer's operational performance. Indeed, by working closely with the supplier to develop unique and bespoke technological solutions the buyer felt that it was able to improve its overall operational effectiveness in ways that allowed it to reduce its overall costs of operations significantly and provide a cost leadership advantage over its own direct competitors.

Given this, the fact that the supplier was making above normal returns was not perceived to be significant at all to the buyer. The buyer was interested more in the functionality that it received rather than in the costs of ownership. This was an ideal position for the supplier to be in, and one that was reinforced by the fact that the buyer realised it would be very difficult for them to alter the situation without a major effort on their part, which they did not wish to make.

Alignment of the buyer and supplier in the relationship

Figure 5.6 demonstrates clearly the alignment that occurred in this case. The buyer was quite prepared for *supplier dominance* to occur, just as long as the finished product (the bespoke and unique flow management technology) was hugely successful in creating cost leadership for them operationally, leading to higher sales revenue growth. Indeed, the buyer was prepared to pay more and give all of their work to the supplying company if they could provide such a successful outcome.

To achieve this outcome the buyer had to undertake an initial *supplier selection* exercise of the available suppliers in the market – none of whom could match the product capabilities of the dominant supplier. This meant that the dominant supplier was *competent but not congruent.* It could offer improved functionality, but with increased costs relative to the other potential suppliers. Once this initial selection decision had been made the buyer recognised that, to achieve the best fit between the supplier's technological capabilities and their own operational requirements, they would have to work very closely with the supplier using a *supplier development* approach. This approach was based on the adoption of a *non-adversarial collaboration* relationship management style.

The buyer was happy to accept this arrangement – with the supplier making above normal returns – because the consequence of the relationship was that the buyer's operational performance improved commensurate with the joint efforts that both parties put into the relationship over time. The buyer discovered that the more that they were prepared to make longer-term commitments to the supplier – without leveraging the supplier on their returns – the more the supplier was prepared to dedicate its best staff to the development of bespoke improvements to the buyer's assembly production processes.

In achieving a situation of *supplier dominance* the supplier in this case demonstrated that they fully understood the desire by the buyer to focus the relationship on process improvement through the purchase of a supply offering that provided *product differentiation* when compared with what was available elsewhere in the market place. Indeed the supplier recognised that if they were able to give the buyer the functionality they required, by proactively working with them to differentiate their assembly processes, they would be able to operate in the *adversarial collaboration* relationship management style and achieve *above normal returns,* while also retaining all of the buyer's revenue flow and locking them into a long-term relationship.

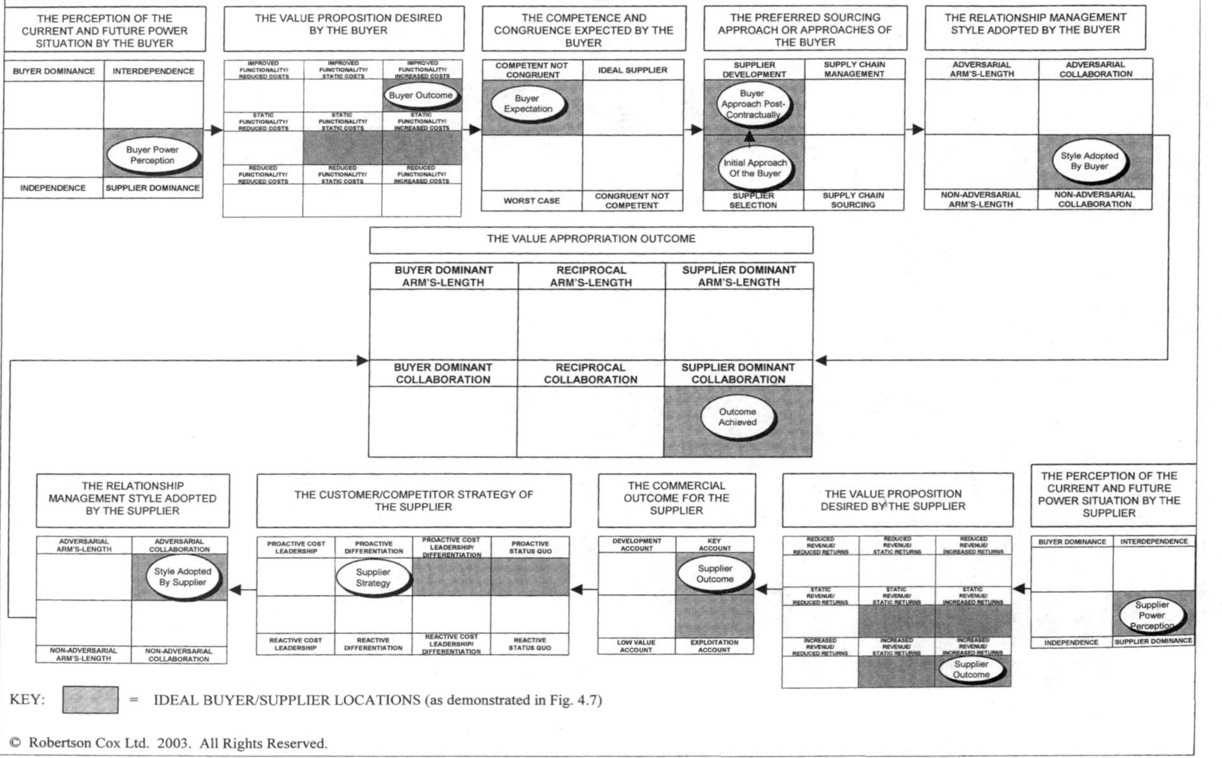

Figure 5.6 Aligned supplier-dominant collaboration in the flow management case

Furthermore, given the success that the buyer received from the innovative process improvements that arose from the use of the supplier's technology, this allowed the supplier to receive above normal returns on a continuous basis. This is clearly a situation of *aligned supplier dominance*.

Sources of continuing tension in the relationship

Despite this apparent alignment there was still tension in the relationship. The tension arose because the buyer understood that the supplier was making above normal returns at their expense and they were only able to make normal returns in their own business model, however much the supplier's technology improved the buyer's relative competitive advantage. This was because the product of the buyer was a basic commodity that could be relatively easily replicated whatever the initial process improvements made in the assembly production process.

This meant that the buyer was well aware that the supplier was achieving above normal returns due to their effective corporate strategy in closing the market to other competitors for the technology they possessed, and the buyer had already planned that when they had the time and resources to do so they would attempt to encourage more competition in the supply market. This was to be achieved by retaining as much technical 'know-how' and expertise as possible about how the supplier's technology operated, so that eventually they would be able to work closely with alternative suppliers to develop their competence in the future.

Unfortunately, for a variety of reasons the buyer was not able to devote the necessary resources to make this increased leverage occur so that, in the short-term, they were forced to accept *supplier dominance*, but with more functionality than they might receive from other suppliers. Whether or not the buyer will ever be able to change this situation of *supplier dominance* is, of course, a moot point, because the spend is of such relatively low significance to them that it is possible that it will never become important enough for them to leverage. This is of course a relatively ideal position for a supplier to occupy.

6

Cases in Misaligned and Sub-Optimal Buyer and Supplier Relationship Management

In this chapter six cases are presented of sub-optimal misalignment in buyer and supplier relationship management. Each case demonstrates how the buyer and supplier relationship was commercially and operationally inappropriate, and how the buyer and/or supplier were able to make relationship-specific adaptations to create a more effective alignment given the power circumstances prevailing.

6.1 Misaligned and sub-optimal arm's-length buyer dominance: the licensing case

This case demonstrates that sometimes buyers can lose their dominance over a supplier if they adopt an arm's-length approach and do not continue to monitor the consequence of their actions in the market over time. In this case the buyer was initially complacent but, after realising this, at the next contract review was able to redirect the relationship with the supplier to one that was more aligned.

The context of the case

The case concerns a car company that has outsourced, under licence, one of its proprietary parts – the gearbox – to a supplier. The company normally designed, specified and manufactured the gearbox in-house, but only for the initial production run of the car model produced. Once the car model had been replaced by another model the production of the gearbox was normally outsourced to a supplier.

The reason for this approach is straightforward enough. Since the car assembler needed to maximise the use of its capital assets, and because the demand for gearboxes is relatively low volume in the after-sales market place, the car company did not want to make relatively inefficient use of its facilities, which it needed for the intensive production of the latest models.

Given this, the car company normally outsourced the production of the established gearboxes for old models to a single source supplier, because there was normally insufficient volume for more than one supplier to operate efficiently. In sourcing the gearbox the buyer normally retained dominance over the supplier by retaining all intellectual property ownership, and by paying the supplier a royalty for the production of each gearbox based on agreed annual pricing review. The buyer also normally insisted that all functional improvements in the design and specification of the gearbox that the supplier made belonged to them.

In this case the buyer had established a long-term relationship with one supplier that had lasted for ten years, but the buyer did not involve themselves actively in the supplier's manufacturing and business processes. The buyer and supplier operated relatively at arm's-length with one another, and the relationship was mainly based on an annual inflation adjustment pricing agreement, with the buyer monitoring any recommended design changes that the supplier indicated it could make to the gearbox. The buyer was aggressive in insisting that when any design changes were made the intellectual property in the design passed to them. The supplier was heavily dependent on the buyer for their business revenue. The supplier's business was located in an area with high unemployment and fierce competition for basic manufacturing capabilities from fairly desperate small and medium sized manufacturing companies.

The buyer, therefore, believed that they were in the *buyer dominance* situation. They owned the intellectual property in the gearboxes, retained all intellectual property in any design innovations and had complete control (or so they thought) over the commercial terms of the relationship. This was because they determined the annual royalty and pricing process. Unfortunately, in this case the buying company eventually came to realise that the supplier was making much higher returns than they were as a company.

When a new head of procurement was appointed at the car company he initiated a review of the gearbox after market relationship with the supplier. The review focused not just on the intellectual property, royalty and pricing structures in the relationship but focused also on the cost base of the supplier, as well as requiring the supplier to adopt an open-book approach to its cost structures and financial returns.

This review turned up the interesting finding that the gearbox supplier had been an early adopter of lean manufacturing and supply processes, and that over the previous ten years it had been systematically improving the functionality and the total costs of ownership of its manufacturing and supply processes.

It soon became clear that the supplier was making a substantial return of between 10 and 12 per cent margin on its business with the buyer. This was a staggering discovery for the buying company because they barely broke even financially due to the fierce market competition that existed globally in the car market. The immediate realisation by the new head of procurement was that the buying company had been excessively complacent in its relationship with the supplier, and that there were significant financial concessions that the supplier could make for them. These potential concessions were based on a better understanding of the supplier's cost base and its relationship to the annual pricing review.

The buying company, therefore, told the supplying company that unless they were prepared to provide them with continuous access to their books, and also provide transparent annual information on their cost base related to pricing, that they would offer the work to other suppliers. The supplier – being heavily dependent on the buyer's business for their survival – eventually decided to comply. The result was that the buyer received an immediate pricing improvement and a rebate against profits made by the supplier in the past. The supplier offered this as a good-will gesture to demonstrate that they were a 'willing supplicant'.

The supplier's argument to the buyer was that since the buyer had not asked them to provide cost information in the past they were simply operating their business as effectively and efficiently as they could. It was clear that they were prepared to accept greater leverage in this case because they had few alternatives and the buyer was their major customer.

Alignment and misalignment of the buyer and supplier in the relationship

As Figure 6.1 demonstrates, the buyer's initial perception was that *buyer dominance* existed in the relationship, and the supplier was providing *improved functionality with static costs*. The initial perception of the buyer was also that they were working with an *ideal* supplier, but after the review they discovered that they were working with a *competent but not congruent* supplier. This failure to properly leverage the supplier was clearly occasioned by the fact that the buyer had adopted a *supplier*

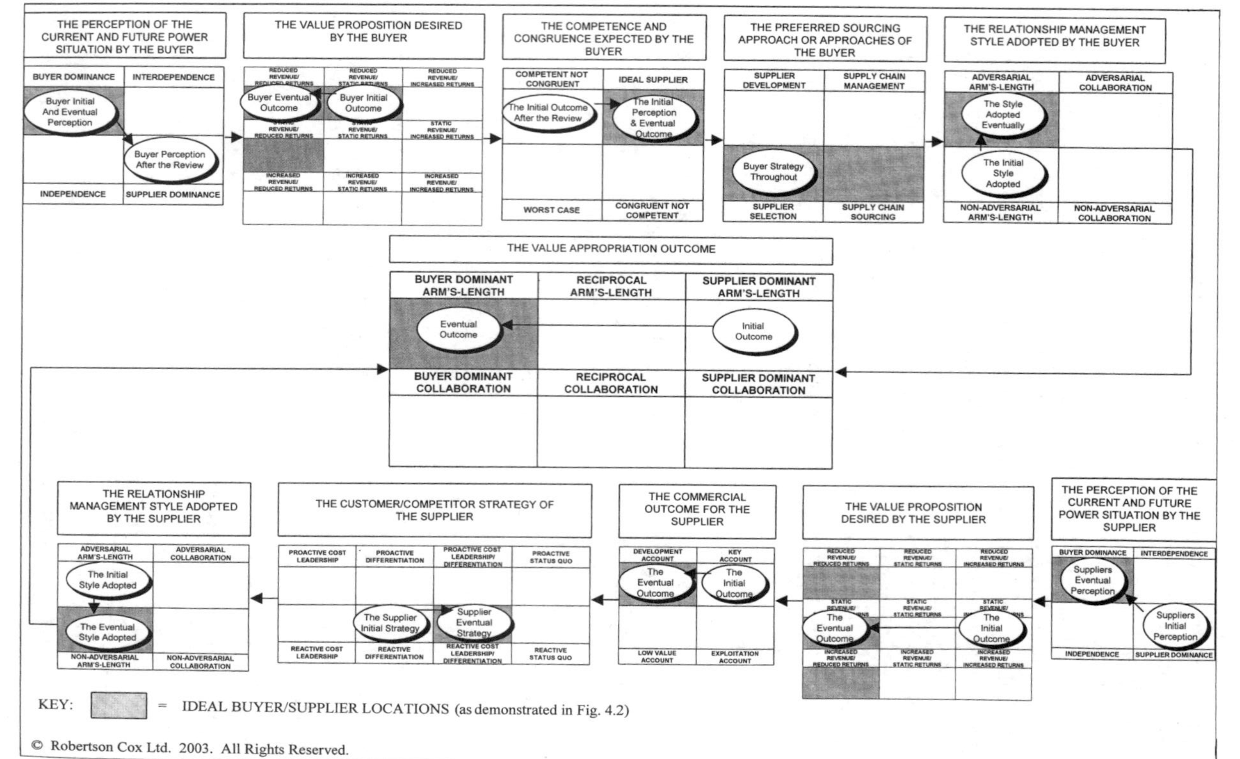

Figure 6.1 Alignment and misalignment in the licensing case

selection strategy but had managed it in a fairly *non-adversarial arm's-length* manner. The result was a *supplier dominant arm's-length* outcome.

This outcome is clearly indicated by an analysis of the supplier side of the relationship. Since the buyer did not review the cost base of the supplier, or its operating margins, what should have been a buyer-dominant situation became in practice a supplier-dominated one. This was because the cost reduction strategies of the supplier allowed them to earn double-digit returns whatever the buyer decided at the annual pricing review. This meant that while the supplier had *static revenue* (it already had all of the buyer's business volume), it also had *increased returns*. This implied that the supplier was managing the buyer in the *key customer account* position, and was only forced to provide a *reactive differentiation* competitive market strategy to the buyer – focused on innovation in design and specification, but not in costs. Overall it was clear that the supplier was pursuing an *adversarial arm's-length* approach.

Strategies for improving relationship alignment

Once the buyer properly understood their own failure to actively leverage their *buyer dominance* situation the appropriate alignment of the relationship was quickly achievable. The supplier was clearly heavily dependent on the buyer, and although they were not very happy about having to reduce their profit margins to below 5 per cent, they had to do so in order to retain the business. Therefore, after the procurement review, the buyer achieved a much more aligned relationship in which they were using objective power resources to drive *improved functionality and reduced costs of ownership* with an *ideal* supplier, using a *supplier selection* and robust performance management approach, based on an *adversarial arm's-length* relationship management style.

The supplier eventually had to accept the *buyer dominance* situation and realign its relationship approach to a value proposition of *static revenue and reduced returns*. This involved them managing the buyer in the *development customer account* quadrant and the adoption of a *reactive cost leadership and differentiation* competitive market strategy, with a *non-adversarial arm's-length* relationship management style.

Clearly, the supplier was not as happy in the relationship as they had been with the previous position that they had been able to obtain due to the complacency of the buyer. Any potential tensions in this relationship were, however, minimised by the fact that the supplier was heavily dependent on the buyer for their business revenue. This meant that the buyer had achieved a more effective leverage in the buyer-dominant position, without causing dysfunctional conflict in the relationship. Obviously the supplier was not as content as they had been but work at a lower margin was clearly more important to them than no work at all.

6.2 Misaligned and sub-optimal arm's-length reciprocity: the air travel case

This case demonstrates that there are often considerable opportunities for buyers to achieve improved leverage of their spend even when they operate in a relatively weak power position. In this case the power circumstance is one of *independence,* with the buyer having few leverage resources over the supplier and vice versa. Nevertheless the case demonstrates that if the buyer is able to improve their current internal management of demand then a misaligned and sub-optimal buyer and supplier relationship can be transformed to the advantage of the buyer, without any necessary loss to the supplier.

The context of the case

This case concerns a company that sourced its travel spend in a relatively unstructured way. The company had many different business units, all of which could decide which carriers they could use to travel by air between London and New York. The company is in the financial services business and when the staff travel across the Atlantic they often do so at short notice, due to commercial pressures that require that deals are agreed and signed on time. Most of those travelling are extremely well paid and used to having all of the perks that are associated with a 'jet-set' lifestyle.

Given this, most of the travel was undertaken in first-class (for the most senior staff) or business class (for everyone else), and all of the staff had historically been allowed to select their own preferred travel agents and/or airlines to book and fly with. Most staff had airline loyalty cards that provided them with advantages from the collection of airline frequent flier programmes. Consequently all members of staff were not willing to countenance any consolidation of expenditure and preferred airline policy within the company and as result the current spend was highly fragmented with over six suppliers being used.

The company had, however, recently suffered serious financial problems associated with the collapse of the dot-com bubble and the ending of the merger and acquisition boom of the late 1990s. The supply market was also undergoing rapid change, with the Internet eroding the position of travel agents and providing airlines with the opportunity of selling direct to customers. There had also been a massive decline in demand for air travel on the Atlantic route, associated with the 9/11 tragedy and the ending of the long-boom of the 1990s. As a result there were numerous carriers facing intensive competition for travellers of all kinds on the New York – London route, all of which were desperate for customers.

Alignment and misalignment of the buyer and supplier in the relationship

As Figure 6.2 demonstrates, the alignment of the buyer and supplier in this relationship was clearly misaligned and sub-optimal. The buyer and supplier could quite easily transform this outcome even though collaboration between the two parties is not required. All that was required for alignment was for a renegotiated arm's-length relationship to be constructed by the buyer and one or two suppliers.

The consequence of the buying company's staff making their own sourcing decisions for air travel was that most of them flew with their own preferred carriers because they were locked-in to the carriers frequent flier programmes. This created a power situation of *interdependence*, despite the fact that in reality the power of the buyer and supplier should objectively be *independence*. This arose because there were many potential buyers and many potential carriers, all of which offer relatively similar packages.

The other reason that interdependence occurred was because the individual corporate buyer was also paying premium prices for air travel. Thus, on the London–New York route the company was normally paying full fare prices even though it had a relatively large spend (when compared with the one-off individual and corporate travellers), with many staff regularly crossing the Atlantic on a weekly basis. This meant that the buying company was, in effect, allowing their staff to maintain their own personally desired functionality, but having to pay an inflated price than would be possible if a more professional approach was taken to sourcing.

The result of the existing sourcing decision was that suppliers were perceived as highly competent by most staff in the buying company but, from a commercial point of view, each carrier was able to make higher than normal returns from their relationship with the buyer given their level of regular spend. Thus the suppliers were all *competent but not congruent* under the existing sourcing strategy. The buyer was therefore operating with an unfocused *non-adversarial arm's-length* relationship management style.

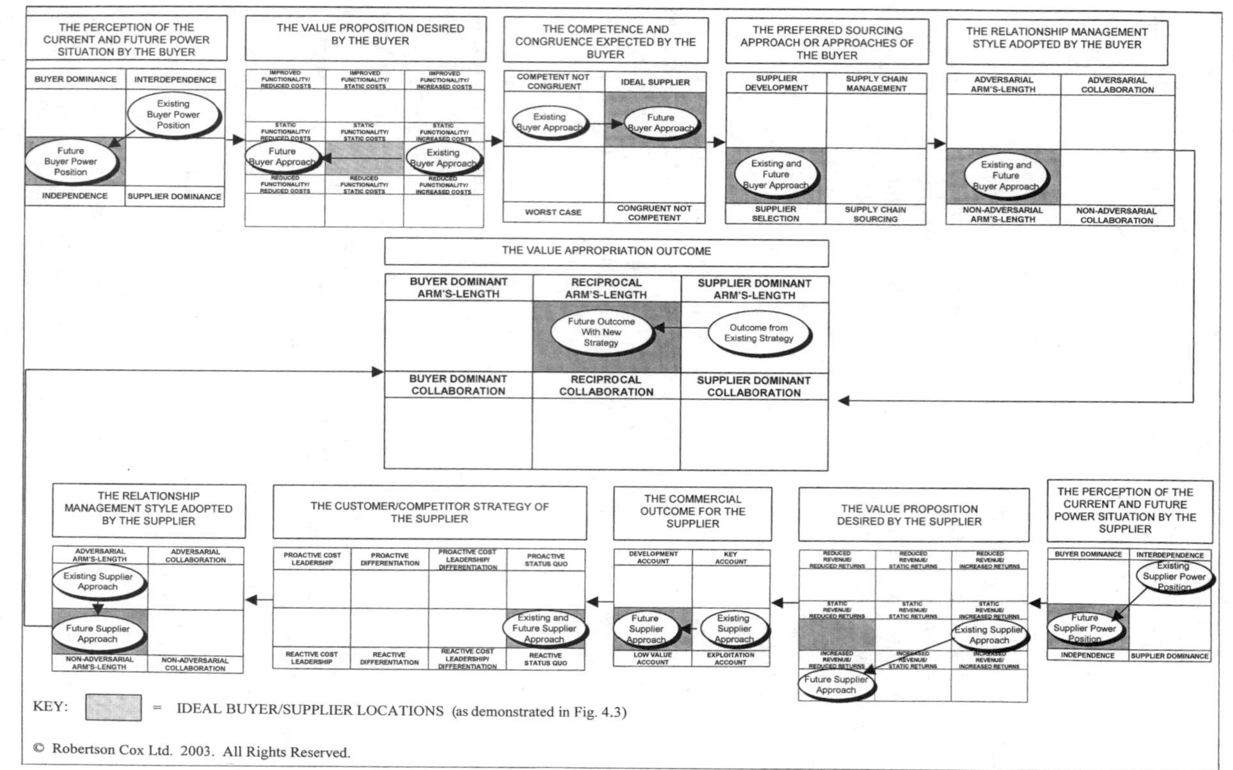
THE PERCEPTION OF THE CURRENT AND FUTURE POWER SITUATION BY THE BUYER
BUYER DOMINANCE
INTERDEPENDENCE
INDEPENDENCE
SUPPLIER DOMINANCE
Existing Buyer Power Position
Future Buyer Power Position
THE VALUE PROPOSITION DESIRED BY THE BUYER
IMPROVED FUNCTIONALITY/ REDUCED COSTS
IMPROVED FUNCTIONALITY/ STATIC COSTS
IMPROVED FUNCTIONALITY/ INCREASED COSTS
STATIC FUNCTIONALITY/ REDUCED COSTS
STATIC FUNCTIONALITY/ STATIC COSTS
STATIC FUNCTIONALITY/ INCREASED COSTS
REDUCED FUNCTIONALITY/ REDUCED COSTS
REDUCED FUNCTIONALITY/ STATIC COSTS
REDUCED FUNCTIONALITY/ INCREASED COSTS
Future Buyer Approach
Existing Buyer Approach
THE COMPETENCE AND CONGRUENCE EXPECTED BY THE BUYER
COMPETENT NOT CONGRUENT
IDEAL SUPPLIER
WORST CASE
CONGRUENT NOT COMPETENT
Existing Buyer Approach
Future Buyer Approach
THE PREFERRED SOURCING APPROACH OR APPROACHES OF THE BUYER
SUPPLIER DEVELOPMENT
SUPPLY CHAIN MANAGEMENT
SUPPLIER SELECTION
SUPPLY CHAIN SOURCING
Existing and Future Buyer Approach
THE RELATIONSHIP MANAGEMENT STYLE ADOPTED BY THE BUYER
ADVERSARIAL ARM'S-LENGTH
ADVERSARIAL COLLABORATION
NON-ADVERSARIAL ARM'S-LENGTH
NON-ADVERSARIAL COLLABORATION
Existing and Future Buyer Approach
THE VALUE APPROPRIATION OUTCOME
BUYER DOMINANT ARM'S-LENGTH
RECIPROCAL ARM'S-LENGTH
SUPPLIER DOMINANT ARM'S-LENGTH
Future Outcome With New Strategy
Outcome from Existing Strategy
BUYER DOMINANT COLLABORATION
RECIPROCAL COLLABORATION
SUPPLIER DOMINANT COLLABORATION
THE RELATIONSHIP MANAGEMENT STYLE ADOPTED BY THE SUPPLIER
ADVERSARIAL ARM'S-LENGTH
ADVERSARIAL COLLABORATION
Existing Supplier Approach
Future Supplier Approach
NON-ADVERSARIAL ARM'S-LENGTH
NON-ADVERSARIAL COLLABORATION
THE CUSTOMER/COMPETITOR STRATEGY OF THE SUPPLIER
PROACTIVE COST LEADERSHIP
PROACTIVE DIFFERENTIATION
PROACTIVE COST LEADERSHIP/ DIFFERENTIATION
PROACTIVE STATUS QUO
Existing and Future Supplier Approach
REACTIVE COST LEADERSHIP
REACTIVE DIFFERENTIATION
REACTIVE COST LEADERSHIP/ DIFFERENTIATION
REACTIVE STATUS QUO
THE COMMERCIAL OUTCOME FOR THE SUPPLIER
DEVELOPMENT ACCOUNT
KEY ACCOUNT
Future Supplier Approach
Existing Supplier Approach
LOW VALUE ACCOUNT
EXPLOITATION ACCOUNT
THE VALUE PROPOSITION DESIRED BY THE SUPPLIER
REDUCED REVENUE/ REDUCED RETURNS
REDUCED REVENUE/ STATIC RETURNS
REDUCED REVENUE/ INCREASED RETURNS
STATIC REVENUE/ REDUCED RETURNS
STATIC REVENUE/ STATIC RETURNS
STATIC REVENUE/ INCREASED RETURNS
Existing Supplier Approach
INCREASED REVENUE/ REDUCED RETURNS
INCREASED REVENUE/ STATIC RETURNS
INCREASED REVENUE/ INCREASED RETURNS
Future Supplier Approach
THE PERCEPTION OF THE CURRENT AND FUTURE POWER SITUATION BY THE SUPPLIER
BUYER DOMINANCE
INTERDEPENDENCE
Existing Supplier Power Position
Future Supplier Power Position
INDEPENDENCE
SUPPLIER DOMINANCE
KEY: = IDEAL BUYER/SUPPLIER LOCATIONS (as demonstrated in Fig. 4.3)

The outcome was a *supplier-dominant arm's-length* relationship. The suppliers were achieving returns that were above what they would have received if the buyer had been able to consolidate the spend effectively internally and focus it on one or two preferred suppliers. In effect the suppliers were providing the basic *reactive status quo* service they were providing to all of their customers, but instead of being forced to provide better value for money they were able to take advantage of the buyer and operate in the *interdependence* power scenario (due to the lock-in of the frequent flier programme) and with an *exploitation customer account* approach. This was because all of the suppliers were achieving higher returns from the same basic supply offering, and operating an *adversarial arm's-length* relationship management style with the individual corporate buyers.

Strategies for improving relationship alignment

Once the buying company came under severe financial and commercial pressure it was obvious that the existing strategy of autonomy for staff would have to be rescinded. The result was a decision at the highest level in the company that all air travel spend would be managed in the future through the agreements negotiated by the procurement function, and that all non-compliant travel would be a direct charge against the budgets of each business unit, with financial consequences for the salaries and bonuses of all staff indulging in non-compliant behaviour.

This immediately focused the minds of the staff internally and provided the procurement function with the capability to offer compliant spend to the air carriers. Having organised a standard tender process with the major airlines the buyer's procurement function was able to negotiate a much cheaper deal by selecting two preferred suppliers, who were guaranteed a minimum of 35 per cent of the buyer's business. This minimum figure for each airline was ascertained by analysing the past consequences of individual sourcing decisions. The cost of business-class travel was reduced by a third and first-class by 20 per cent with both carriers on the London–New York route, and all of the staff were awarded the highest level of frequent flier club membership.

This case demonstrates that although the buyer could not move out of the *independence* power situation, by consolidating their spend and using this to leverage the existing suppliers in the market, they were able to achieve a significant improvement in alignment and savings. The successful suppliers were therefore forced to accept lower returns and a non-adversarial relationship management style. In return, of course, each supplier was guaranteed a much higher share of the available revenue from the buyer. This implies a better value for money deal for the buyer aligned with higher business revenue, with lower returns (a potential source of tension in the future) for the supplier.

6.3 Misaligned and sub-optimal arm's-length supplier dominance: the pipeline case

This case shows how a dominant supplier can sometimes lose control of its power position, and significant revenue opportunities, by adopting an arm's-length approach to relationship management with a customer, who is then able to use the supplier's infrastructure to build a successful business on the back of the supplier. The case also demonstrates that the supplier merely has to negotiate a flexible pricing agreement on the use of its infrastructure to achieve control over the buyer's behaviour.

The context of the case

This case involves the operator of a pipeline. The pipeline was the only source of oil for the capital of a country. The pipeline connected the oil terminals on the coast with the capital, and it was 300 miles long. It had a capacity that was double the capacity requirement of the operator, who needed the oil for the generation of electricity in its own nationally owned power stations. The operator was a quasi-public utility power company that worked with the national government to set electricity prices in the country. These prices were effectively set by the price of oil on the world market (which is highly volatile), the taxation levels set by the government, plus a bureaucratic charge set to cover the costs of the power company that operated the pipeline.

The country had no oil industry of its own and had to import all oil and gas from overseas for domestic use. The power company built an over-sized pipeline in anticipation of an increasing population, requiring the import eventually of more oil for use in the power generation business. The power company recognised that the under-utilised capacity represented a potential revenue opportunity because of the need to ship oil to the capital for other uses, and it had entered into an exclusive five-year agreement with an oil company to allow them to use the pipeline capacity. This had been set at an agreed fixed price for use, with the oil company operating on the assumption that they would pay for full use of the available capacity, even if full use was not required.

The supplier in this case – the power company – believed that they were in the *supplier dominance* position because they had a five-year agreement that guaranteed them revenue, even if the buyer did not use the pipeline. Unfortunately the supplier was not aware of the real profitability for the oil company of having access to the pipeline. The benefit of the pipeline access for the buyer was the fact that the population of the capital of the country was expanding rapidly and its disposable income was increasing. This led to a continual rising demand for the use of oil products, in the form of car use and for industrial manufacturing uses. The oil company, therefore, effectively dominated the supply of oil to the capital and also had a major chemicals production facility located close to the capital which was dependent on the pipeline for the supply of raw materials for its own manufacturing processes.

These factors, plus the fact that the costs of building an alternative pipeline or shipping oil to the capital by road was so prohibitive, created effective barriers to market entry for other oil companies. The capital costs required to build an alternative pipeline would take so many years to repay that the cost of oil shipped would always be much higher (or profits much lower) if other oil companies attempted to enter the market. This meant that the pipeline effectively provided a monopoly source of oil for the capital, for car and manufacturing industry use.

Although the supplier felt they were dominant, because they had a reasonably long-term agreement to provide oil at a fixed price, in fact the power structure was buyer-dominant. The power company had not appreciated that the price agreed by them at the beginning of the five-year agreement had been set at the lower end of the oil price cycle. The oil company had negotiated a deal for use that was based on the oil prices in the market at that time, which were historically low, and there was no mechanism in the contract to flexibly adjust pricing if the oil price increased. Furthermore, the power company had placed no stipulations in the contract to force the oil company to reveal the profitability of its operations on a quarterly or even annual basis. The result was that, due to rising oil prices and the quasi-monopoly supply position that the oil company enjoyed, it was earning profit margins in the 20 to 30 per cent range.

The supplier eventually came to understand that it was not in the *supplier dominance* situation when it employed a consulting company to review its negotiating position when the five-year contract came up for renewal. The consulting company quickly demonstrated to the supplier that the buying company was making large profits because of the increase in oil prices relative to the original pricing structure put in place. Performance data also demonstrated that the oil company had been using the pipeline at full capacity.

In the contract negotiation preparation period it also became apparent that the customer in this case was very keen to sign a very long-term deal on the same terms as initially agreed. Indeed, the buyer was happy to sign a twenty-year deal if this was acceptable to the government and the power company. This clearly demonstrated that the buyer recognised that they were in the *buyer dominance* position with an uninformed supplier, who did not fully understand the true value of the assets they managed.

Once the true value of the pipeline was explained to the supplier it was possible to move the relationship very quickly to a situation of *supplier dominance*. This was achieved with the acceptance (however reluctant) of the buyer, and demonstrated that the supplier had been significantly under-utilising their power and leverage resources against the customer. The power company only offered an extension of three years to the buyer and insisted that they accept a flexible pricing structure based on the movement in the oil price. This was monitored on a weekly basis and prices where adjusted accordingly. The supplier was also forced to accept payment for full usage even if they did not use the capacity, as they had in the past. The national government also reserved the right to charge windfall taxes on the oil company if their profit margins rose above 10 per cent. This required the oil company to declare its local profits in the country for the business division involved, using an open-book costing and pricing approach.

Alignment and misalignment of the buyer and supplier in the relationship

As Figure 6.3 indicates, the initial position of the supplier in this case was based on significant misperceptions about its power position and the type of relationship it had with the buyer. The supplier clearly thought that it was operating in *supplier dominance* when, in fact, the oil company had them in the *buyer dominance* position.

This failure of leverage resulted in the supplier receiving *static revenue with static returns* and meant that they were operating sub-optimally in the *development* customer account management position. The supplier was simply providing a standard *reactive status quo* competitive market strategy to the customer, because they only provided the basic pipeline. They were, however, now effectively managing the relationship with a *non-adversarial arm's-length relationship* management style.

This resulted in an *arm's-length buyer dominance* outcome in the relationship, in which the buyer received *static functionality but with reduced costs of ownership* compared with what the supplier could have imposed

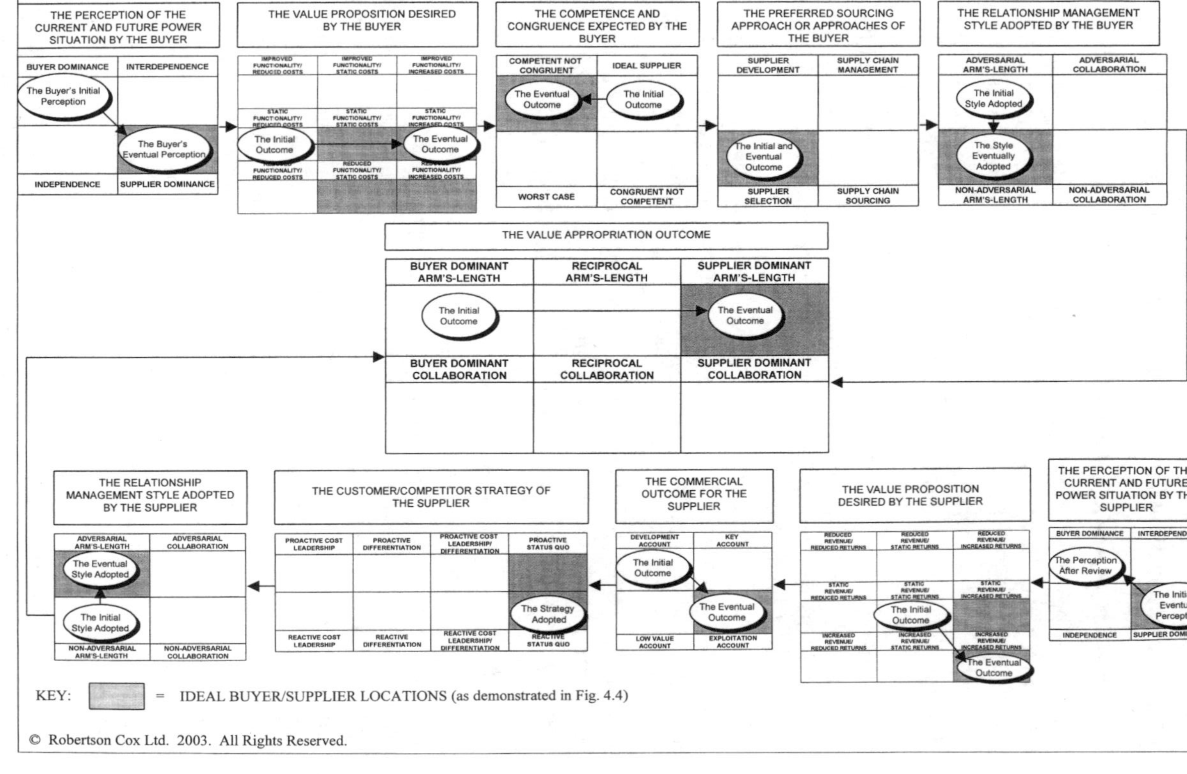

Figure 6.3 Alignment and misalignment in the pipeline case

upon them. This meant that the supplier was *ideal* from the buyer's point of view because they allowed them to make very high profit margins. This was achieved with minimal effort by the buyer who adopted an *adversarial arm's-length* relationship management style after *supplier selection.*

Strategies for improving relationship alignment

Once the supplier was apprised of their myopia and the opportunity for them to leverage their power resources more effectively, a more aligned relationship, given the objective power circumstance, was created during the contract renewal process. Essentially the supplier was able to shift the power relationship into the supplier dominance by the threat of exiting from the relationship and inviting the oil company's competitors to bid. This ensured that the buyer was prepared to pay far more for the right to have a three-year monopoly use of half of the pipeline capacity. This resulted in higher prices and therefore *increased revenue and increased returns* for the supplier.

Furthermore, this meant that the supplier was effectively moving the relationship outcome into the *exploitation* customer account management position. This was demonstrated by the commitment to a short-term contract and the introduction of flexible pricing reviews and windfall taxes on the buyer's profits. The operational strategy of the supplier remained in the *reactive status quo* position, but it was now managed by a much more *adversarial arm's-length* relationship management style.

The buyer was forced to accept the shift from *buyer dominance* to *arm's-length supplier dominance* because even at the lower profit levels it was still better for them to have a quasi-monopoly position for three years, which they could deny to their competitors. Thus, the buyer was willing to accept *static functionality with increased costs* and recognise from their perspective, that the supplier had moved, to *competent but not congruent.* The buyer also had to accept that it would have to adopt a *non-adversarial arm's-length* relationship management style after the contract was signed because the supplier was effectively selecting them rather than the other way around.

6.4 Misaligned and sub-optimal buyer-dominant collaboration: the construction case

This case demonstrates that sometimes a buyer can over-leverage a supplier to the detriment of their own operational and commercial performance. In this case the buyer had achieved a buyer-dominant position through the use of long-term and highly collaborative relationship management strategies, but then attempted to force the supplier to take more risk. This resulted in the supplier exiting from the relationship and, after an abortive attempt to work with another supplier, the buyer was forced to realign their strategy and work with the supplier on a more mutually beneficial – if still buyer-dominant – basis.

The context of the case

This case concerns a property development and management company that builds and manages large distribution trading estates that are used by large multiple stores as regional distribution centres. The core competencies of the property management company are land purchase and development, and negotiation with public regulatory bodies and multiple stores. Post construction of the distribution estates – which involves the construction of large storage facilities and offices – the property company normally manages the completed development, after selling it to insurance companies and/or pension funds as a long-term investment.

This business was very profitable for the property company, who were able to consistently earn above normal returns. One of the major ways in which these high returns had been made was through focusing on the high-value aspects of the development and estate management process. The lower-value construction competencies were always outsourced to third-party suppliers. In order to leverage continuous improvement in construction, and because this was a regular business for the property company, it had been decided to use long-term collaborative relationship management sourcing strategies with two preferred suppliers.

The buying company in this case realised that, in general, regular clients in the construction market have considerable potential leverage over the multitude of suppliers operating in what is normally a highly contested market. The construction market has many short-term clients, with a multitude of suppliers, all bidding aggressively for any work that is available. Given this, the buying company realised that if they could offer longer-term commitments to two suppliers they would be able to insist on open-book transactions and train their suppliers to be highly competent and 'willing supplicant' suppliers. The buyer did not want to single-source so some uncertainty remained in the minds of the two parties about whether they might lose work. To encourage them even more, a third pre-qualified supplier was normally kept on the books just in case any of the two incumbents eventually had to be removed for poor performance.

The relationship between the property company and its two preferred suppliers became very close and highly collaborative, with the staff of the two construction companies sharing the same office space on the estate developments as the property company. Over many years the two suppliers also became quite close in their relationships, even though there was still some competitive tension in the relationship. As a result, over five years of highly successful relationship management the buying company had achieved significant continuous improvement in cost reduction and on time completion for all its works. The buyer normally paid the two suppliers on a cost-reimbursable basis, with a 3 per cent guaranteed margin. Eventually the buyer decided to increase the leverage in the relationship. This was to be achieved by passing ground risk on all projects to two suppliers.

The thinking by the buying company was that the suppliers had earned reasonable returns (for the construction industry) and it would be appropriate for the suppliers to shoulder more of the unforeseen risks on projects as the price of their continued preferential treatment. Unfortunately for the buyer in this case, one of the suppliers experienced serious ground risks on the first two projects operated under this new, more leveraged, relationship approach. After losing a considerable amount of money on the two projects the supplier informed the buyer that they could not continue to work with them on this basis, and that unless they were prepared to return to open-book and cost-reimbursable contracts, with guaranteed margins, they would have to exit from the relationship.

The buyer decided to let the supplier exit from the relationship and brought in the third pre-qualified supplier. Unfortunately this supplier was not able to 'hit the ground running' from an operational point of view. The problem for the buying company was that over the five years of the original relationship they had become quite dependent on the staff of the supplier companies and their own staff were not in a position to manage construction projects any more. This meant that the property company had serious operational problems when it introduced the new supplier into the business. Eventually the buying company had to recognise that it had a misaligned and sub-optimal relationship management approach with the new company and with the company that had been forced to exit from the relationship.

Alignment and misalignment of the buyer and supplier in the relationship

As Figure 6.4 indicates, there was considerable evidence of misalignment in the relationship with the initial supplier and with the new supplier.

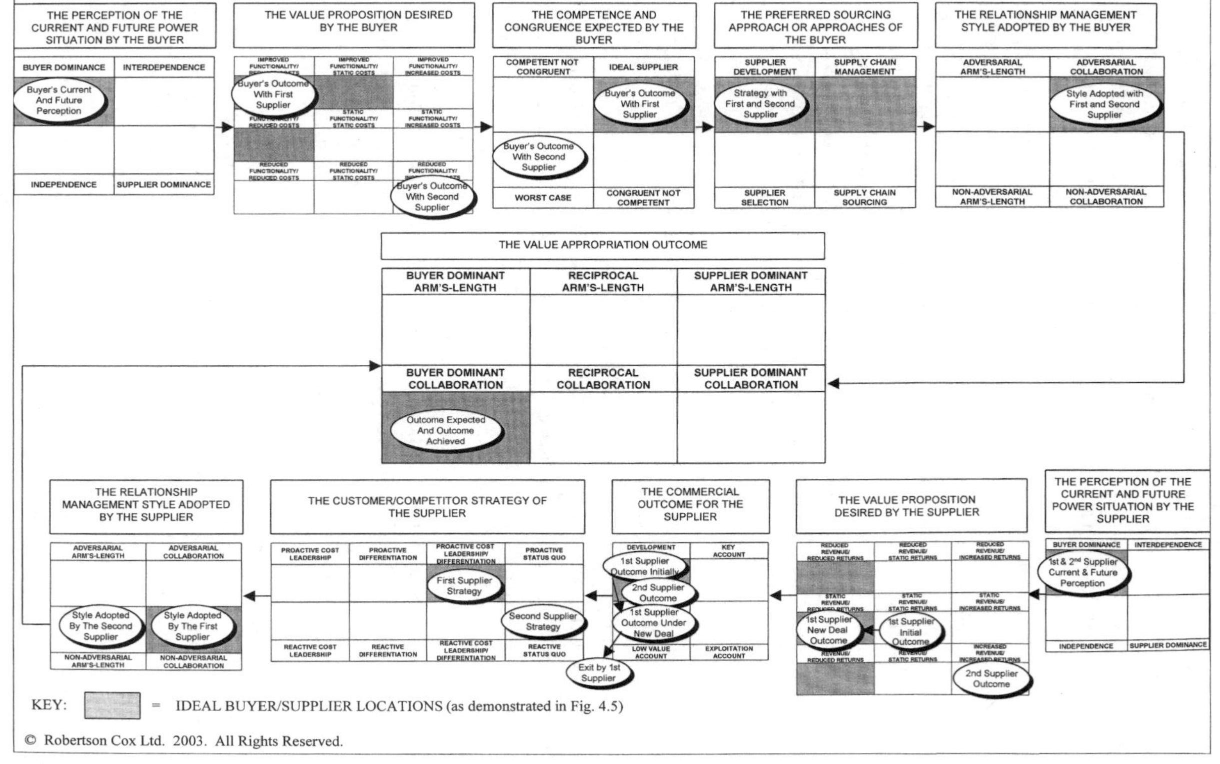

Figure 6.4 Alignment and misalignment in the construction case

The buyer recognised that the power situation was one of *buyer dominance* and this view was accepted by the two suppliers that were involved in this case. The problem for the buyer was that while some aspects of the relationship approach were aligned with both suppliers, other aspects were not. The buyer was clearly adopting the right approach by attempting to undertake *supplier development* sourcing strategies with both suppliers, and by adopting an *adversarial collaborative* approach with them.

The problem for the buyer was that even though they retained a *buyer dominant collaborative* outcome with both of them, the two suppliers did not have the same capabilities. Initially the buyer had received increased functionality and reduced costs from the first supplier, but had undermined this relationship by passing too much of the commercial risk to the supplier. The problem for them was that the second supplier could not meet the high operational performance of the first supplier, or their low operational costs. This meant that the second supplier was a *worst case* supplier compared with the first supplier who had been *ideal* in competence and congruence terms. This was not because the second supplier was completely incompetent. It was a result of the fact that the first supplier had developed a close and highly collaborative approach with the buyer over five years. It would take the second supplier many years to attain the same level of rapport.

It is clear on the buyer's side of the relationship that a serious misalignment had occurred, both with the first supplier and now with the second. This was mirrored on the suppliers' side of the relationship. While both suppliers recognised the buyer was dominant, the value proposition of the two suppliers was not the same. The first supplier had been providing a fairly *static revenue and returns* performance for the buyer (which was still *highly competent and congruent*). The problem was that the buyer now wanted to increase the leverage so that the first supplier would have *static revenue with reduced returns* if ground risk occurred – which it did.

This meant that although the first supplier had historically managed the customer in the *development account* position, over time it was forced into the *low value* account situation and then to *exit* completely from the relationship. This was a major problem for the buyer because the supplier had been pursuing a highly successful *proactive cost leadership and differentiation* strategy, based on a *non-adversarial collaborative* relationship management style. This had provided considerable benefit to the buyer over the previous five years.

The second supplier could not match this performance. From its point of view the new relationship provided an opportunity, at least initially, to *increase revenue* and, given the poor profits they were receiving elsewhere, *increase returns*. The supplier was therefore prepared to work with the buyer in the *development* position, but their problem was that they only knew how to work with customers on the basis of the *reactive status quo* approach they had been using with other clients. This approach was operated normally on either an *adversarial* or, in this case, *non-adversarial arm's-length* basis.

Strategies for improving relationship alignment

It is clear from the analysis above that the buyer had created a serious short-term commercial and operational problem. While it was possible to work with the new supplier to improve their performance the buyer recognised that this would take time. The buyer did initially actively try to work with the new supplier to bring them up to the performance level that was desired, but the property company's staff did not have the competence to show the new construction supplier how to improve.

After three months the buyer in this case decided that they had caused the relationship misalignment to occur. The buying company recognised that they had pushed their commercial leverage too far and that this was having a detrimental impact on their own commercial and operational performance. Given this, the buyer decided to reinstate the first supplier and return to the old cost-reimbursable model, with guaranteed margins, and with the buyer taking all responsibility for ground risks. Once a properly aligned buyer-dominant collaborative relationship had been established with the two willing but supplicant suppliers, the buyer's operational and commercial performance returned to the level it had been operating at within a very short time. The case demonstrates clearly, however, that even 'willing supplicants' cannot be pushed too far, and that no supplier can work for customers for very long if they do not make reasonable profits.

6.5 Misaligned and sub-optimal reciprocal collaboration: the IT outsourcing case

This case demonstrates that when operating in the *interdependence* power situation it is imperative that one party to the exchange (in this case the buyer) does not allow the other party (in this case the supplier) to use collaboration to shift the power circumstance into one of dominance. By the judicious use of the threat of exit it is possible for the buyer to force the supplier to moderate their behaviour and behave in a less adversarial manner.

The context of the case

The buyer in this case is a financial services company, involved in the retail banking and credit card business in the US and elsewhere in the developed world. The buyer is heavily reliant on fast and accurate communications in order to operate its business operationally. Furthermore, the company uses its communication connection with its customers not only to advise them of the state of their current financial balances, but also as a means to sell new product offerings to them whenever they call. The efficiency and effectiveness of the IT system is therefore critical to strategic and operational performance. It is a means of sales and revenue generation; it impacts directly on the responsiveness by which the customer compares the company's performance with its competitors; and the efficiency of the IT and call management impacts directly on the company's operational costs of ownership.

The buyer in this case had historically insourced the IT systems and processes that it required. This meant that the buying company had an extensive array of high-end and mid-range servers, as well as desktop and lap-top PCs, all serviced by an internal software development, maintenance and support and call-centre staff. As the company's business grew, and as the pace of technological innovation in the IT industry increased in the 1990s, the buying company began to realise that it could not keep up with the pace of change because of the heavy sunk and switching costs in its existing IT hardware. Furthermore, the company recognised that the costs of headcount staff in the IT function were also growing, but that the staff were not necessarily being fully utilised all of the time. Neither the software development nor the call centre and maintenance and support staff were required in the business all of the time – they were needed only some of the time.

Given this, the buyer decided to consider outsourcing its software development, call-centre and maintenance and support requirements to the supply market. Initially this required an internal analysis of the relative criticality of the three areas of spend and of the risks and benefits of make/buy. Once this analysis had been undertaken the buyer decided that since software development was critical to the strategic differentiation of the company the ability to create new algorithms around new software requirements should remain insourced. The actual writing of any software programmes was not, however, considered critical and the company decided to outsource this element to the supply market using a list of pre-qualified preferred suppliers – all of these were relatively small players who would highly value the buyer's business.

The buying company sourced the call-centre and maintenance and support service requirements differently. Since the company believed these activities were not strategically but only operationally critical it was decided to source these in the growing IT outsourcing market. After an initial tendering process the company decided to bundle both the call-centre and maintenance and support services to a single supplier using a seven-year non-adversarial collaborative relationship approach. The supplier was a major global provider of IT outsourcing services, with a reputation for high-quality performance.

The fit between the buyer and supplier was initially perceived as ideal, since the supplier was very positive about the functionality and cost improvement targets set by the buyer. The buyer was keen on increasing responsiveness and reducing the costs of ownership of the maintenance and support and call-centre services. In the contract bidding process the chosen supplier offered to reduce the costs of ownership by 50 per cent and increase responsiveness performance twofold over the life-time of the seven-year contract. In order to achieve this the buyer had, of course, to agree to transfer its insourced high-end and mid-range servers, and its call-centre and maintenance and support staff to the supplying company, as well as providing a seven-year contract.

Alignment and misalignment of the buyer and supplier in the relationship

The buying company recognised that since the outsourced services would be operationally critical, and because they were outsourcing their own personnel and internal competence, they would be creating some dependency on the chosen supplier for the seven-year term of the relationship. The buyer felt, however, that if the supply market remained contested post-contractually, that they would still be able to switch to other suppliers if they were not satisfied with the incumbent supplier at the end of the contract. The buyer was also a highly prestigious account for the supplier to win and the buyer's volume requirements placed it in the top two customers of the chosen supplier.

This, plus the promise of a twofold increase in responsiveness performance and a 50 per cent cost reduction led the buyer to believe that, although they would be creating some short-term switching costs and relative dependencies, this was an *interdependence* power situation. The buyer expected that in this situation they would receive improved *functionality with reduced costs*, from a mainly *ideal* supplier, who they should work with in a *non-adversarial collaborative* manner, using a supplier development strategy whenever possible. The buyer's perception was that this was a *reciprocal collaboration* sourcing outcome.

In the first three years of the contract the buyer received virtually all of the improvements that had been promised. Responsiveness increased as expected and the company not only received an initial cost of ownership prize from outsourcing expensive headcount to the supplier, but the supplier was able to manage the improved service delivery within the financial and cost reducing operational terms of the agreement. Despite the initial high expectations and the early benefits that were achieved at the commencement of the relationship, gradually the buyer began to receive sub-optimal performance from the supplier. By the end of the third year the supplier's responsiveness performance was substandard and there were a growing number of requests for increases in wage rates, due to a failure by the supplier to be able to deliver high-quality staff at the rates initially agreed in the contract.

These developments coincided with a change in the supplier's position in the market. Over the three years of the contractual relationship the IT outsourcing market had grown quite rapidly, as had the business of the supplier. Now, while the buyer's business was still highly prestigious and one that the supplier wished to retain, the supplier was experiencing difficulty in serving all of its accounts with highly qualified and trained personnel. There had also been a boom in wage rates in the US market place, and better-quality staff – especially in the maintenance and support areas – were able to earn much higher wage rates than the supplier had agreed to pay in its initial contract. This meant that to service the buyer's account the supplier was starting to use less-qualified or able staff. This was partly because the 'A Team' staff were being used for customers who were prepared to pay more and provide the supplier with higher returns than those earned from the buying company in this case.

It is clear from this that, as Figure 6.5 demonstrates, the initial *interdependence* between the buyer and supplier had over the three-year period moved into one of growing *supplier dominance*. This provided the opportunity for the supplier to begin to leverage the buyer over the price for agreed, or any required increase in, functionality, thereby allowing the supplier to increase not only its share of revenue but also returns. As a result the buyer had to rethink its sourcing strategy in light of the changed power circumstances.

Figure 6.5 demonstrates that initially both parties accepted that they were in a situation of *interdependence*. The buyer was one of the supplier's top two customers and the supplier accepted that it was a *key*

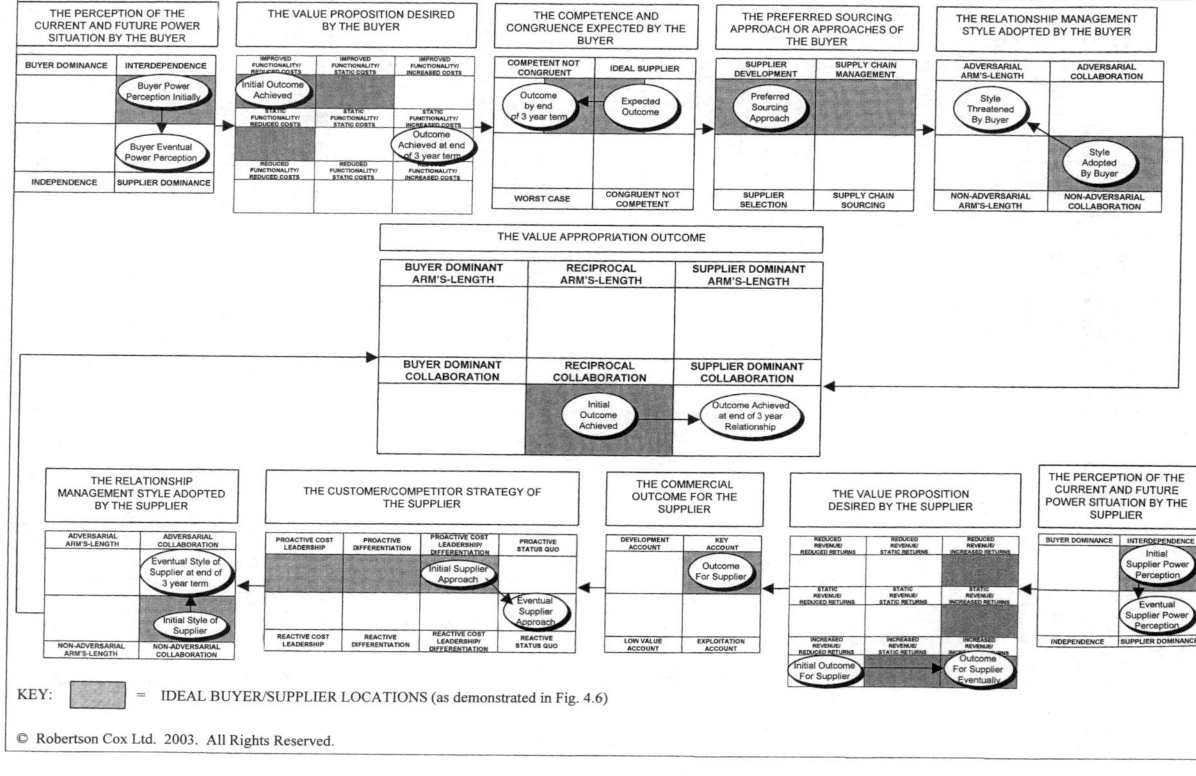

Figure 6.5 Alignment and misalignment in the IT outsourcing case

account. As a result the buyer achieved many of the gains they had expected from the relationship – especially in terms of improved functionality and reduced costs of ownership.

There was, however, always a problem in the relationship. This arose because, in order to win the business, the supplier had been forced to bid low against fierce competition in the market from other potential suppliers. This meant that when entering into the relationship the supplier was expecting to *increase revenue*, but this would have to be done initially with *reduced returns*. In effect the supplier would be working with the buyer using a *proactive differentiation and cost leadership* approach. This was because they were providing best in class responsiveness performance and at a currently low price, with a negligible profit margin. This meant that, initially at least, the supplier started to operate in the *non-adversarial collaboration* style.

Over time, as Figure 6.5 demonstrates, the relationship changed. This was bound to happen because of the strategic approach adopted by the supplier. The supplier was offering the buyer a seven-year deal in order to lock them into the relationship. Furthermore, by de-skilling the company (by insourcing all of the buying company's IT staff) they hoped that over time the buyer would become increasingly dependent on the supplier. The supplier was gambling that if technical innovation continued at the same rapid pace as in the past in the IT market they would eventually be able to provide the same functionality at a much lower cost than that agreed in the initial contract. Eventually, the hope was also that they would create switching costs that were so high that they would be dealing with a relatively uninformed buyer at the end of the contract.

The problem with this approach was that the supplier's own business grew exceptionally strongly in the short term, and, in part, as a result of having won this highly prestigious customer account. As the supplier's business grew and it became more difficult to service all of their accounts it became a source of some frustration in the supplying company that they were using their best staff on an account that paid negligible returns. As a result, the supplier decided that it was now in a stronger position than it had been when the contract was signed and that, given the buyer's operational dependency on the supplier, they could begin to leverage them at the end of the third year of the relationship. This demonstrated clearly to the buyer that their existing approach was misaligned and sub-optimal. The supplier had moved into *supplier dominance* and was now pursuing *adversarial collaboration* and offering a *reactive status quo* approach unless the buyer was prepared to pay more for the functionality originally specified.

Strategies for improving relationship alignment

Given this post-contractual shift in power circumstances it soon became apparent to the buyer that they would have to act differently in the relationship if they were to force the supplier to return to the initial *non-adversarial collaboration* approach that had been agreed by both parties at the outset. To achieve this the buyer had at their disposal a number of potential power levers.

The first lever was their brand name in the market place, which made them a highly prestigious customer, and the fact that they were still one of the top two accounts for the supplier. The final, and potentially most effective lever, was the fact that the supply market was not fully consolidated and the cost of switching from the present incumbent to another supplier was not impossible, even though it would be painful for both sides. The buyer would have to incur operational disruption and a new learning curve with an alternative supplier. The supplier's reputation would be severely damaged if the market became aware that they had lost a highly prestigious account for under-performance and excessive leverage.

The strategy chosen by the buyer to discipline the supplier and to bring them back to a more reciprocal trading relationship of *interdependence* was to threaten exit if the existing terms of the initial agreement were not met. This signalling behaviour – using the threat of exit – was intended to demonstrate to the incumbent supplier that they either had to accept that *interdependence* and *non-adversarial collaboration* was the best way to manage the relationship or they would source from another supplier. Eventually the supplier had to relent and meet the performance and cost targets agreed in the original contract. The buyer had called the supplier's bluff and demonstrated a willingness to incur the short-term switching costs that would be necessary if they exited from the relationship. This signalling behaviour quickly focused the supplier's mind and forced them to stop behaving opportunistically against the buyer.

6.6 Misaligned and sub-optimal supplier-dominant collaboration: the bio-materials waste case

This case demonstrates that buyers can sometimes improve the value for money they receive from dominant suppliers if they first accept their own relative dependency and focus more of their spend on the dominant supplier. Second, if the buyer provides this incentive for the supplier, and also focuses internally on the processes that are sub-optimal and create unnecessary demand requirements, it may be possible to work collaboratively with the supplier to develop both their own and the supplier's capability. In this way the buyer and supplier become more aligned, with the buyer improving operational performance while still allowing the supplier to make significant commercial returns.

The context of the case

This case involves a company in the food processing industry that has a waste disposal requirement from the creation of its consumer products. The waste disposal requirement is controlled by government regulations that ensure that the supply industry is relatively limited due to high HSE requirements. There is also a history of consolidation in the supply industry. The buyer's power situation is further weakened by the fact that it is not a key account for the supplier and there are many other producers that the supplier could choose to work with.

This low switching cost for the supplier was exacerbated for the buyer by the fact that the supplier was also one of the few suppliers that was also a potential customer for the buyer. The buyer creates some bio-materials that can be sold for re-use and the supplier is one of the few combined waste removal and bio-material re-users in the industry. This means, therefore, that the supplier was not only a source of waste removal but also a source of revenue for the buyer.

Given this, it was not surprising that the relationship was in the *supplier dominance* position. The buyer had few alternative choices that met both of its requirements for HSE-compliant waste disposal and a revenue source. Furthermore, the buyer was unaware of the prices that the supplier could charge for re-usable bio-material to its own customers, and, as one of the major suppliers of waste disposal services, the supplier had relatively perfect knowledge of the state of demand and pricing from buyers of waste disposal services in the buyer's industry. This meant that information asymmetry favoured the supplier not the buyer in this case. Finally, the buyer also had to protect their brand image in what was a highly sensitive and fickle consumer market place for processed foods. This meant that the ability of the buyer to use highly innovative and emergent new suppliers was a very high-risk strategy, forcing them to source from well-established and HSE-compliant suppliers to protect their brand image and reputation.

Alignment and misalignment of the buyer and the supplier in the relationship

As Figure 6.6 demonstrates, there were significant areas of sub-optimal relationship misalignment in this case, most of which were based on

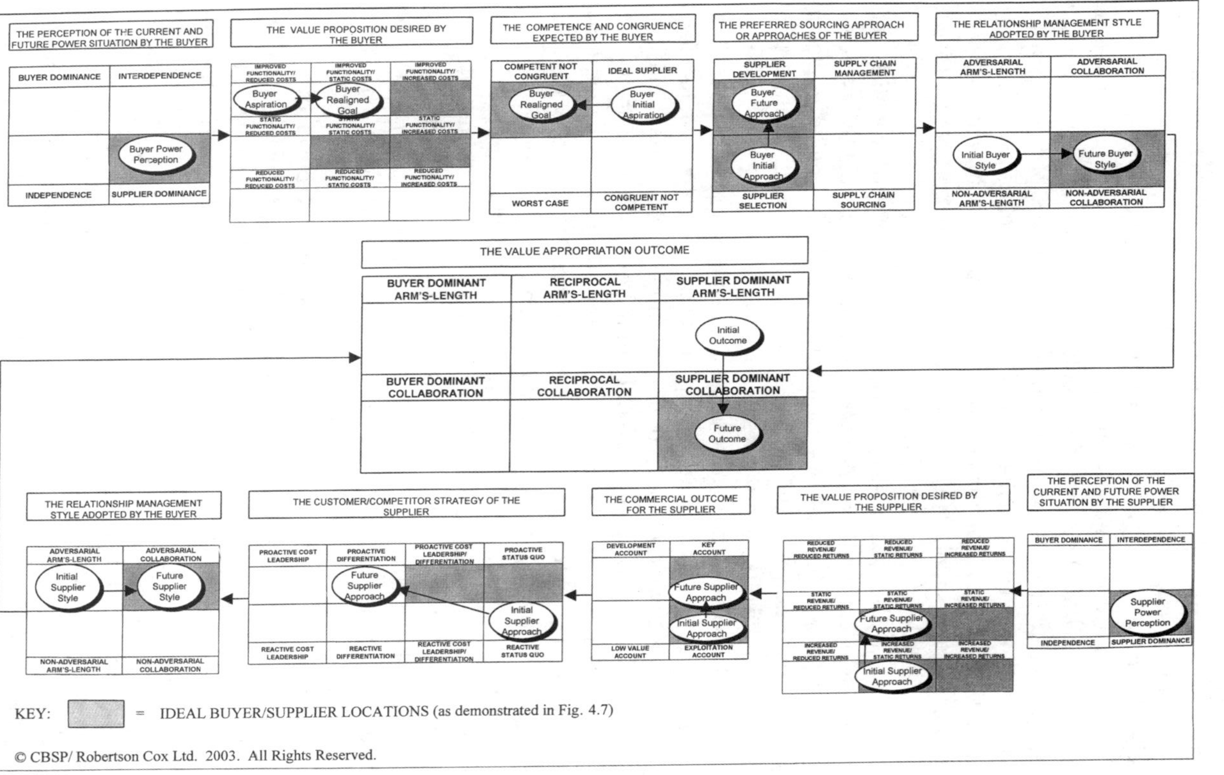

Figure 6.6 Alignment and misalignment in the bio-materials waste case

the buyer initially not understanding the potential scope for them to use collaboration with the supplier to reduce their own internal operational inefficiencies. There was therefore a failure to recognise that *supplier dominance* does not necessarily mean that the two parties to the exchange must operate at arm's-length from one another. Indeed, in this case, it was clear that while collaboration would not necessarily allow the buyer to reduce the commercial leverage of the supplier it would allow them to achieve significant improvements in their own internal processes. The buyer also provided more of its waste disposal demand to the supplier to provide them with a commercial incentive to work more closely with the buyer operationally.

Figure 6.6 also demonstrates clearly that the buyer recognised that they were operating in the *supplier dominance* power situation, as did the supplier. Despite this, the buyer initially hoped to be able to find alternative suppliers who could be leveraged on functionality with reduced costs of ownership. Eventually this goal was perceived to be unrealistic because the buyer came to realise that the incumbent supplier was *highly competent, if not congruent*. This is what buyers normally have to accept when they are working with a dominant supplier who understands that they have control of quality and price in the exchange relationship.

It was clearly unrealistic, therefore, for the buyer to seek an *ideal supplier* in the competence and congruence sense. The desire to seek one was not an error but the current market structure did not provide the basis for effective leverage of suppliers in this way. Given this, it was clear that the existing approach of the buyer to relationship management with this necessary and highly competent supplier was sub-optimal. The buyer was undertaking a highly *reactive supplier selection* sourcing approach and, post-contractually, working with them in a *non-adversarial arm's-length* manner.

This was sub-optimal when it was realised by the buyer that their greatest opportunity was not to seek to end the relationship with the supplier or to challenge their commercial dominance. On the contrary, the buyer came to recognise that any improvement in the value for money they received could only come from acknowledging their own dependency and, as a result, incentivising the supplier to work more collaboratively with them on operational matters. The gains for the buyer were seen as not coming from commercial leverage of supplier prices and returns, but from commercial and operational improvements internally within their own business.

The major problem in the buyer's business was that it had many independent consumer-product-focused business units, all of which were managing their own waste disposal requirements independently of one another. This led to many different dysfunctional operational and variable commercial pricing relationships with the same supplier, allowing the supplier to operate a 'divide and rule' approach to the relationship. In other words, the supplier recognised that since this was not one of its major customers and did not currently provide opportunities for them to grow revenue, it was best to manage them as an *exploitation account*.

In this approach, the supplier was providing a fairly *reactive status quo* approach, with high returns for what was a highly fragmented and internally unfocused buyer. This implied that the supplier was not really interested in collaboration but was operating an *adversarial arm's-length* approach. The buyer received limited operational and no real commercial leverage from this arrangement, although it did have an HSE-compliant supplier who was also a revenue source.

Strategies for improving alignment

Obviously, if the buyer could make themselves more attractive to the supplier it would be possible to encourage them to collaborate on activities that were of benefit to the buyer without causing any commercial or operational cost to the supplier. The way that this was achieved was by the buyer recognising that their own internal demand management processes were sub-optimal, and that rather than trying to leverage the supplier they should recognise their mutual dependency and reinforce it in return for proactive collaboration.

To achieve this the buyer could provide a higher percentage of their demand to the supplier and on a longer-term basis. This provided a credible commitment to the supplier that they would receive *increased revenue even if returns were static*. This would be an incentive for the supplier when compared with the current *static revenue and returns* being achieved. In return the buyer would now be in a position to ask the supplier to adopt a proactive differentiation approach and move over time from the *exploitation* account management approach towards a *key account* approach.

This transformation involved the supplier accepting that the short-term opportunistic approach adopted in the past should be replaced by a joint exercise to help the buyer understand how to consolidate their demand requirements and reduce unnecessary process inefficiencies. The supplier also had to accept that in return for more guaranteed work with high returns, they would stop acting opportunistically over pricing for the buyer's individual business units. As a result of this change of approach the supplier still operated adversarially and the buyer still operated non-adversarially, the major difference being that both parties agreed to collaborate operationally.

This case demonstrates clearly that it is possible for a buyer to cooperate operationally with dominant suppliers, but only if the buyer can provide the supplier with a sufficiently significant incentive (in this case a guaranteed share of the buyer's volume with high returns) to do so. There are, however, still tensions in this type of relationship. The buyer would still ideally prefer a collaborative situation of *interdependence* or *buyer dominance,* and the supplier must therefore accept that the buyer will continue to search for more commercially conducive opportunities. This can involve a continuous search for alternative suppliers, substitutes or opportunities to insource and/or forward integrate against the supplier. The buyer also must accept that the level of operational collaboration that the supplier will be prepared to provide will also be limited by the fear of forward integration and the desire to protect sensitive commercial and operational information.

7
Cases in Dysfunctional Buyer and Supplier Relationship Management

In this chapter six cases are presented of dysfunctional misalignment in buyer and supplier relationship management. Each case demonstrates how the buyer and supplier relationship was commercially and operationally inappropriate, and why the buyer and/or supplier needed to find alternative partners in order to achieve their commercial goals.

7.1 Dysfunctional arm's-length buyer dominance: the telecommunications case

This case is about how a buyer was able to take advantage of a supplier due to the way in which the supplier performance managed its marketing and sales staff. The case demonstrates that from the supplier's point of view the customer they ended up with, although providing them with a significant revenue opportunity, was not the ideal relationship partner. The case also demonstrates that, sometimes, if a buyer has more commercial understanding than the supplier, then the buyer can obtain exceptional terms over and above what one might expect given the objective power situation in place.

The context of the case

The case involves a food processing company wishing to select a supplier to provide them with an outsourced telecommunications service that was critical to the operational and commercial performance of the company. The buyer wanted to outsource because telecommunications were not a core competence and they could not afford the regular investment necessary to upgrade their systems whenever technology changed. The company's thinking was that if they outsourced to a major telecommunications supplier – of which there were a number – then it would be possible for them to achieve better operational performance in information management and storage – aspects that were critical to operational performance.

The buyer was aware, however, that while the telecommunications spend they could offer to a major supplier was reasonable it would be a relatively small share of the supplier's overall business revenue, and that this would be true for whichever supplier they chose. Given this, the buyer decided that rather than focusing on the objective power circumstance of the buyer and supplier – which they correctly assessed to be on the cusp of *independence* and *supplier dominance* pre-contractually, but which might be moved to *interdependence* post-contractually – they decided to operate in a much more opportunistic sourcing manner.

The project leader in the buying company was a very able commercial individual who had operated both as a buyer and a supplier, and understood the rules of the game better than most. The buying company, therefore, asked all of the potential suppliers (of which they short-listed three) to attend individual meetings to discuss the way in which the relationship would work if they were successful. This was a formal meeting in which the buyer explained the operational risks they needed to manage and the suppliers universally expressed their interest in running the outsourced service for the buyer. All of the suppliers expressed a desire to have a five-year relationship. Every supplier offered to beat the current functionality (service levels) and cost performance of the in-house service.

The real purpose of the meeting with the suppliers – all of whom the buyer recognised were competent – was to discover which of the suppliers was the most congruent (or the most desperate for the work). The result of this process was that one of the suppliers appeared to be much more willing to meet the buyer's stretch targets than the other suppliers. The buyer ascertained that the sales team from the supplier in question was extremely keen to strike a deal because they were just one deal short of winning the annual bonus for best sales performance in their company. The buyer correctly judged that the sales team would do anything to win the business.

Given this, the buyer created its specification for the operation of the outsourced service and set the base level service (against which the supplier would have to perform before earning any money) at a level that was 10 per cent higher than the buying company's in-house service was currently able to perform. This was a level that was also way in excess of the performance level that the company required to operate efficiently and effectively. If the supplier winning the contract did not hit the basic performance levels they had to pay financial penalties to the buyer; if they achieved performance levels above this level (which was highly unlikely given existing technology) they would receive incentive payments.

It was expected that there would be a bidding war on the cost of delivering the service and the willingness to accept the performance service levels. The buyer was correct, and eventually the bidding war was won by the sales team that was desperate to win their company's best sales team performance bonus. When the project management team from the successful supplier entered into the delivery phase of the contract they quickly realised that they were not able to deliver against the service level agreements entered into.

The overall consequence was that the supplier had to provide the outsourced service with substantial penalties and with no profits over the terms of the five-year deal. The buyer, despite, at best, being in the *interdependence* power situation, employed their superior commercial skills to use the supplier's performance measurement system against it to achieve an exceptional deal. This was because the supplier gave the buying company outstanding service and was able to significantly improve on the previous performance of the in-house service. The only problem was that in doing so the supplier was consistently penalised because of the terms that the original sales team had accepted.

The sales team of the supplying company were measured by revenue (sales) numbers not on the profitability of the sales made. This short-sighted internal performance measurement system in the supplying company allowed the buyer to take advantage of what should have been an *interdependence* power situation and turn it into *buyer dominance*. The only downside for the buyer was that the frustration of the supplying company's project management team regularly spilled over into dysfunctional conflict as they constantly tried – unsuccessfully as it turned out – to renegotiate the terms of the contract. As one might expect, when the contract came up for renewal the incumbent supplier declined to bid for the new contract. They did not wish to work with a buyer who had been able to leverage them so effectively.

Alignment and misalignment of the buyer and supplier in the relationship

As Figure 7.1 demonstrates, the buyer in this case was correct in the perception of the possible power relationship that could be created by the use of superior commercial leverage skills, but the supplier was not. Indeed the supplier's project management technical team had

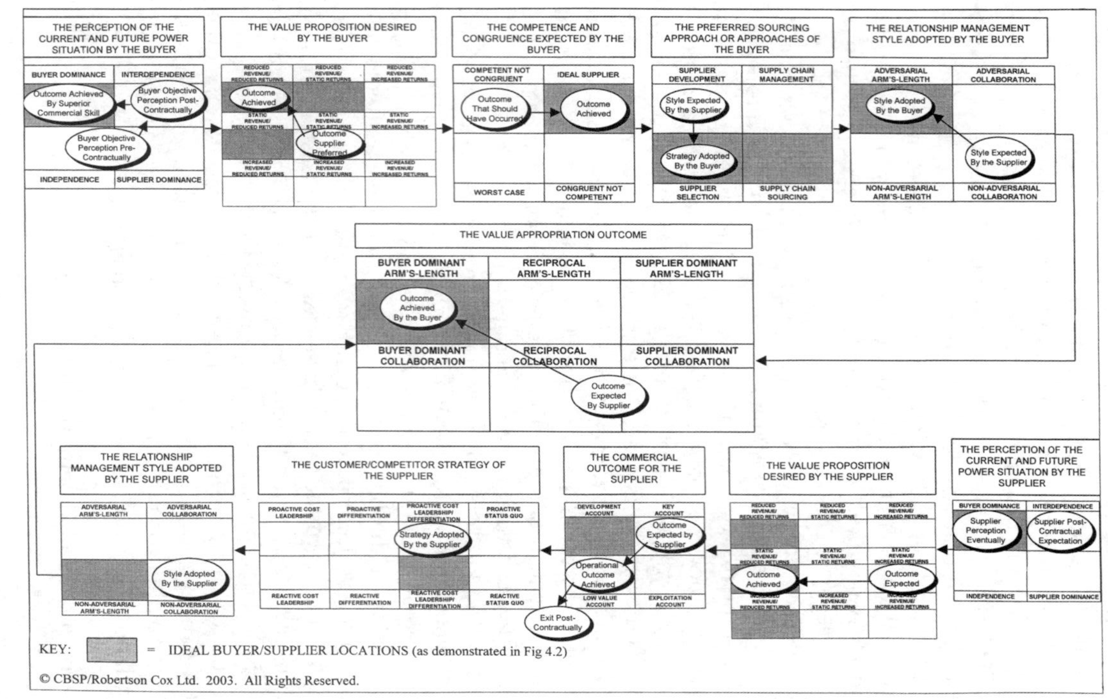

Figure 7.1 Alignment and misalignment in the telecommunications case

a completely misguided view of what the relationship entailed – once the sales team of the supplier had agreed the terms of the deal with the buyer – and was unable to align the relationship effectively.

The buyer recognised that there would be an *interdependence* power situation post-contractually because the two companies would need to work closely together, and the supplier would seek to create switching costs in the relationship. The buyer's revenue would, however, still remain important to the supplier. The buyer was able to improve on this situation in the contract negotiations by setting the minimum service levels agreement at such a threshold that the supplier would almost certainly be forced to make penalty payments.

This situation would, however, provide *increased functionality with reduced costs* overall for the buyer. This was because the supplier would be forced to strive to increase functionality (service levels) to avoid penalties and to make profits for themselves, but they were unlikely to do so because they had already provided a guarantee of lower costs in the initial contract – which would now be even lower because of the penalty payments. The supplier was therefore unable to achieve their minimum desired goals of *static functionality and static costs*.

This meant that the buyer had an *ideal* supplier, even though the supplier had expected to be operating more in the *competent but not fully congruent* quadrant. The supplier also expected that the buyer would work within them in *supplier development*, using a *non-adversarial collaborative* relationship management mode rather than in the *supplier selection* and *adversarial arm's-length* mode that was adopted. This caused the supplier to realise that, rather than *reciprocal collaboration* tending over time to *supplier dominant collaboration* being the relationship outcome, in fact they were operating in a *buyer dominated arm's-length* situation.

The supplier's relationship management strategy was therefore completely misaligned, given the strategy of the buyer. They had expected to operate in *interdependence* and achieve *static revenues, with increased returns* over the five-year term of the contract. In fact they received *static revenue and reduced returns* due to the leverage exerted by the buyer. Similarly, the supplier had expected that they would be operating in a highly profitable *key* account customer mode, but eventually discovered that they were operating in the low-value account position – which eventually encouraged them to exit from the relationship at the end of the contract. The problem for the supplier was compounded by the fact that in order to make any returns at all the contract forced them to operate a *proactive cost leadership and differentiation* strategy, with the supplier operating in the *non-adversarial collaborative* mode. But the buyer was operating in the *adversarial arm's-length* position. This was hardly conducive to collaborative ways of working.

Strategies for improving relationship alignment

It is hardly surprising, therefore, that this relationship did not continue beyond the length of its initial term. The buyer was not really interested in developing a long-term working relationship with the supplier. In fact the buying company was only really interested in finding the most gullible supplier in order to achieve the most effective commercial leverage it could against a large supplier who they knew could absorb any loss on this particular account because they had many opportunities to achieve acceptable profits from other, less commercially astute, customers. This is why the buyer chose only larger companies to bid – they always intended that they would use naked commercial leverage if they could do so. The buyer was also keen to avoid long-term lock-in to any specific supplier and so wanted to avoid collaboration and make the relationship a difficult one for the supplier.

So from the supplier's point of view the relationship was a disaster from start to finish. The problem for the supplier's technical project management team that had to implement the agreement was that there was no way that they could deliver a profit for their company against the contractual terms agreed. Furthermore, the buyer was not interested in working with them to resolve the problem because they had a tight contract that gave them everything they wanted. The real problem for the supplier was their naive performance measurement process which allowed their sales team to enter into a disastrous long-term agreement. The relationship had considerable dysfunctional conflict but the buyer had expected this and they were still able to receive exceptional performance from the supplier at a much cheaper price than they might have expected to pay.

This indicates that sometimes it is impossible to resolve relationship misalignments, however hard one party might try. The supplier in this case clearly wanted to improve the relationship but the problem was that the buyer was more than happy with the relationship that had been created and had no incentive to do so. In such circumstances relationship misalignment is not remediable.

7.2 Dysfunctional arm's-length reciprocity: the reverse auction case

This case is fairly straightforward and demonstrates how new technology can sometimes empower a buyer in their relationship with a supplier when they are operating in the *independence* power situation. In this case the use of reverse auction technology provided a mechanism by which the buyer was educated to the fact that their preferred supplier for a basic commodity had clearly been taking advantage of them for many years. This led to the termination of the relationship and the establishment of a new, but much shorter-term relationship with a much lower priced provider.

The context of the case

The buying company in this case required bottled gases for its manufacturing processes. The historic problem for the buying company was that, while it needed bottled gases on a regular basis, even if it consolidated all of its demand – which it did – its position in the market place was not very significant from the perspective of the major bottled-gas suppliers. The buyer recognised, therefore, that they were operating in the *independence* power situation and decided that the most effective way for them to reduce the total costs of ownership – given that most suppliers can provide an acceptable quality product – was to focus on reducing their internal transaction costs.

The company had decided many years before to work with only one of the major chemical gas suppliers and negotiate prices with them on an annual basis. When they negotiated with the preferred supplier – who provided acceptable delivery and quality standards throughout the relationship – they benchmarked them against other comparable sized suppliers in the market. The buying company was reasonably content with this arrangement because they had established a long-term relationship with what was, for them, a highly competent supplier who appeared to provide them with best in class pricing and performance.

When the new reverse auction technology was introduced into the market the buying company was highly sceptical of its utility, but after attending an auction organised by one of their subsidiary companies they were surprised at the savings that were achieved. They eventually decided to utilise the technology to test the market for bottled chemical gases. To achieve this they brought in consulting advice because, although they knew the major suppliers in the industry, they were intrigued to know if there were any other potential suppliers in the market. The consulting team located many potential suppliers, but a large number had to be eliminated because they did not have the scale to meet the locational deliveries required by the buyer.

Despite this, the buyer was able to conduct a reverse auction with six suppliers, two of whom were unknown to the buyer, although they had passed all of the pre-qualification tests conducted prior to the auction. The auction was conducted and, to the surprise of the buyer, their incumbent supplier was the highest priced. Interestingly enough this supplier's price offerings were not that dissimilar from those of the three other suppliers against whom the buyer normally benchmarked the preferred supplier. The auction had in fact created a real contest between the two unknown suppliers, one of whom was eventually awarded a short-term contract to supply the commodity required at a cost that was 12 per cent below that normally provided by the incumbent supplier.

This outcome caused considerable consternation in the buying company and led them to conduct research into the causes of this result. The buyer eventually discovered that their preferred supplier was a major multinational company with very high overheads and needed to make relatively high returns for its shareholders. When compared with the two smaller and more entrepreneurial companies who had participated in the auction the major players in the market had very high overhead and profit requirements. The smaller and more aggressive companies were nationally rather than globally based, privately owned and happy to work for much lower margins.

This clearly demonstrated to the buying company that, while the long-term relationship with the initial preferred supplier had provided the buyer with an opportunity to reduce internal transaction costs, the supplier was not providing them with best in class pricing. Rather, the supplier was allowing the buyer to believe that they were receiving the equivalent of best in class pricing because they only benchmarked prices against equivalent large players in the market.

The supplier knew there were other players who offered much lower prices but used the high search and negotiation costs that the buyer would have to incur to understand this fact as a form of information asymmetry against the buyer. By doing so the supplier was able to move the power circumstance in their favour so that they could achieve higher than normal returns in this particular market. When the buyer became aware of the reality of the situation they were perfectly happy to work with the smaller suppliers – if they could provide the required functionality required.

Alignment and misalignment of the buyer and supplier in the relationship

By making this decision it is clear that the buyer had recognised that they were being commercially leveraged by their preferred supplier, and they were operating in a sub-optimal power circumstance. This is demonstrated clearly in Figure 7.2.

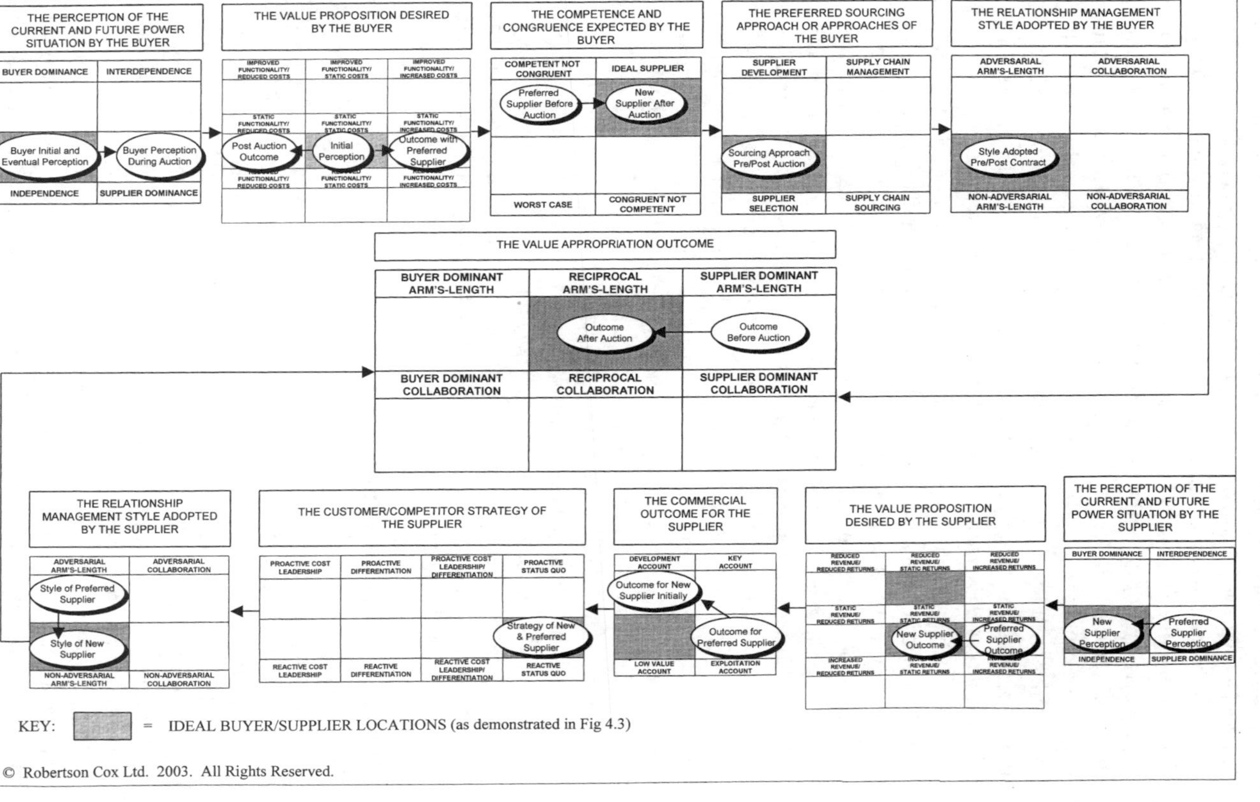

Figure 7.2 Alignment and misalignment in the reverse auction case

The buyer in this case initially believed that they were operating in the *independence* power situation although, during the reverse auction, they came to understand that they were in fact operating in the *supplier dominance* position. The buyer had also assumed that by providing the supplier with long-term commitments they would receive *static functionality and static pricing* – in other words, they would receive the functionality required at the best in class price currently operating in the market for companies with their type of demand and volume. In fact they were paying more than they should have, and were operating in effect with *static functionality with increased costs* with their preferred supplier.

This meant that, although they thought they had an *ideal* supplier, in fact they had a *competent but not congruent* supplier. This problem had clearly been created by the fact that the buyer did not devote dedicated resources to the regular analysis of market trends in this area, and operated a fairly *non-adversarial arm's-length* relationship management style after *supplier selection.* It was not surprising, therefore, that the relationship outcome was clearly in the *supplier dominated arm's-length* position.

The strategy of the preferred supplier confirmed this fact. The supplier clearly understood that it was operating at higher prices than the smaller players in the market and was, therefore, relatively speaking, in the *supplier dominance* power position with the buyer. This allowed the supplier to make *static revenue, with increased returns.* From the buyer's perspective this meant that the commercial outcome of the supplier was that they were being managed in the *exploitation* account position and receiving only a *reactive status quo* supply offering. The supplier was clearly using an *adversarial arm's-length* relationship management style focused on exploiting the benefits of information asymmetry.

Strategies for improving relationship alignment

As soon as the buyer became an informed customer during the reverse auction process the game was up for the preferred supplier. After the buyer had conducted intensive research into the reasons for the price discrepancy, it was clear that the supplier had been operating in a commercially opportunistic manner. Given this, despite attempts by the preferred supplier to explain the discrepancy away on the basis of higher operating costs and the need for larger margins than smaller players, the buyer could not be convinced and the relationship was terminated.

The case demonstrates that opportunism when discovered will normally lead to dysfunctional conflict, which means that there is little chance for the opportunistic party to convince the other party that they can be trusted in the future. The preferred supplier in this case did try to introduce uncertainty into the mind of the buyer by making dire warnings about the inability of smaller suppliers to meet the buyer's functionality specifications. The buyer was not convinced by this argument, and decided that even if this was the case they would rather use any other of the major suppliers in the future than the preferred supplier who had broken their trust.

The overall outcome was that the buyer was eventually able to achieve a relationship alignment with one of the smaller suppliers. This supplier accepted that the buyer should be managed in the *independence* power circumstance and did not attempt to move them into the *supplier dominance* position. The new supplier provided *static functionality at reduced costs* (when compared with the preferred supplier). So the buyer perceived them to be an *ideal* supplier who allowed an ideal alignment of *arm's-length reciprocity*.

This was supported by the supplier's strategy of *static revenue and static returns*, managed in the *development* customer account position, using a *non-adversarial arm's-length* relationship management style for a basic commodity product. For the new supplier this was a major opportunity because, for them, this was a major customer who might provide them with the opportunity to grow their own business against the major suppliers. Therefore they were not interested in behaving opportunistically against the buyer.

7.3 Dysfunctional arm's-length supplier dominance: the insourcing case

This case demonstrates the problems for suppliers who become too powerful and begin to believe that they can take advantage of a buyer with impunity. The case shows how, if the buyer is financially capable and technically competent, it is possible for them to respond by insourcing the supply item completely and competing directly against the supplier. This is clearly one of the most undesirable consequences of dysfunctional conflict in a relationship – especially for a supplier.

The context of the case

This case concerns the relationship between the manufacturer of telecommunication switching gear and the supplier of a critically important component. The manufacturer had historically made the component, but over many years had recognised that this was not core to their business and had decided to outsource this to an emerging highly competitive market. In fact the buying company had assisted many of the new entrants by encouraging them to enter the market and working with them to develop their capabilities.

Over time, however, the market place increasingly consolidated and eventually one company became the leading player. At the same time this major supplier developed some innovative technology, especially related to the connections between the buyer's switching gear and the supplier's components. These connections were far more effective than those offered by other suppliers and this meant that the supplier established a dominant position with the buyer.

Each year the supplier began to leverage the price of the components against the buyer, who was their biggest customer. Eventually the buyer decided that they should have a meeting with the supplier and seek to agree a fair price for the components.

While the buyer had not retained many of the original staff who had produced the components in-house there was still enough embedded knowledge in the company to understand what the basic make-up of the components was, and the buying company had begun to undertake a cost build-up of the product to try to become better informed about the profits that the supplier was now making from them.

The buyer hoped to be able to align the relationship by establishing a power position of *interdependence* with the supplier because they felt that, since they were the supplier's biggest customer, and because their components was of little value without the sales of the switching gear, the two parties should work collaboratively together and share the value created in a non-adversarial manner. Unfortunately the supplier was not interested in working in *reciprocal collaboration* with the buyer and refused to participate in transparent open-book working relationships. Instead the supplier continued to increase the price of the components.

The response of the buyer to this was, initially, to continue its internal work to understand the cost build-up and profitability of the component supplier's business, and also to look at alternative suppliers in the market to ascertain whether any of them could be encouraged to move into this higher-technology area to compete with the dominant supplier. Unfortunately none of the existing market players proved willing or capable of crossing the technology barrier.

Given this, and having understood that the profit margins being earned by the dominant supplier were between 60 and 80 per cent, the buyer decided to insource the component manufacture themselves. It took them eighteen months to achieve the required quality and consistency of production, but once this had been achieved the relationship with the supplier was immediately terminated and the buyer re-entered the market as a direct competitor to the formerly dominant supplier.

Eventually the supplier had to exit from this niche of the market in face of the fierce competition from the buying company.

Alignment and misalignment of the buyer and supplier in the relationship

Figure 7.3 indicates clearly that there was significant misalignment in this case. The buyer understood that they were currently operating in *supplier dominance* but wished to arrive at an accommodation with the supplier in the *interdependence* power position. The buyer's reason for wanting to achieve this was clear enough. They were constantly being leveraged by a supplier that they had helped to establish in the market and were receiving only *static functionality with increased costs*. This meant that, from the buyer's perspective, they had a *competent but not congruent* supplier in return for their current *non-adversarial arm's-length supplier* and *supplier selection* approach.

The supplier fully understood that they were operating in *arm's-length supplier dominance*. This was indicated by the fact that they were receiving *static revenue with increasing returns* from the buyer. Essentially this meant that they were operating in the *exploitation* customer account position, and only providing a *reactive status quo* supply offering. The supplier was clearly operating with an *adversarial arm's-length* relationship management style. This was indicated by the very high profit margins being made.

Strategies for improving relationship alignment

The buyer tried to work transparently with the supplier but found that the supplier was extremely arrogant and felt that they had nothing to fear, either from their direct competitors in the market or from the buyer. It was surprising that the supplier did not think about the threat of the buyer insourcing the component, given that the buyer told them that they were actively involved in undertaking a cost build-up to try to understand the profitability of the supplier's business. Furthermore, the supplier must have known that the buyer had historic competence in this area of manufacturing and might consider insourcing if the supplier pushed their aggressive leverage too far.

Once overtures to the supplier had been rejected it was not very long before the buyer concluded that the relationship with the supplier was dysfunctional and conflictual, and that the supplier would not relent unless effective competition entered the market. The buyer realised that the supplier was not at all interested in any halfway-house accommodation, and since the buyer had the financial resources and the technical competence it was not a difficult decision for them to insource.

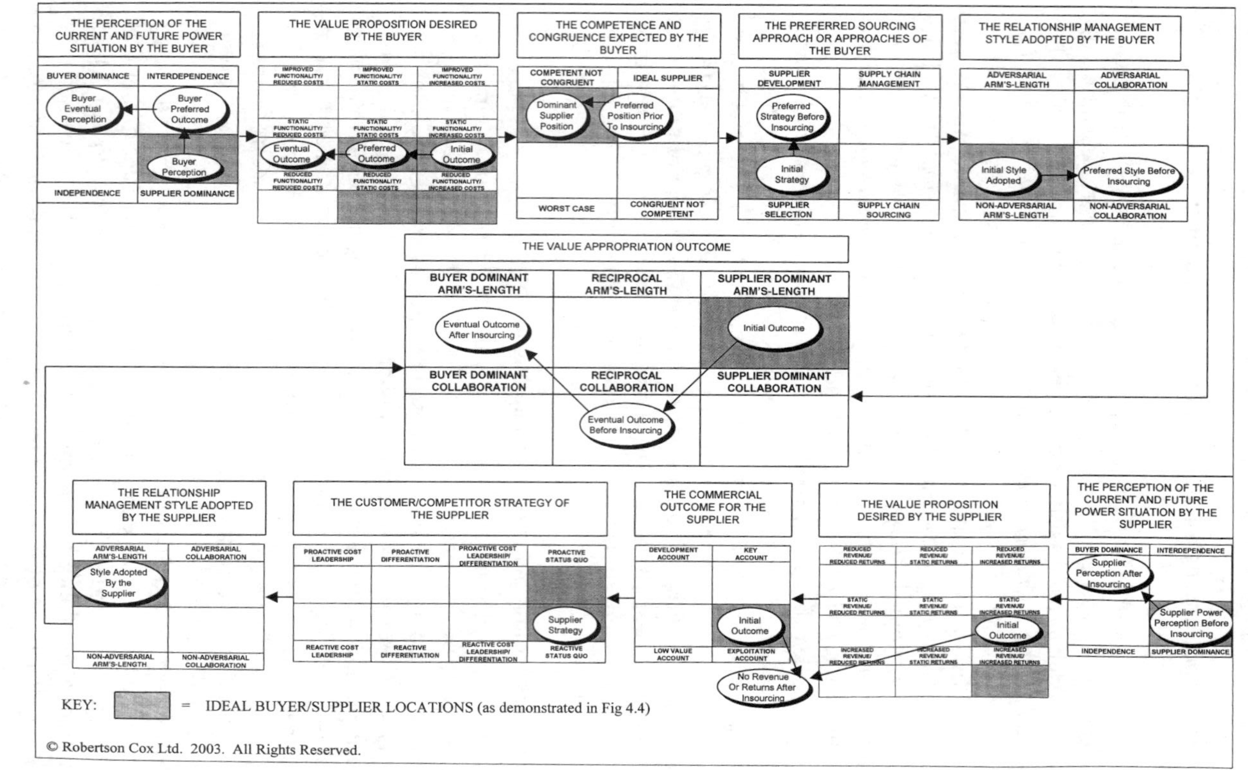

Figure 7.3 Alignment and misalignment in the insourcing case

This case demonstrates that suppliers who aggressively leverage large buyers who have financial resources and technical know-how may very well end up regretting their actions, especially if the buyer eventually decides to teach the dominant supplier a lesson. The case also shows that the major reason for dysfunctionality in relationships is the conflict that occurs over commercial rather than operational issues.

7.4 Dysfunctional buyer-dominant collaboration: the rings and prismatics case

Sometimes it is possible for buyers to achieve short-term benefits in functionality and the costs of ownership, even though they are in misaligned relationships. In the long term, however, the strategy of the buyer can only be achieved if they eventually recognise the need to align their commercial and operational goals with suppliers who have the appropriate power capabilities to deliver what is required.

The context of the case

This case involves a large manufacturing company spending approximately £ 70 million on rings and prismatics for their finished products. These components are made by machinists, who make rings and prismatics from the metal sub-components received from forging and casting houses. These components are necessary but not critical in terms of value add for the buyer's finished products. The company currently buys with limited standardisation and has many different divisions and teams sourcing independently in the same supply market.

The supply market is highly contested with many potential suppliers, with relatively low switching costs between them. Few suppliers are dependent on this company for their business revenue, but if the company could work with a few suppliers their relative dependency would increase somewhat. The company had over seventy such suppliers and one of the major sourcing teams decided to increase its commercial leverage by reducing the number it worked with to seven. The new deal put in place with each of them was for five years, with the expectation that they would work proactively on a *supply chain management* sourcing strategy to bring continuous improvement over time.

Alignment and misalignment of the buyer and supplier in the relationship

As Figure 7.4 demonstrates, the commercial strategy of the buyer was to *increase functionality* (better quality and delivery) and *reduce the costs of*

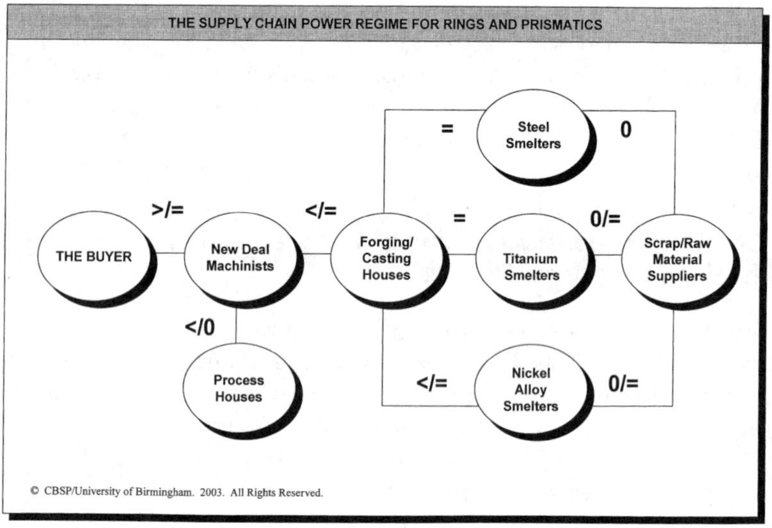

Figure 7.4 The supply chain structure

ownership by working with fewer preferred suppliers, who would accepted *buyer dominance* in the future. The buyer's assumption was that the current suppliers were *not ideal*, but if they worked with the buyer on *supply chain management* activities they would eventually become more competent and more congruent. This, it was expected, would lead, through the development of an *adversarial collaborative* relationship management style, to the buyer achieving *buyer-dominant collaboration.* The buyer expected to achieve continuous improvement in functionality and reductions in the costs of ownership.

The buyer was relatively uninterested in the returns that the supplier achieved, at least at the first stage of the relationship, and wanted the supplier to become somewhat more dependent on the buyer's business. This implied that the buyer was happy if the supplier *increased revenue and returns*, but only if the supplier provided better functionality and lower costs of ownership.

It is clear from our analysis of this case that the supplier actually came close to achieving initial alignment with what the buyer required, expect in one crucial respect. There is no question that the suppliers who were eventually selected were prepared to accept a relatively higher level of dependence on the buyer, and to accept that the power circumstance would be in the *buyer dominance* quadrant. The decision by the buyer to ignore returns, at least initially, ensured however that the supplier's perception of this position would be somewhat less clear than that of the buyer.

This in itself did not create a significant misalignment in the relationship. Indeed, if the buyer decided to focus on returns later, then the supplier would be moved into the buyer's perception of dominance. The commercial outcome the suppliers were able to adopt demonstrates this fact also. The suppliers were able to operate in the *key account* situation because they were able to make high returns. If the buyer was able to leverage returns in the future it is likely, however, that they would have the resources (relative dependency) to force them into the *development account.*

There was, however, a major operational misalignment when the customer and competitor strategy of the supplier is considered. The ideal alignment of the supplier in a *buyer dominant collaboration* relationship is *proactive differentiation and cost leadership.* In this case the best that the suppliers were able to deliver was short-term *reactive cost leadership.* The evidence for this was that when the sourcing strategy was put in place the buyer received an initial 10 per cent cost reduction, but very little improvement in functionality in the first year. Quality was acceptable if not at the level that was hoped for, but delivery performance did not meet the standards expected and there was little improvement coming from suppliers further down the supply chain.

This clearly demonstrates that the buyer's approach had improved short-term leverage in the supply market. This came about because the buyer consolidated the spend and gave higher volumes to a few suppliers, who were able to provide short-term economies of scale to the buyer, while still retaining the level of returns they desired. Unfortunately, better quality and delivery standards were not achieved, so any improvement in this area could only occur through the supplier undertaking either a *proactive differentiation* strategy or *proactive differentiation and cost leadership* strategy with the buyer, to improve the performance of the supply chain as a whole. This would require the supplier to work towards the development of *non-adversarial collaboration.*

Unfortunately, they opted instead for *reactive cost leadership* approaches with either an *adversarial or non-adversarial arm's-length* relationship management style, because the machinists were small companies lacking the internal resources and competencies to undertake proactive collaboration with the buyer and certainly not with the supply chain as a whole.

The real cause of misalignment in this relationship with machinists was not due to the unwillingness of the suppliers to accept *buyer dominance*, nor was it occasioned by their unwillingness to *reduce the costs of ownership*, at least initially, once they had been given more volume. The main cause of the misalignment was that the buyer had failed to appreciate the relatively weak position of the machinists (the first-tier suppliers) to bring about the continuous improvements in the supply chain that the buyer's strategy required. While the machinists were able to work on their own shortcomings in operational delivery and quality, their ability to align the supply chain behind a lean continuous improvement strategy was negligible.

Figure 7.5 demonstrates why this was the case. The machinists receiving the 5-year new deal had limited effective leverage over the forging and casting houses at the second-tier that they were highly dependent on for their own requirements. This limited power capability was occasioned primarily by the fact that there were a limited number of suppliers at the second-tier, who had achieved differentiation for some proprietary products and relative superior competence in some complex production processes. These advantages, plus the relatively high financial barriers to market entry, closed the market to increased contestation. This meant that the machinists were not in a position to leverage improvements in functionality or costs from their relationship with the forging and casting houses.

Furthermore, further down the supply chain the smelters (in particular those involved in nickel alloys) were also in a powerful position to resist supply chain management strategies – especially if the machinists were initiating them. At the raw-material stage the relatively small volumes required also made it unlikely that the raw-material and scrap-metals suppliers would see any commercial advantage from participating in lean supply chain management sourcing strategies.

Given all of these constraints it is clear that the strategy of *buyer dominated collaboration*, with proactive *supply chain management*, could not succeed – especially if the machinists were supposed to drive this strategy through the supply chain. The power regime that existed was simply not conducive for this approach and it was therefore an inappropriate strategy. This is true, even though the buyer initially received some significant cost improvements from reducing the number of suppliers. In the long term, however, the machinists were not in a position to deliver continuous improvement commercially for the buyer. They lacked the power resources upstream in the supply chain and this was bound to lead to conflict over what was achievable over time. This tension could only increase, because attempts to leverage continuous supply chain improvement can only occur when there is

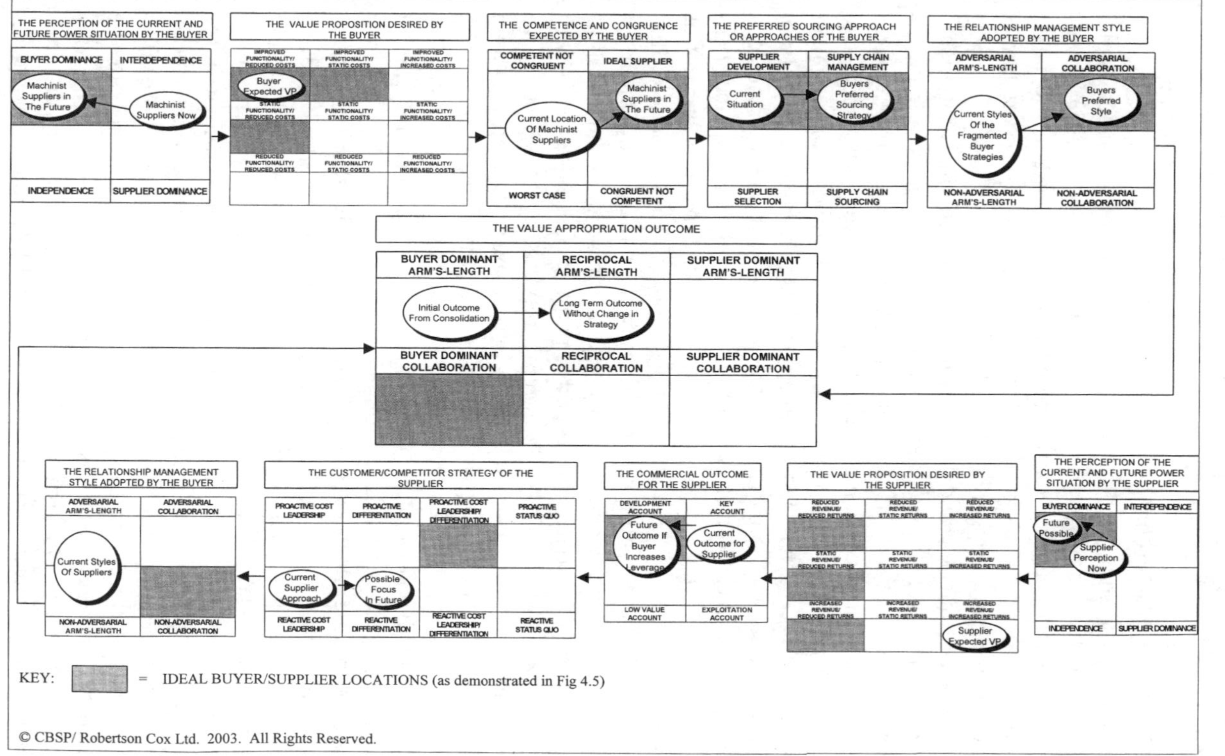

Figure 7.5 Alignment and misalignment in the rings and prismatics case

either *buyer dominance* and/or *interdependence* throughout the chain (Cox *et al.*, 2003).

Strategies for improving relationship alignment

What this case shows is that it is impossible to resolve fundamental misalignments in a buyer and supplier relationship – especially if they result from an inability of the supplier to deliver what the buyer requires further down the supply chain, due to a lack of power resources on the part of the supplier.

Clearly alignment could have been improved in this relationship between the buyer and supplier by focusing in the short term on operational issues, but only at the first-tier. The buyer could, for example, decide that supply chain management strategies were not appropriate and focus instead on more reactive approaches, limited to joint supplier development work targeted on functionality performance gaps (sub-optimal quality and poor delivery). The problem with this approach was that it is only likely to deliver short-term and limited commercial benefits for the buyer. This might still provide some benefits but not as many as would have been achieved if the buyer had been able to find an alternative and more appropriate supply chain management partner.

It seems obvious, given their key role in the supply chain (both as dominant supplier to machinists and as partners in *interdependence* with many of the smelters), that the forging and casting houses would be more congenial partners for the buyers in this case to develop long-term collaborative relationships with. Even though the forging and casting houses had many other customers, the buyer's business was potentially highly attractive because of the brand and reputational benefits of working with this particular customer.

Furthermore, if the buyer was prepared to recognise that *interdependence* is all that could be achieved with these second-tier suppliers, then the adoption of a *reciprocal collaboration* approach with them would probably have paid more dividends than the previous preference for *buyer dominant collaboration* at the first-tier. By working closely with the second-tier suppliers it might also have been possible for the two players to leverage the performance of the first-tier machinists more effectively than if the buyer tried to do this on their own, without the support of the forging and casting houses.

It would appear, therefore, that in this case the buyer had an unrealistic sourcing strategy with suppliers who could not deliver what was expected of them. Such an arrangement inevitably leads to conflict in business relationships, even after short-term benefits have been achieved. A more effective commercial strategy was either for the buyer to change their commercial expectations and align these with the power capabilities of the first-tier suppliers, or for them to find more appropriate partners at the second-tier with whom to leverage continuous supply chain improvements.

7.5 Dysfunctional reciprocal collaboration: the engine controls case

This case demonstrates that sometimes buyers enter into relationships expecting to achieve significant commercial benefits by using *reciprocity* (give and take) in the relationship, but end up in a supplier dominant position. At best, in this situation the buyer is unable to achieve the improvements in functionality and cost reduction desired and conflict is endemic in the relationship. At worst the buyer can become so dependent on the supplier that they can be forced to pay more for the same level of functionality, or even find themselves threatened by forward integration by the supplier as technology changes.

The context of the case

This case is based on the sourcing of a control system for a high-value, and technologically complex, engine. The engine is produced as a component for a product that is sold into a restricted customer market. There are only three major providers of this type of engine in the world and a limited number of potential customers for the final product. The buyer's business position is reasonably assured in what is a currently difficult global market for the end-users of the finished product. This difficulty is manifest for the buying company in continuous demands from its own customers for aggressive cost reductions, but with very high-quality standards. The buying company currently, therefore, only makes normal returns.

The control system makes up approximately 5–10 per cent of the cost of the engine and it is mission critical, in the sense that it provides the means by which the engine operates effectively and efficiently when in use. The control system is in effect an engine management system, providing the functionality required by the final customer, by helping all of the other sub-components in the engine assembled by the buyer to work effectively. In this sense it is both critical operationally for performance, and provides one of the key mechanisms by which the buying company differentiates itself from its competitors. This means it is also of high commercial criticality.

The buyer outsources the integration and assembly of the control system to a single first-tier supplier, so that it can focus on its core competence of final assembly of the engine as a whole. The rationale for this sourcing decision is that control systems are not a core competence, and that by allowing one supplier to have all the spend it would be possible to create an alliance or partnership based on *reciprocal collaboration*. One major problem for the buyer is that there are only a few potential suppliers with the competence to deliver what it required, and there is increasing consolidation in the market. An additional problem is that the switching costs in the relationship with any supplier are high. In addition it would take up to three years to source from an alternative supplier.

Alignment and misalignment of the buyer and supplier in the relationship

It is clear in this case that the buyer and supplier were not aligned and that there is *dysfunctional conflict* in the relationship. Clearly, as Figure 7.6 demonstrates, the buyer believed that they were operating in an *interdependence* power situation and should be seeking a *reciprocal collaboration* outcome. The supplier, on the other hand, realised they were operating in *supplier dominance* and did not need to pass very much value to the buyer and could pursue *supplier dominant collaboration*.

The buyer's view of the relationship was that both parties needed one another and, as a result, they should jointly make dedicated investments in the relationship and work proactively together. Thus the buyer, by single sourcing, provided a commitment to the supplier that it hoped would be reciprocated in the form of increased functionality and reduced costs of ownership. Functionality would be improved by close and continuous operational ways of working between the buyer and supplier. The buyer's own 'stretch' differentiation strategy required that engines would be built within 40 days, with long-lasting components to minimise repairs and a total care approach to customer after-sales service. Costs of ownership would be reduced through greater transparency over 'hidden costs' in the supplier's internal and external supply chain production processes.

The buyer's view was that the power relationship would be one of *interdependence* and that both sides should use *non-adversarial collaboration* as a way of working. This relationship management style should be focused on *supplier development* and, if possible, *supply chain management* sourcing approaches. The buyer anticipated that, while the relative restricted supply market would not allow them to leverage the supplier fully on costs and returns, over time they would become a more *ideal supplier* than their current position as just about competent, but not very congruent.

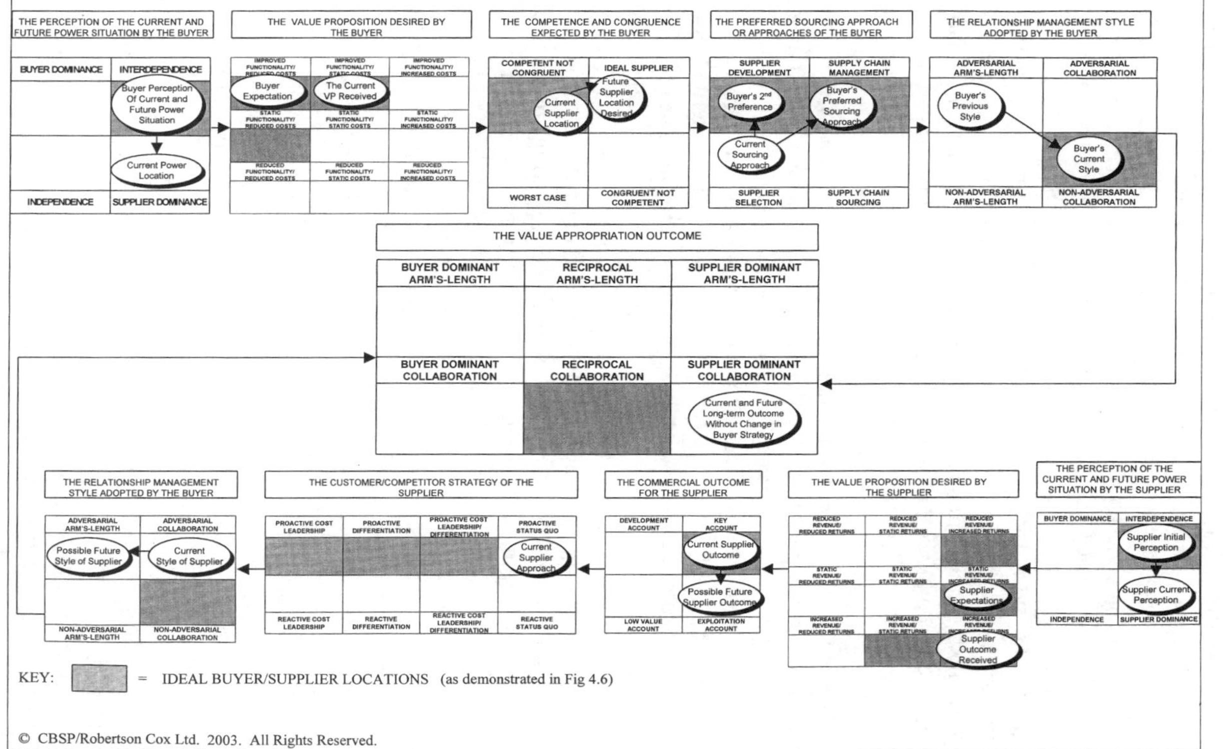

Figure 7.6 Alignment and misalignment in the engine control systems case

Given these targets the performance of the supplier in the relationship was less than ideal. Although the supplier demonstrated excellent performance in certain aspects of the relationship the expected improvements from the *reciprocal collaboration* approach did not fully materialise. In general terms the supplier was better at meeting functionality performance targets than at meeting commercial targets, although it was not excellent in all aspects of functionality.

The supplier performed well against the buyer's on time delivery performance requirements and sometimes was even better than the buyer's targets. The buyer also judged the supplier to be very good at manufacturing and assembly responsiveness; replacement turnaround times in manufacturing; and support responsiveness in the after-sales market. The supplier was, however, judged to be less good at meeting quality improvement and cost reduction targets. The supplier was one of the buyer's three worst performers on defect rates, and although the buyer had set a target of year-on-year annual cost reductions of 5 per cent the supplier's performance had been below target and was now zero.

Overall, the buying company felt that they were being taken advantage of by the supplier commercially, especially in the after-sales service market where the cost of parts is often up to ten times higher than the original equipment price, allowing the supplier to make very high returns. Attempts by the buyer to develop commercially transparent projects – such as open-book costing and value engineering – were also rebuffed by the supplier. Furthermore, the buyer was sometimes forced to take sub-optimal parts from the supplier rather than best of breed. This was because the buyer was dependent on the supplier for the integration of the control system as a whole, and could not always specify exactly what they required from the supplier.

The buyer had misunderstood the post-contractual power situation that would be created after the initial single source decision had been made. The supplier, because of the high switching costs and the restricted supply options available for the buyer, recognised that they were in a *supplier dominant* situation for the current generation of control systems. In this situation their ability to create either *increased revenue and increased returns* (if the buyer achieved more sales for the engine) or *static revenue with increased returns* (if they did not) was guaranteed.

Furthermore, in order to achieve these returns the supplier realised that while the buyer was a *key account* currently there was limited leverage available to the buyer to force the supplier either to reduce their returns to reduce the buyer's costs of ownership, or to pass value to the buyer through increased differentiation (functionality). As a result it was obvious that the supplier was happy to work closely with the buyer operationally but was not prepared to do so commercially. This equates to a *proactive status quo* customer and competitor strategy by the supplier. Overall the supplier was operating an *adversarial collaboration* relationship style rather than the transparent and *non-adversarial collaboration* approach expected by the buyer.

Strategies for improving relationship alignment

There was therefore a significant misalignment between the buyer's perception of the power circumstance and that of the supplier. Furthermore, the buyer, while understanding what the ideal sourcing strategies and relationship management styles ought to be for a *reciprocal collaboration* to work successfully, failed to understand that the supplier must have the same perceptions. The supplier must also be prepared to adopt the appropriate relationship management strategies and styles on their part for the relationship to work successfully.

This case demonstrates the problem of the 'fundamental transformation' or post-contractual moral hazard (Williamson, 1985). This is a situation in which pre-contractually there is significant power and leverage for the buyer, but post-contractually the dedicated investments in the relationship eventually favour the supplier rather than the buyer and create a situation of *supplier dominance* over time. In such circumstances it is inevitable that there will be misalignment in the relationship and dysfunctional conflict. On the one hand, the buyer is attempting to operate with an equally dependent supplier in a non-adversarial manner. The supplier, on the other hand, is operating in the *supplier dominance* situation and attempting to find a buyer who is happy to work with them non-adversarially, while they are providing only limited improvements in functionality and costs of ownership.

At one level the relationship between the buyer and supplier in this case could be made to work, but only if the buyer is willing to be a 'willing supplicant' to the supplier's dominance and work collaboratively and non-adversarially, while the supplier maximises their appropriation of revenue and returns from the relationship. The relationship could persist, therefore, in a permanent state of tension with the buyer accepting a dependent situation and working on limited operational improvement gains, without expecting commercial improvements through significant functionality improvement or cost reduction.

The problem in this case was that the buyer was under severe cost pressures from their own customers, with their own margins under pressure. Given this it is unlikely that this relationship can persist over time without conflict. This is because the operational and, in particular, the commercial goals of the buyer cannot be satisfied given the current power situation and the lack of need by the supplier to pass value to them. In such circumstances the buyer has only two choices. The buyer can either build long-term relationships with more dependent and supplicant suppliers, or it can insource the required competencies and undertake the cost and functionality improvement itself.

This latter (insourcing) approach might be the most desirable option in this case due to the relative commercial and operational criticality of the control system to the engine. The control system in an engine is fundamental to product differentiation in engine assembly and outsourcing it may not be the safest approach in an environment of rapid technological change in the electronics component industry. Indeed a worst-case scenario might be that the control system supplier could eventually have the technological differentiation to allow them to forward integrate against the buyer. This could occur if the control system became the fundamental competitive differentiator in the engine.

7.6 Dysfunctional supplier-dominant collaboration: the logistics case

Buyers can sometimes be too trusting of suppliers, especially when they operate in circumstances where there is a significant risk of post-contractual moral hazard. In this case the buyer decided to work closely with a supplier and outsource all of their logistics services to them under a five-year contract but then found that they had very high switching costs at the end of the contract. This resulted in the buyer operating in a power position of supplier dominance induced by misguided collaboration on the buyer's part.

The context of the case

This case involves an oil company that had historically insourced the fleet of tankers that delivered petrol to filling stations. Eventually the buying company decided that the oil tanker fleet was not core to their business and that it could be safely outsourced to a major multinational supplier of logistics services. The buying company awarded the logistics supplier a five-year contract and put in place tight performance requirements. The reason for doing this was because the oil company relied on the prompt delivery of petrol to the filling stations as one of the major sources of operational revenue. Thus, while the ownership of the fleet of tankers was not regarded as core, the need for revenue was operationally and commercially critical.

After the five-year contract had been signed between the two parties, the supplier offered the buying company an additional and unsolicited benefit as a demonstration of its commitment to *non-adversarial collaboration*. This was an offer to replace the antediluvian logistics software systems currently being used by the oil company's internal staff and to train their internal staff in the use of the logistics company's software system and processes. This software provided sophisticated order tracking technology but required that, for it to work effectively, the buyer adopted this new proprietary system throughout their business. The logistics supplier offered to provide the software and training at no additional cost to the buyer.

The buyer was clearly impressed by this offer and believed that they were operating in the *interdependence* power circumstance with the supplier. This misperception lasted until about nine months into the contract when the supplier began to miss key performance targets. The buyer instituted an enquiry into why the supplier was not meeting the performance targets agreed under the terms of the contract and found that the supplier was having difficulty obtaining qualified drivers at the rates agreed in the contract. This led to serious conflict between the buyer and the supplier, especially as the delays in deliveries began to affect the performance of the filling stations and had a detrimental impact on the revenue flow of the company.

This problem persisted for many months until eventually the supplier requested an increase in the rates in the contract in order to pay for better-qualified staff. One of the major problems was that the supplier claimed that it could not recruit and retain reliable staff at the rates agreed in the contract. Eventually, after considerable conflict and a review by the buyer of the cost of exiting from the relationship, it was decided that they would have to agree to a significant rate increase. This did not, unfortunately, completely eradicate the problem of unreliability and poor delivery performance amongst tanker drivers, even with the new rates in place.

What was clear was that the new rates had been primarily used to inflate the profits of the logistics company rather than increase the rates of the tanker drivers. At the end of the contract the buyer had the opportunity to exit from the relationship with the supplier but they eventually decided they would have to stay with the incumbent supplier even though their performance was far from perfect. This decision was taken because of the major cost of replacing the, by now, fully embedded logistics software system and the cost of retraining the in-house staff in a new one.

Alignment and misalignment of the buyer and supplier in the relationship

As Figure 7.7 indicates, the buyer in this case had misunderstood the power circumstance they had entered into. The buying company clearly believed that they were creating an *interdependence* power situation based on *non-adversarial collaboration*, in which they would receive improved *functionality and reduced costs of ownership* from an *ideal* supplier, whose competence would be improved by the buyer working with them on *supplier development*.

What the buying company eventually received was far from this ideal. In fact it received *reduced functionality with increased costs*, provided by a supplier who was *not fully competent nor congruent*, and who was not interested in *supplier development* activities and rebuffed the buyer's attempts to collaborate to improve operational performance. The outcome received by the buyer was hardly the *reciprocal collaboration* intended but was in fact *supplier dominant collaboration*.

The strategy of the supplier also fitted perfectly into a supplier-dominant collaboration framework. The supplier received *static revenue, with increased returns*. This was because the supplier already had all of the buyer's business and eventually was able to force them to increase the rates they paid for drivers. This implied that the supplier was actually operating in the *exploitation* not the *key* customer account management approach expected by the buyer. The buyer had hoped for a *proactive differentiation and cost leadership* approach, but eventually had to accept a *reactive status quo* supply offering from the supplier. The supplier also adopted a one-sided *adversarial collaborative* relationship management style. It was one-sided because the supplier collaborated only with the buyer to lock them into a permanent dependency on the supplier, not to improve logistics delivery performance.

Strategies for relationship improvement

The buyer consistently attempted to work collaboratively with the supplier in this case but found that the supplier was only interested in one-sided collaboration, as explained above. This meant that by the end of the five-year term the buyer was fully aware that they had made a significant error in allowing themselves to become locked-in to the supplier's software offering. It was this technology, and its embedded nature, that created very high switching costs for the buyer and forced

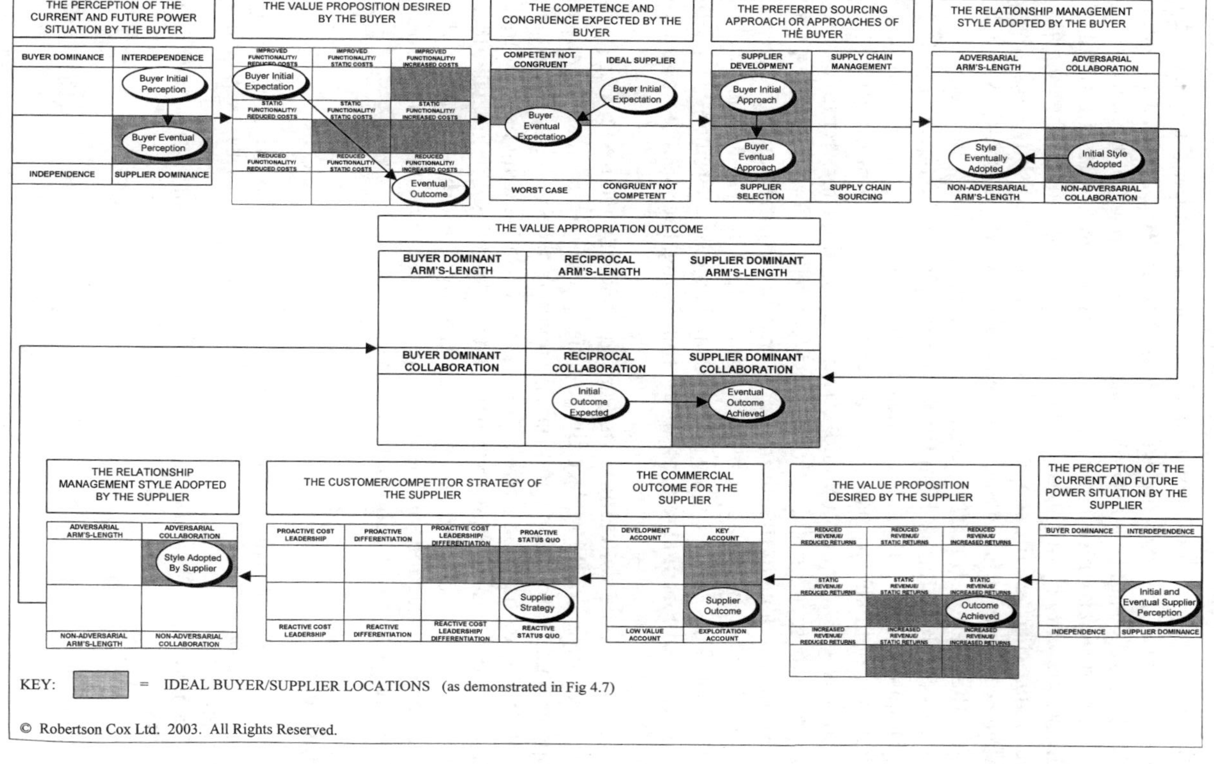

Figure 7.7 Alignment and misalignment in the logistics case

them into the lesser of two evils when it came to contract renewal. The lesser of two evils was to continue the unsatisfactory relationship with the supplier on a rolling annual contractual basis rather than incur the costs of changing out the whole logistics process and software and retraining the staff in a new in-house or new supplier's offering.

The buyer recognised that in continuing to work with the supplier this would only be possible in a power circumstance of relative *supplier dominance*, because the supplier was able to leverage the buyer on driver wage rates since it knew that the buyer would find it difficult to switch from the relationship. This allowed the supplier to make above normal returns for the industry from the relationship with the buyer.

Despite this, there were still significant tensions in the relationship that were not likely to disappear quickly. The buyer definitely wanted to terminate the relationship and was merely waiting for technology to improve to such an extent that the increased performance from the software available in the future would make the switching costs acceptable, when taken into account with significantly improved delivery performance. This meant that, while the supplier was able to use lock-in to leverage above normal returns for the time being, the supplier was walking a tightrope.

As soon as the switching costs were substantially reduced it was clear that the buyer would replace the supplier because of their sub-optimal operational performance and naked commercial leverage of the situation that they had engineered. Once again this case demonstrates that the primary cause of relationship breakdown and dysfunctional conflict is the commercial leverage of one party by the other party in the exchange transaction, although in this case the poor operational performance was also a contributory factor.

References

Cox, A., Ireland, P., Lonsdale, C., Sanderson, J. and Watson, G. (2003) *Supply Chain Management: A Guide to Best Practice* (London: Financial Times/Prentice Hall).

Williamson, O. E. (1985) *The Economic Institutions of Capitalism* (New York: Free Press).

Part III

Decision Support Tools for Improving Business Relationships

8
A Way Forward for Managers

We hope that theoretical discussion and empirical case evidence provided in this volume has explained why it is that many business relationships fail to deliver what was expected. The problem for mangers who engage in buyer–supplier exchange relationships is that there are many variables that must be in place before a relationship can be successfully aligned. Indeed, the discussion in previous chapters has emphasised that misalignment of business relationships is a common occurrence. This is true whether misalignment occurs because of unavoidable conflict over the commercial goals of the two parties to the exchange, or because there is a 'remediable' misalignment occasioned by misperception on the part of one or both parties to the transaction.

In this final chapter we provide further evidence of the complexity that must be managed internally by both the buyer and the supplier if alignment is to occur in any relationship. Following that, we provide a simple decision-tree checklist for managers to use when they try to align relationships whether acting as buyers or suppliers. In the final section of the chapter we discuss the problem of opportunism in relationship management and indicate what some of the predictable outcomes of opportunism by buyers and suppliers are likely to be under different power and leverage scenarios. The first part of this final chapter is, however, devoted to a discussion of the problem of winning internal support for any external relationship management strategy.

8.1 Winning internal support for relationship management strategies

The need to win internal support for external relationship management strategies is self-evident, whether one focuses on the buying or the supplying company. In all of the cases of alignment discussed in Chapter 5 it was evident that there was a high degree of internal support within both the buying and supplying companies for the external relationship strategies that were being proposed. This does not mean that there was no internal conflict as the strategies were developed internally; rather it implies that the strategies had been properly discussed and debated internally and that there was, eventually, a high degree of common understanding within the buying and supplying companies about what the relationship involved. This is another way of saying that both companies had achieved internal buy-in for the strategy, which also facilitated the pre- and post-contractual relationship.

In the cases of misalignment discussed in Chapters 6 and 7 there was nearly always evidence, in either one or both of the companies analysed, of a lack of understanding amongst key players internally about what the buyer–supplier relationship being proposed implied for the business, which in almost all cases led to serious internal conflict post-contractually. There is considerable evidence, as a result, of a failure to win buy-in within the company by managers seeking to develop external relationship strategies. When this occurs it can lead either to sub-optimal relationship management strategies being put in place pre-contractually, or to serious internal conflict once significant sections of the company are affected by the relationship outcome post-contractually.

Given this, it seems sensible for managers to focus just as much effort on achieving internal support as on achieving external support for their buyer–supplier relationships. There are many cases in which buyers and suppliers are not able to adopt the most appropriate relationship management strategy because of the internal power structures that they have to confront in their own companies, not just those of their potential external relationship partners.

When a manager has to develop business relationship management strategies this will normally require that managers in other functions and divisions of the company also fully understand the impact of the proposed strategy on their own responsibilities. If these managers, who will be affected by, or who need to be involved in assisting with the implementation of an external business relationship, do not fully understand what they must do, or how they will be affected, then it is likely that they will contribute to either pre- or post-contractual relationship misalignment. It is therefore incumbent on managers to fully inform their colleagues about the consequences of any proposed strategy, and how they need to be involved to make it work.

It would be easy enough for managers if this problem was the only one that needed to be addressed. There is considerable evidence, however, that potentially beneficial relationship management strategies are stymied within companies because other actors simply do not understand what is being proposed, often because they think it is irrelevant to their responsibilities and do not attend meetings, or send junior staff who have little awareness of the real implications of what is being considered. As well as an ability to understand the complexities, any proposed external relationship strategy therefore requires the willingness of managers to cooperate with one another.

There is also evidence in our research that managers within companies have varying levels of willingness to be cooperative with those managers who have to devise and operate buyer–supplier relationships. Many examples were found in the case studies of managers who though needing to work in a cross-functional manner to make the relationship successful were not being cooperative. Added to this problem is the further issue of the internal power of particular managers and functions within organisations. Our research demonstrates that there are power structures internally within organisations that can be understood quite simply by reference to whether or not particular internal actors and managers have initiation and/or veto capabilities.

As Figure 8.1 demonstrates, individual managers (and the functions they represent) can have the ability to initiate new strategies, and they can also have ability to constrain or veto the strategies that others may initiate. Logically, an organisational actor who is able to initiate without

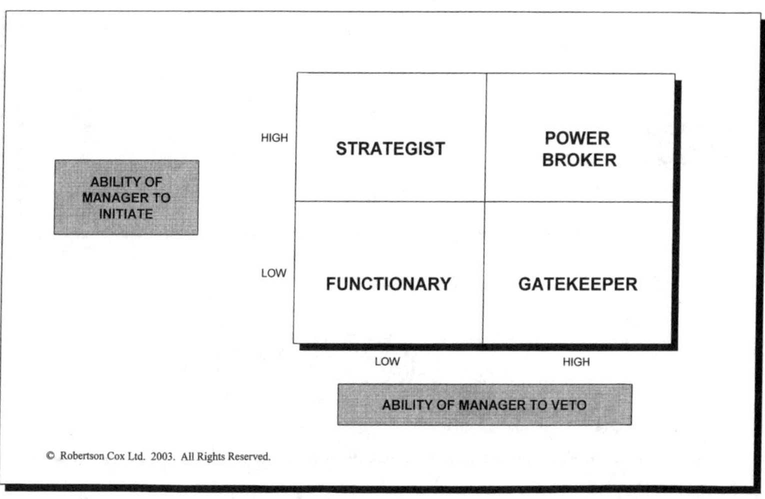

Figure 8.1 The power of internal actors

constraint and also to veto the initiatives of others is likely to have high power attributes in an organisation. These are the *power brokers* in an organisation. Similarly there will be many organisational actors – *functionaries* – who cannot initiate very much and have no ability to veto or constrain the actions of others. Such actors are likely to have low power resources. Obviously there may be intermediary power positions where individuals can initiate but not veto (*strategists*), or veto but not initiate (*gatekeepers*).

Putting all of these variables together provides a way of thinking (outlined in Figure 8.2) about the problems that managers normally face internally when they initiate new relationship management strategies. Managers face complex and shifting coalitions of different actors, all of whom have varying degrees of understanding, internal power capabilities and willingness to be cooperative. In seeking to implement successful external relationship management strategies it is our view that managers often pay too little attention to the need to create stable coalitions of their own colleagues, or fail to address the need to move those colleagues who do not understand and who are currently uncooperative into more cooperative and understanding situations.

It is obvious that if managers are to have innovative relationship management strategies adopted they will have to recognise the need to work with those cooperative managers internally (*key ally* and *ally*) who have high organisational capability to build coalitions with *potential key*

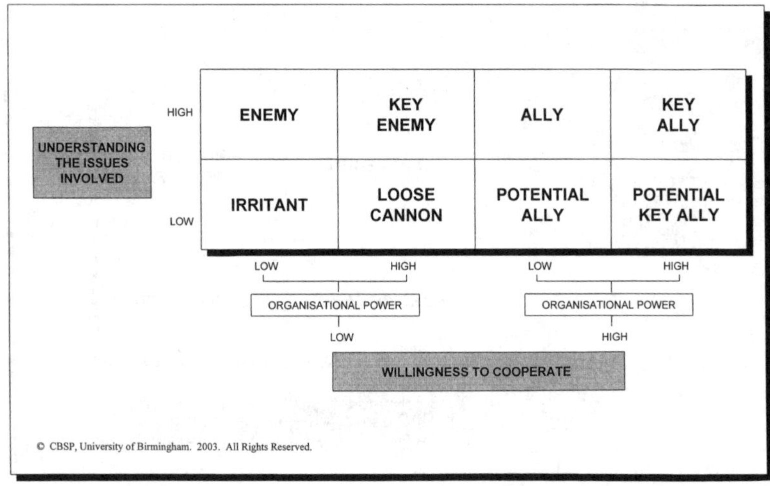

Figure 8.2 The structure of internal power and support in organisations

ally, potential ally, irritant and *enemy* organisational actors. The aim of such a strategy is always to build a coalition to either isolate, or change the mind of, the *key enemy* organisational actors. Our research has demonstrated that this internal aspect of business relationship management is not as fully addressed in the literature as it could be and we believe this will be a fruitful area for future business relationship management research.

There is, however, one further internal factor that must be understood, and that is the issue of whether or not there are any insurmountable internal obstacles to the development of a particular relationship management strategy. Clearly, these obstacles are likely to be most pronounced when a buyer and supplier are thinking about developing longer-term collaborative relationships which involve the creation of dedicated investments and relationship-specific adaptations to existing processes and systems. To undertake the creation of these types of technical bonds, companies have to invest considerable time and resource in the development of new ways of working. Sometimes companies do not have the financial, human or technical capabilities available to allow them to actively undertake a particular relationship management strategy, even though there may be widespread internal support for doing so (Cox *et al.*, 2003).

Given this, for any external business relationship approach to be capable of successful implementation, it is normally necessary for both parties to the exchange to have internal buy-in for the desired strategy to work. As Figure 8.3 indicates, for buy-in to occur there must be both internal support and an absence of serious internal financial, human and technical impediments. If these two factors exist and there is external alignment then overall relationship alignment ought to be possible.

8.2 A decision-tree for aligning buyer–supplier relationships

It should be clear from this brief discussion of the problem of achieving internal buy-in, and from our more extensive analysis of the factors that must be aligned externally for successful relationship management, that business relationship alignment is a complex and time-consuming activity. To assist managers to think about the choices they have to make and the issues that must be addressed for successful relationship alignment to occur Figure 8.4 provides a decision-tree for understanding relationship alignment and misalignment.

As the decision-tree demonstrates, buyers and suppliers have to think not just about their own requirements but also those of their exchange

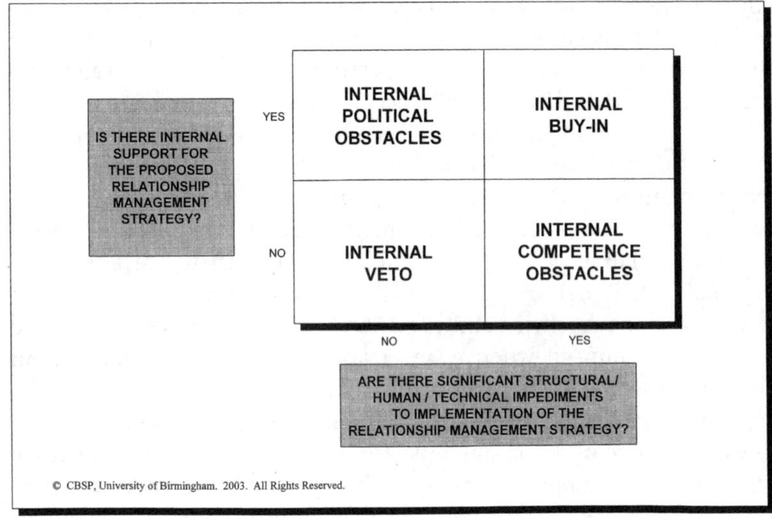

Figure 8.3 Understanding internal buy-in

partners if relationship alignment rather than misalignment is to occur. The decision-tree demonstrates that while each side in the transaction needs to pursue their own strategies they must also be aware of what the other side is doing, and make sure that both parties have the internal and external alignment that is necessary for a successful outcome.

The decision-tree shows that relationships tend to be 'remediable' when the misalignment occurs as a consequence of a misunderstanding operationally that is not based on conflicts over commercial goals. It is also possible, however, that misalignment will occur that is not 'remediable' because of the different commercial drivers that each party may have in the relationship. Given this it seems obvious that managers should focus their attention on overcoming those relationship misalignments that arise from an operational lack of understanding, rather than those that arise from a clear difference in commercial drivers.

This is just another way of saying that managers should first understand the power circumstances they are in and select the customers or suppliers that are most aligned with their commercial goals. One of the most surprising results of the case study work reported here is that there were many circumstances when buyers and suppliers had selected dysfunctional and conflictual exchange partners that could not be aligned effectively. This leads inevitably to the conclusion that all managers are not equally competent in understanding commercial and operational

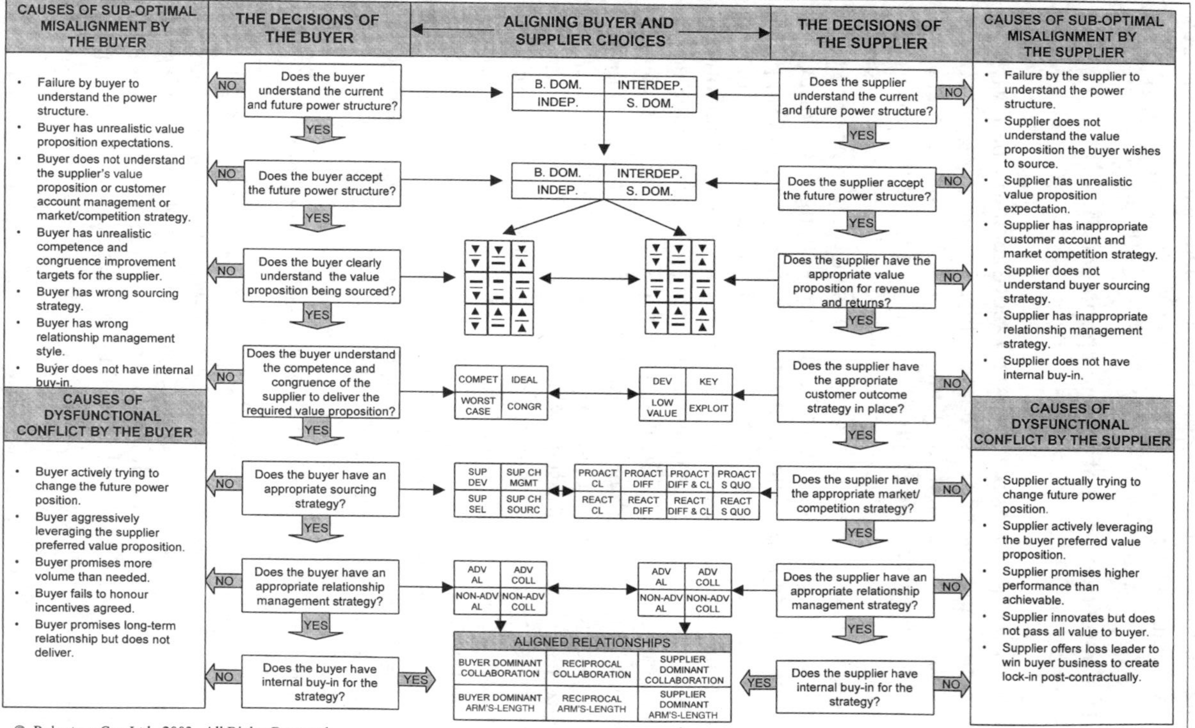

Figure 8.4 A decision-tree for relationship alignment

realities, which provides scope for more competent managers to take advantage of those who suffer not only from bounded rationality but also from commercial myopia.

8.3 The outcomes of relationship opportunism in different power scenarios

The problem with much of the discussion above about the best ways for managers to align their business relationships is that managers always operate with bounded rationality (Simon, 1997). This means that managers operate with varying levels of understanding of the power circumstances that currently do exist, or could exist in the future, as well as varying levels of awareness of how to measure competence and congruence, attractiveness and returns, and with varying levels of awareness of the relationship management choices that buyers and suppliers can make in terms of strategy and style. This is just another way of saying that some managers are more competent commercially than others, and this is true whether they operate in buying or selling companies.

This is an interesting insight because our discussion in this volume has been based on providing an ideal template against which a buyer and supplier can align themselves in order to understand what makes a relationship work successfully. It has also tried to provide a way of understanding why any relationship is misaligned, whether or not it can be aligned, or whether or not it is impossible due to non-commensurable commercial conflicts of interest. We believe this is a valuable way for managers to think about relationship alignment, but we also have to accept that opportunism (self-seeking interest with guile) is a permanent reality in business life (Williamson, 1985). This does not mean that all managers are equally opportunistic but that it is almost impossible to tell in advance of any relationship whether or not any manager or company is likely to be more opportunistic than another. Clearly some people and some companies may have a much greater propensity than others to behave opportunistically.

Given this, and recognising that buyers and suppliers will often be driven by their need to maximise shareholder value whenever possible, it is safe to assume that managers will behave opportunistically against the other side in a business relationship if they understand the power circumstances (both currently and potentially in the future) better than the other party. Furthermore, it has been our experience that buyers and suppliers will normally take advantage of their exchange partners if they perceive that the other side has a high level of bounded rationality that allows them to be taken advantage of either pre- or post-contractually. Given this, we provide a simple way of thinking about the probable outcomes of any business relationship if one side understands the rules of the game around power and leverage better than the other.

As Figure 8.5 demonstrates, if the current power position between a buyer and supplier is one of *buyer dominance*, and if both sides understand the rules of the game of commercial power and leverage, then the most likely outcome is that the buyer will remain dominant over time. On the other hand, if the buyer does not understand the rules of the game, especially those that operate post-contractually, and there is scope for supplier opportunism based on buyer myopia and incompetence, then the supplier may be able to move the power situation to *independence* or *interdependence* or, if the buyer is particularly incompetent, into *supplier dominance*. Either of these outcomes would be, from the supplier's point of view, a better result than could realistically be expected from the objective power circumstance currently prevailing.

If the current power situation is one of *independence*, then, if both parties understand the rules of the game, and there is no desire by either party to enter into a long-term relationship of *interdependence*, then the most likely outcome will be that the power situation remains in *independence*. If, however, the buyer understands the rules of the game better than the supplier, then it may be possible for the buyer to move the power situation to one of *buyer dominance*. On the other hand, if the supplier understands the rules of the game better than the buyer, then it is possible that the power situation will move to one of *supplier dominance*. In these cases either the buyer or the supplier would be achieving a better than expected result given the objective power circumstance prevailing.

In circumstances where the current power circumstance is *interdependence* and both sides fully understand the rules of the game, then the most probable outcome, assuming no other structural changes in the power of either party, is that the relationship will remain in *interdependence*. If, however, the buyer understands the rules of the game better than the supplier then it is possible that they will be able to move the relationship into *buyer dominance*. On the other hand, if the supplier understands the rules of the game better than the buyer then it is possible that the power situation will shift to *supplier dominance*. In both cases either the buyer or the supplier would once again be achieving a better then expected outcome given the objective power circumstance.

In the final circumstance, if the power situation is one of *supplier dominance*, and both parties understand the rules of the game then it is

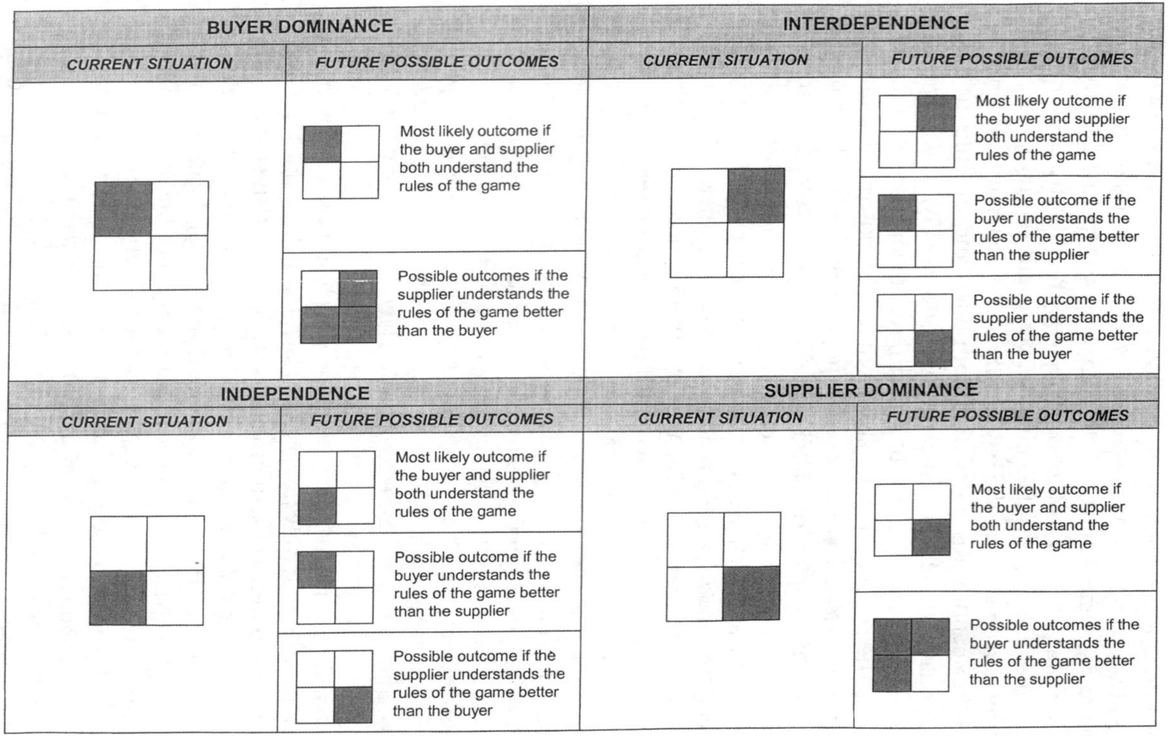

BUYER DOMINANCE

CURRENT SITUATION

FUTURE POSSIBLE OUTCOMES

Most likely outcome if the buyer and supplier both understand the rules of the game

Possible outcomes if the supplier understands the rules of the game better than the buyer

INTERDEPENDENCE

CURRENT SITUATION

FUTURE POSSIBLE OUTCOMES

Most likely outcome if the buyer and supplier both understand the rules of the game

Possible outcome if the buyer understands the rules of the game better than the supplier

Possible outcome if the supplier understands the rules of the game better than the buyer

INDEPENDENCE

CURRENT SITUATION

FUTURE POSSIBLE OUTCOMES

Most likely outcome if the buyer and supplier both understand the rules of the game

Possible outcome if the buyer understands the rules of the game better than the supplier

Possible outcome if the supplier understands the rules of the game better than the buyer

SUPPLIER DOMINANCE

CURRENT SITUATION

FUTURE POSSIBLE OUTCOMES

Most likely outcome if the buyer and supplier both understand the rules of the game

Possible outcomes if the buyer understands the rules of the game better than the supplier

Figure 8.5 Relationship outcomes under conditions of symmetric and asymmetric competence

probable that the power situation will remain supplier dominant. If, however, the buyer understands the rules of the game much better than the supplier then it is possible that the power situation will be moved into *independence, interdependence* or even *buyer dominance*. In these circumstances the buyer would be achieving a better outcome than could have been expected given the objective power circumstance.

It is clear, therefore, that while relationship alignment is a desirable goal the objective of competent business managers is not always to accept the prevailing power circumstance. On the contrary – it is normal for managers to seek to achieve better than predictable or probable outcomes if they can. If one party to a business relationship is therefore more competent than another and understands the rules of the game better than the other it is likely that the more competent party will operate opportunistically against the other. This can be seen – as it is by many academic writers – as short-term thinking which will ultimately rebound on the perpetrator. This is because the party taken advantage of can normally be expected to seek to punish those that are eventually discovered to have been behaving opportunistically.

While there is undoubted truth in this view an opportunistic manager must also measure this predictable response against two factors. The first is their perception of the capability of the other party to eventually discover that they have been taken advantage of, and the second is how long it will take. It seems reasonable to conclude that, in circumstances where the opportunistic party believes the chances of the other party achieving competence are low, or where it will take them a long time, managers will behave opportunistically. As John Maynard Keynes is famous for saying: 'In the long-term we are all dead.' Given this fact, many hard-pressed managers faced with the need to make short-term quarterly results will behave opportunistically, if they can, in order to meet the targets that senior managers set for them.

Thus we must recognise that while there is always a need for managers to understand the objective power circumstances they are in, it is clearly possible that the objective power circumstance is also shaped by the subjective perceptions of power that buyers and suppliers hold. This fact immeasurably complicates the recommendations that one might make to managers. On the one hand, it is possible to argue that managers should seek always to understand power circumstances and align business relationships accordingly. On the other hand, it is also perfectly respectable to argue that managers should not educate the other side in a relationship and should seek to achieve better than expected outcomes from the myopia and incompetence of others. This pursuit of opportunism is clearly at the heart of all business practice and complicates the way in which recommendations for relationship management might be framed.

8.4 Conclusion

The discussion above leads us to conclude that however hard one tries to enlighten managers as to the most appropriate ways to manage and align relationships there will always by asymmetry in competence, and scope for some managers to achieve relationship outcomes that are better than they ought to be given the power circumstances. This is because not all managers have the same time, resources or level of knowledge and understanding as others about commercial and operational realities. This means that a substantial part of the teaching of effective business strategy must always be about the development of an understanding of how to take advantage of others under conditions of bounded rationality (Cox, 2005).

Despite this, it is still a useful starting point in the development of competence in business relationship management for managers to understand what conditions must be in place for relationship alignment to occur. By understanding the ideal, it is possible for managers to see why their current strategies are misaligned and also to what extent this misalignment is a result of operational misunderstandings by either party, or the result of dysfunctional and non-commensurable commercial goals. Furthermore, by understanding how alignment is achieved it is also possible for managers to educate themselves to the sources of opportunism by others in any relationship.

The basic argument of this book has been that business relationships cannot be made to work effectively unless there is a joint understanding by the buyer and the supplier of the need to align their commercial and operational goals both internally and externally. This allows us to specify some of the key conditions that must be in place for successful relationship alignment:

- The first condition for successful relationship management is that the buyer and supplier in any relationship understand the power circumstance between the two parties, both currently and in the future, and are both comfortable with this outcome.
- The second condition is that the buyer and supplier must have commensurable commercial strategies. For the buyer this involves the selection of an appropriate value proposition about use value and

the cost of ownership, that is commensurable with the supplier's value proposition for revenue and returns. Both of these choices must also be linked to an acceptable supplier competence and congruence for the buyer and an appropriate customer account management strategy by the supplier.

- The third condition is that buyers and suppliers must have commensurable operational strategies. For the buyer this involves the selection of an appropriate sourcing strategy that is commensurable with the competitive market strategy being pursued by the supplier.
- The fourth condition for successful relationship management is the ability for the buyer and supplier to be able to differentiate between relationship styles and select one that is most appropriate for them given the power circumstance, commercial goals and operational strategies of each party in the transaction.
- The fifth condition of successful relationship management is the need for there to be internal buy-in from within both the buyer's and the supplier's organisation.

Our work has demonstrated that success normally occurs in relationship alignment when these five factors are in place, and that relationship misalignment normally results when any of the five factors are not in place. Our work also demonstrates that sometimes it is possible to remedy misalignments – especially if they occur through an operational misunderstanding by either party, where there is no real conflict over commercial outcomes.

Unfortunately, it is not always possible to remedy the misalignments that occur in business relationships. These normally arise as a result of clear conflicts of interest associated with non-commensurable commercial goals, or non-commensurable leverage strategies over current and future power positions. When exchange partners discover that they have such conflicts of interest, usually the relationship cannot be aligned and it must either be endured until a better alternative is found, or ended as soon as possible. If this volume allows managers to understand when they can or cannot remedy misaligned business relationships, as well as what is the most appropriate way of aligning relationships under different power and leverage scenarios, then it will have served its purpose.

References

Cox, A. (2005) *The Rules of the Game: How to Capture Value in Business* (Helpston, UK: Earlsgate Press).

Cox, A., Ireland, P., Lonsdale, C., Sanderson, J. and Watson, G. (2003) *Supply Chain Management: A Guide to Best Practice* (London: Financial Times/Prentice Hall).

Simon, H. A. (1997) *Administrative Behavior* (New York: Free Press).

Williamson, O. E. (1985) *The Economic Institutions of Capitalism* (New York: Free Press).

Index